WOODSQUEER

WOODSQUEER

Crafting a Sustainable Rural Life

GRETCHEN LEGLER

TRINITY UNIVERSITY PRESS   San Antonio, Texas

Trinity University Press
San Antonio, Texas 78212

Cover design and illustration by Caitlin Sacks / Notch Design
Book design by BookMatters
Author photo by Jaime Lynn Photography

ISBN 978-1-59534-959-0 paper
ISBN 978-1-59534-960-6 ebook

Trinity University Press strives to produce its books using
methods and materials in an environmentally sensitive manner.
We favor working with manufacturers that practice sustainable
management of all natural resources, produce paper using
recycled stock, and manage forests with the best possible
practices for people, biodiversity, and sustainability. The press
is a member of the Green Press Initiative, a nonprofit program
dedicated to supporting publishers in their efforts to reduce
their impacts on endangered forests, climate change, and forest-
dependent communities.

CIP data on file at the Library of Congress

26   25   24   23   22 | 5   4   3   2

CONTENTS

Woodsqueer

With the Animals

The Tyrant and the Apple Tree

WOODSQUEER

Woodsqueer I

The cabin sat in a dark glen along what was once the main trail to Mount Blue, shaded by second-growth Maine pines, hemlock, and birch, within easy earshot of a bubbling stream that hikers, led there by the old trail, once stopped beside for rest and water. The hiking trail up this popular mountain in western Maine, however, had long since been rerouted, and now the derelict log structure with its falling-in tar paper roof and leaf-strewn porch was hunkered down in the woods just off a short, rarely trod spur path.

My partner Ruth and I had recently moved to Maine from Alaska where we'd spent the first two years of our couple-hood, me teaching at the University of Alaska Anchorage, and Ruth working as an electrician and fire alarm technician. In Maine, we'd bought eighty acres of wooded land with a house and barnlike shed and had launched ourselves into growing our own food, something we'd both done before we met but put our backs into now with renewed effort as a couple, hoping our gardens would grow to provide most of our food year-round. I suppose you could call it homesteading, but with none of the sod-busting and wilderness-taming of times gone by. In the 1970s it was called "going back to the land," when waves of urban-born, politically motivated young people moved to rural Maine, inspired by the likes of Helen and Scott Nearing and their book *Living the Good Life: How to Live Sanely and Simply in a Troubled World,* which chronicled the couple's move to rural Maine in 1932 and their twenty years restoring soil, gardening, farming, and engaging in political activism on behalf of the earth. Ruth and I were both fascinated by people who chose to live close to nature, so of course we couldn't resist taking the detour off the hiking trail to look at the cabin.

We were hiking with Ruth's sister Elaine, Elaine's husband Dave, their son Jake, and a nine-year-old summer guest who was visiting us from Manhattan as part of the Fresh Air project, which has been bringing city kids to the woods for more than a hundred years. We all trooped into the woods to take a closer look at what had apparently once been the forest ranger's residence. What we saw were piles of dirt and leaves blown into the corners, spiderwebs hanging from the beams, a stained mattress that some squirrel had pulled apart for a warm winter nest, a torn shirt or pair of pants in a rotten pile, a rusted woodstove, a pot with a hole in it, a broken-down bookshelf, a wooden chair with only two legs, and some beer bottles and hamburger bags. Too bad; it seemed like once upon a time it was a sweet place.

Back on the trail, two hikers came sweating up behind us, exclaiming loudly, "I *knew* that old cabin was here *somewhere*." The pair was an older woman and a younger one, perhaps a mother and daughter. The older of the two, huffing and puffing, said she had hiked this mountain many times in her younger days and remembered the old trail going by the stream and past the cabin door, so that you could have a chat with the ranger—if the ranger was in, that is, and not at the rocky, windswept top of the three-thousand-foot mountain in the fire tower watching closely for puffs of smoke from the dark, rolling ranges of tree and rock that stretched for many miles in all directions.

While we rested companionably beside the trail we got to talking about living in the woods. Living in the woods, in a cabin such as the abandoned one behind us, was not hard to imagine. Sweep it out, seal the cracks, haul up a cot and a table, install a little gas cookstove, put in a pump that would bring the stream water right to your countertop, light up the woodstove, and voilà! You would have a cozy place to live, away from the noise of cars and sirens, machines in general, and people. In my youth, I had stayed for summers in places like this when I worked for the U.S. Forest Service in Utah and Wyoming. All my life I'd wanted to live in a cabin in the woods just like this one. I often felt I should have been born in a different time, when things were slower—when people traveled by horse, by boat and on foot, sent letters, went to bed when it got dark, grew their own food, kept diaries, danced and made music for entertainment.

I looked longingly at the derelict cabin and said, "That would have been a nice place to be a forest ranger." Ruth and I told the hikers about a friend of ours who had lived in the woods for eight years, keeping watch from a fire tower at Allagash Lake in Maine's Allagash Wilderness. This was one of the first things we learned about our friend, Marilyn, and something that impressed us deeply. Anyone who could do that, live in the woods alone for eight years, was a person with inner resources beyond those available to most of us.

Maine is famously the home of what some have called "the last true hermit," profiled in the popular book *The Stranger in the Woods*, by Michael Finkel, who writes about how twenty-year-old Christopher Knight headed off into the woods in 1986, spending almost thirty years without talking to nearly a single human being. He was raised in Albion, Maine, by what sound like emotionally distant parents who, by the way, never reported him missing. The woods Knight built his camp in were not really the deep wilderness some news accounts make them out to be, but woods not much different from those surrounding mine and Ruth's farm, where there are lots of places among the boulders and knolls one might set up a secret camp. News stories tell of Knight's "capture," his rustic camp and how he survived the Maine winters, stealing propane canisters and other supplies, including books, from nearby seasonal cabins. He cut his hair, took baths with melted snow, concealed his tracks, stockpiled so he didn't have to travel in the winter and leave telltale footprints. Finally caught and charged with multiple petty burglaries, which had perplexed camp owners for many years, Knight was sentenced to time in jail, charged with a fine, and served probation.

In interviews he was hard-pressed to offer motives for his actions, but he did express remorse for stealing and likened himself to contemplatives like Ralph Waldo Emerson and Thomas Merton, saying that solitude "bestowed" upon him increased perception. When he applied that perception to himself, his ego fell away. "I lost my identity," he said. "There was no audience, no one to perform for.... I was completely free."

I think he knew things, or came to know things, that many of us long to know—namely, how to be at peace in this world, live in harmony with what is, consume only what we really need, and be satisfied with what we have rather than long for what we don't.

For a while Ruth and I, our hiking companions, and our trail mates debated the merits of such a life as one lived in the rustic cabin beside the stream, sipped our water, and snacked on crackers and raisins. "Well," one of the women said as we set off again, "I think I'd go a little soft in the head if it was me, you know. I'd go… what was it they used to call people who'd been in the woods too long?" She paused and then suddenly recalled the term: "Woodsqueer!" I looked at Ruth and she at me, and we smiled at one another over those two lovely words joined together.

I suppose there are people who think Ruth and I are a bit woodsqueer. We are those geeks you see snooping through the woods in nylon quick-dry cargo shorts, the pockets full of binoculars, bird books, wildflower guides, and a pocketknife. I always pack a raincoat, at least one water bottle, a snack, a flashlight, some matches, a compass, a whistle, a hat and a bandana, toilet paper, a knife, and usually a small bag to carry foraged edibles and other treasures in. I don't know when I set out what will be in that bag when I return, but there is usually something out there worth bringing home. Sometimes it will be mushrooms, other times a handful of ripe wild raspberries, edible flowers, seeds I'd like to try planting in my garden, or maybe I'll ditch the bag altogether and fill my water bottle with blueberries. I never know what I'm going to find in the woods—it's a queer place. We're the hikers you see wandering off the trail, and you wonder, *Who are those freaks and what are they doing?* We like to reassure people by saying, perhaps a little too self-consciously, "Hi! We're just looking at flowers!"

We often played a game when we hiked. It was called *What If We Got Lost and Had to Spend the Night Outdoors?* To us it was wildly entertaining. We'd start with the essentials. Fire. Check. We had matches in our backpacks and a bit of dry paper, and we could always find something to stoke a fire with, even in the rain. Water. Check. Water bottles full and stream nearby. Food. Check. There were all the above fresh foods, plus berries, and of course the extra crackers and cheese in our packs. What if we didn't have any food? We'd have to kill a squirrel or a vole. Or catch a fish. How? The game would go on until we got tired of it.

When I feel boggled by the pace and sometimes overwhelming variety and abundance of everyday life in twenty-first-century America, I play another game called *How Did We Get Here?* I keep going back and back and back until I am there in the woods with bow and arrow or a spear and a birchbark pot, a strong will for survival, and enough knowledge about what grows wild around me so that I won't poison myself or starve. That's how it all started, with people making do. Everything else—electricity, the lightbulb, the washing machine, the toaster, the grocery store, the icebox, the shower, the hair dryer, the dishwasher—that was all gravy.

It's commonplace for those worried about the state of our planet and the state of our souls to speak of the "nature illiteracy" of most of today's Americans. One test of nature literacy is whether you can name ten common plants and animals from your geographical region. I delight in testing myself. Western Maine. Mammals: moose, black bear (mostly gone now, but my neighbor Steve Bien saw one recently), bobcat, deer, raccoon, porcupine, skunk, weasel, beaver, coyote, fisher, vole, mouse. Birds: spruce grouse, wild turkey, raven, crow, mallard, chickadee, barred owl, pine grosbeak, purple finch, Baltimore oriole, loon, eagle. How about edible plants? Mallow, chickweed, wild cress, cattails, wild leek, willow, blackberries, blueberries, raspberries, wild strawberries, thistle, coltsfoot, acorn, lamb's-quarter. Insects? Mosquitoes, deer flies, ticks, dragonflies, no-see-ums, butterflies. This is where my ignorance shows. What kinds of butterflies? What kinds of dragonflies? Fish? Trout, bass? My knowledge is getting thinner. Trees? Pine, hemlock, white birch, yellow birch, silver birch, red maple, sugar maple, silver maple, beech, wild cherry, hawthorn, popple, oak. I start my list with confidence, but by the end I run out of knowledge.

Even though I do pretty well at my own queer games and quizzes, I hate to pass judgment on others. After all, we're not all crazy about the same things. Some knowledge just doesn't seem pertinent anymore to the modern urbanite, such as how to make flour from acorns, or how to skin and cook a wild duck that happened to fly into the side of your car and break its neck. What interests me more than shaming or judging someone who doesn't know a juicy chanterelle from a deadly jack-o-lantern mushroom is the question of what joys we might all be missing out on by not knowing more about the plants and animals that share our intimate lives with us—not only those in hard-to-get-to wild places but also in our backyards, front flower gardens, parks, vacant lots, roadsides, even cracks in the sidewalks.

There's been a lot of conversation in recent decades about "species loneliness." Part of that loneliness comes from increasing extinction rates among nonhuman species—we are more and more alone as a species as other forms of life expire.

I think part of that loneliness also comes from not knowing many other "other-than-humans"—such as birds and their songs, spiders, flowers, trees, and other lively beings. It's kind of like living in a neighborhood or an apartment building where you don't know any of your neighbors. It's not only less fun to live in your own bubble, but it can be boring and sometimes frightening when you feel cut off and alone. There's a relationship between knowing the names of your human and nonhuman neighbors, caring about them, and doing what you can to help them thrive. Just like we do with other humans, we can start with knowing the names of our plant and animal neighbors, saying hello when we pass by, and checking up on them once in a while. That said, of course there are other ways of tuning in to where you live by getting to know the human-built environment with all its beauty, complexity, creativity, and grace. I had a colleague whose son was, I suppose you could say, the urban equivalent of woodsqueer—he'd memorized the entire Boston subway system map. I have another friend who's crazy about architecture and can name every architect behind every building in America's major urban centers.

But back to the question of whether you could live in the woods by yourself in a little cabin by a stream with no other people around for thirty years (like the Maine hermit) or eight months, or eight weeks or eight days, or whether you could make your home in a small house on eighty acres of wooded land in the Western Mountains of rural Maine and grow your own food for the rest of your life. Would you go woodsqueer, or would you have to be woodsqueer to start with? And what would you gain or lose? And what would you come to know about yourself and the world?

Minding the Fence

Before I built a wall I'd ask to know
What I was walling in or walling out,
And to whom I was like to give offense.

—Robert Frost, "Mending Wall"

"Good fences make good neighbors," says the supposedly backward farmer in Robert Frost's poem "Mending Wall." One day each year the speaker walks the stone wall that borders his farm and his neighbor's, each replacing the boulders that have rolled out of place, establishing again a firm boundary between the two men and their lands. The speaker, the supposedly thoughtful one, wants to know what the stone fence is walling in or walling out, suggesting that fences are not as simple as they might seem—they restrain animals, sure, and establish property lines, but they also restrict creativity, ideas, and lives.

My education in walls and fences—what they are good for, what they wall in, and what they wall out—began in earnest when Ruth and I got our small herd of French Alpine goats: an older doe named Dora, her baby Paulette, and a young wether (a castrated male goat) named Hickson. Back then, neither of us knew much about fences. I inherited fencing supplies from Stephen Levine, a colleague in the history department at the university where I teach, who, like me, had launched into goat-owning with little experience. He had recently upgraded from a homemade electric fence to an expensive professionally

**Broken stone wall
& barbed wire fence along old field**

installed model. As Stephen was transferring the fencing materials from his barn to my pickup truck, he told me, rather offhandedly, that it might not matter what kind of fence I built—if a goat wanted to get out, it would, no matter what. Unlike cows and horses, he said, goats didn't "mind a fence" well. His goats seemed to intuit when the electric fence was on or off and tested it routinely for places to slip between the wires. With a smile, he related to me how they'd jump through the wires to greet him when he arrived home from work.

Nevertheless, goat owners still strive for the perfect fence. Some recommend page wire—a strong wire net impossible for all but the tiniest goats to sneak through—topped by an electrified strand at about four feet. The most cost-effective fence, most experts agree, is electric. Some suggest charging every other wire, some just the bottom, some just the top. Some recommend a five-strand wire fence, while some say a seven-strand is best, just in case you have "jump-ers"—goats that don't bother slipping through the wires but sail right over the top. The odds of that, my friend said, were slim. He'd never had a jumper in his herd. In the end, you can debate the particulars and tinker away all you want and come to nothing, because an elec-tric fence, one source notes, is more of a psychological barrier for a goat than a physical one.

In Frost's poem the speaker suggests that the luggish neighbor wants the fence just to have a fence, but where goats are concerned, there are some excellent reasons for fences.

First there's the "for their own good" reason. There are plants, including rhododendron, chokecherry, domestic sour cherry, milk-weed, and rhubarb that are poisonous to goats. The first year we kept goats I let our small herd out in the fall after the flower gardens had died back so that they could roam around the yard and nibble away. It was charming to see the goats wandering about and sweet to hear their bells ringing out in the fall air. The next morning the baby goats were shivering in a corner of the barn, green slime frothing from their mouths, the barn walls covered in diarrhea and vomit. A call to our vet, Doc Cooper, brought him barreling up the dirt driveway in his red pickup truck. He pumped their stomachs with charcoal and gave them injections of aspirin and instructed us to make sure they got enough water. "They ate something that disagreed with them," he said, in his characteristically understated way. Dora, for her larger size, seemed unaffected, but the little ones could have died.

The next best reason to keep goats on their side of the fence is that they like to sample different foods. Contrary to myth, however, they do not eat just any old piece of trash, although they have been known to eat tar paper and poison ivy. For us, their illicit nibbling meant our pear trees, our perennials, our arborvitae, our vegetables, and our lilac bush. They also don't care where they drop their little pellets, and they might just put their hooves through your screen door or picture window to satisfy their curiosity and their desire to be social.

Our hilly, rocky woods are crisscrossed with old fences made of stone and barbed wire. Ruth and I like to follow the stone walls through the forest, sometimes hopping up on them to carefully walk the walls deep into the trees, then to turn around and follow them back home. The rock walls are vestiges of a time, nearly a century ago, when this land, now a chaos of pine, hemlock, beech, maple, and oak, was mostly pasture—the flip side of the dense forest it is now—not just here but all over New England. We use the stone walls to map our property and our meanderings upon it. At the end of one stone wall, for example, we stop and turn left, search for a copse of tall white birch, and are sure to find there, at the right season of the year, black trumpets, one of our favorite wild mushrooms.

Another stone wall runs parallel to a deer crossing. I've used a chink in that wall to hide and wait for deer during hunting season. I've sat on yet another stone wall, which marks the top boundary of our property, during deer season, as it provided an excellent perch to look down into a ravine where I knew deer to travel. On that wall I met my first fisher—an allegedly fierce, weasel-like creature about as large as a beaver, notoriously shy of humans. It ambled along the wall toward me, coming close enough that I was prepared to defend myself with the butt of my gun; I'd heard that although they were people-shy, fishers were viciously assertive if confronted. When it looked up from its own intense purposes, the fisher held my gaze for a time, then calmly turned and walked the other way along the top of the wall until it disappeared among the hanging hemlock boughs.

I set up my electric goat fence in June, during the hottest and buggiest time of the year, making myself nearly sick from the physical effort of clearing a path through the woods for the fence line, felling trees with a chainsaw, driving eight-foot-tall metal fence posts into the rocky ground with a sledgehammer, sinking the copper ground rods, nailing plastic insulators onto the trees, then stringing the wire—tripping through the forest carrying a heavy spool with a stick through the middle so that the wire would pay out as I stumbled along. Ruth was working in the field as a river geologist that summer, so I was doing the work on my own. In the end I had something I had put up by myself that cost us only a few hundred dollars. When I plugged the fence into the solar charger (which I'd also inherited from Stephen) and tested it by grabbing hold with an ungloved hand, it sent a prickly shock through my arm—nothing like the "throw-you-on-your-butt" jolts I got when, as a curious tomboy, I tested the wire fence around my grandfather's Minnesota cow pasture, but a buzz sufficient to deter a goat. Or so I thought.

Our first three goats arrived in the back of a Subaru wagon, delivered by Stephen and his wife, Alison. The fence was up, and I'd made stalls in the barn and purchased leather collars with cute brass bells, black rubber grain pans and grain, hay, water buckets, and even a brush. Despite my careful preparations, it took Dora, the big doe, five minutes to find the place on the fence where I'd spliced in a gate using yellow plastic insulated hooks. Out she went, followed directly by her baby. Getting her back in gave me respect for her power and that famous goat orneriness; I grabbed her collar to haul her back to the barn, and she proceeded to drag me across the yard, my hat flying off as I bumped along, just like in a cartoon.

Daunted, I went in search of advice. A website recommended another copper ground rod. Another source suggested that the fence wasn't conducting electricity because we'd received so little rain that spring and the ground wasn't wet enough. I asked Darrell, the woodcutter and farmer who lived at the end of our road, what his trick was. He had been raising goats for several years and seemed to have a well-behaved flock. Their pasture was right next to the road, Darrell's fence didn't look any tighter than mine, and yet the goats seemed to mind *his* fence.

"How do you keep them in?" I asked.

He explained that the fence was electrified.

"Mine is too," I said.

Then he let me in on the big secret. He sold the goats with "bad attitudes."

Jack, an excavator, substitute teacher, and tax accountant who also helped us dig ditches and move big rocks, said when he was young they'd "educate" their goats by wetting them down with water and touching their noses to the charged fence wire. The water helped conduct the electric shock. Another trick, he explained, was to put their goats' grain bowls just out of reach near the charged fence wire, so they'd get shocked if they went too far. I put all the advice in my mental filing cabinet.

Our eighty acres of land, along with a small Cape-style home and a large shed that we converted into a barn, came cheap by today's standards, at less than $100,000. The charming post-and-beam house was built by the previous owners in the late 1970s. The architectural plans for the house, they told us, were a copy of the Prince House, an original Cape that was part of the Plymouth Colony. That explained the low ceilings, deep knee walls, steep roof, thick dark hemlock beams, rustic woodwork, wainscoting, and primitive stairs. From the beginning, we set about transforming the cavelike interior into an airy, colorful space; we knocked out walls, opened up ceilings, replaced the plywood floor with bright wide pine boards, painted the walls and cupboards whimsical greens and shades of lavender. Like most do-it-yourself projects, this one was slow to complete, but now and then, when we got motivated, we moved along with whatever piece of the project was still in motion. When we got tired of working in the house, we worked in the yard. Three years after moving in we planted apple trees. Later we added several perennial gardens. Then we completed a writing cottage for me and a music studio for Ruth. Eventually it would all get done—inside and out. We knew that we were in it for the long haul, so we were in no rush.

In the second year of owning goats, we acquired two new French Alpine babies. We named them Ponette and Felix, after our favorite characters in two French films. That was about the same time that we learned that French Alpines were notoriously high-strung and willful goats, and that we might be better off with a more docile breed— Nubians, or Saanens, or Oberhaslis. Disregarding this information, when Ponette was old enough, we bred her to an Alpine buck, and the following spring we were blessed with twin baby goats, both brown and white like their mother. We named them Trillium and Peeper after the three-lobed spring flower that blooms in our woods and the little frog, the spring peeper, that signals the end of winter in the Maine woods.

Each morning Trillium and Peeper, with their perky ears and tiny hooves, were locked in their stall, curled up beside their mother or nursing eagerly. By noon they were in the yard nibbling the wild-flowers or bleating pathetically outside the barn door to be let back inside. How did they get out of their stall? How did they get outside the barn? How did they get through the fence? One day, after we found them in the yard, we decided not to let them back into the barn, thinking this would teach them a lesson; they'd get so hungry for their mother's milk and company that they'd never sneak out again. By evening they'd somehow managed to circumvent the locked barn door and had found their way back to their mother's side. How they accomplished this would become my summer's work to solve.

We redesigned the fence: five super-tight, super-charged strands instead of seven wimpy ones. We swapped out the solar charger for an electric one that sent out six thousand volts of electricity, starting with the bottom strand of wire. We bought wire stretchers to keep the fence tight. I walked the fence line, tightening wires, driving extra posts, lodging rocks and tree limbs under the bottom wire where I thought the twins were slipping under. On the advice of a neighbor, I tied orange marking tape on the wire strands, under the assumption that the goatlings didn't know that the fence was there and were running through it by accident. My fervent hope was to catch them in the act so that I could finally seal off their escape route.

Then one day it happened—there they were, in midair, suspended for a split second in the dappled green of the woods behind the barn. The little goats had turned out to be jumpers!

As punishment we confined them to their stalls in the barn, only to find that they enjoyed leaping onto the stall rails like circus acrobats, jumping from the rails to the tops of the grain cans, and climbing the stairs to the hayloft. Attempts to catch them resulted in a graceless slapstick routine punctuated by the sound of our swearing, the bang and clash of turned-over grain cans, their excited *baa-ing*, and the clatter of their hooves. The example set by her rambunctious twins convinced Ponette that the fence was irrelevant as well, and we'd routinely find the three of them on our side of the fence, happily munching the phlox or the rosebushes.

Of all the stone fences on our land, I have my favorites: the one that runs along the edge of our goat meadow, trailing off into the woods as it wanders away from the yard; the one that runs along the road, breaking where our driveway cuts through it; and the one along the backside of the house that we are now able to see more clearly after cutting some of the scrubby maple and pine that had grown up to hide it. The shapeliness of the stones attracts me, their gray color, speckled with green, white, and orange lichen. The stone walls got their start 500 million years ago, when heat and pressure melted minerals into bedrock deep beneath the earth's crust. As the weight of eroding land above the bedrock lessened, the bedrock lifted slightly, creating bumps. When glaciers crept slowly down from Canada across New England, the icy giants bumped into the lumpy bedrock and picked up boulders, some of which they smashed into sand, some of which they deposited as huge glacial erratics the size of houses, and some they crushed into stones just the right size for a wall. Over time, soil covered this barren, rock-strewn postglacial landscape, hiding the stones beneath fertile earth. When European immigrant farmers began to clear land of trees, a combination of bare soil and cold climate served to heave the stones upward, so that they would (as they still do) appear on the surface anew each year, as if conjured by a fairy in the night. New England farmers in the nineteenth century moved the rocks by hand and with oxen and horses, piling them as nearby as possible, creating crude walls. Another turn in history around the middle of the nineteenth century sent New England farmers off to cities and factories, or in search of easier land to till, and their stone walls, once the borders between fields and pastures, became hemmed in by woods, tumbled by time, raided by those in search of boulders for bridge abutments or gravel. Today, fashionable icons of New England rural life that they are, the walls are being dismantled and moved across the country by land-scapers in search of lichen-covered stones. It is easy to imagine, as I walk along the tops of the walls that punctuate our woods all tumble-down and camouflaged by balsam, a farmer and a son, hot and dirty, prying the rocks out of the ground, hoisting the boulders up to their places in the wall—the grunting, the sweat, the flinty smell of the rock itself.

One day, finally taking Jack's advice, I set out to teach Ponette and her twins a lesson. With a pail of water I wetted the first twin down, held her between my legs, and forced her nose to the fence. She shrieked and bucked, wriggling out of my arms, then stood beside me, wet and quivering, her tongue hanging out of her lips. The shock that went through her also went through me, setting my arm afire. I felt sick to my stomach at the violence of what I was doing, but also perversely vindictive. I repeated the routine with Trillium's little brother, then with Ponette herself. The goats' cries terrified all of us—goat and human alike. What was I doing? Was it that important that they mind the fence? It felt cruel, like beating a child who had misbehaved. They were just being themselves, after all. In the end, it didn't even work. The babies went sailing over the fence again that afternoon.

Eventually we sold the delinquent twins at a nearby livestock auction. But Ponette stayed with us, and kept getting through the fence. It was frustrating enough to be funny. As a joke, Ruth made a "wanted" poster, using Photoshop to dress an innocent-looking, big-eyed Ponette in prison stripes with the headline "Wanted: Ponette Houdini" and a description that included a suspected addiction to electric shocks. Finally, fed up, I placed an ad in *Uncle Henry's*, our regional buy it and sell it guide. "Sweet French Alpine doe for sale. Still milking. A great addition to your dairy herd or nice pet." When the first buyer called and asked why we were selling her, my conscience got the better of me.

"She won't mind the fence," I said.

"Oh," the caller said. "Then I guess that's not so good. We wanted her for a pet."

"No," I said. "She'd be a handful."

When the second buyer called, I told them I'd changed my mind. For good or ill, Ponette was our young doe now; she'd given us beautiful twins and tasty milk. She was a good mother and had, as Darrell said, "a pretty little udder." I wanted to give her one more chance.

One day I was visiting with our neighbors, the Turners, who owned an organic dairy farm a mile down the road. I was going on about the problem of Ponette, the goat who wouldn't mind the fence. "Why don't you put a poker on her?" Marilyn Turner said. I thought she meant I should buy an electric prod. She explained: "You know, you get a crotched stick and you make a top for it and you put it around her neck." She fetched a farm supply book from the back room and showed me a modern version, a collar of crossed metal rods. When the goat put her head through the strands of fence, the ends of the rods would catch her and give her a shock or, in any case, tangle her up enough to discourage her.

Ponette wearing a "poker"

I designed a poker made of sticks held together with wire, like a rustic Elizabethan collar, in which Ponette looked decidedly silly, but it worked—until she knocked it off against a tree. She would go on to have another set of pretty twins the following year, and they too would turn out to be jumpers, and in the end all three of them went to auction.

When we finally had enough money, we tore down the electric fence and had a sturdy page-wire fence installed, topped by one electrified strand. The wire squares at the fence top graduated down to smaller and smaller squares at the bottom to prevent baby goats and chickens from sneaking out, and foxes from slipping in. Our make-shift wire gates were replaced with heavy metal pasture gates that we could swing wide open. The new fence ended the drama that had occupied us for so many years. When we left for a weekend, we no longer had to worry about whether the goats would break out, eat the peas, destroy the rosebushes, trample the lettuce patch, or eat the cherry leaves and throw up all over the barn. I no longer had to torture them under the guise of educating them about the fence.

Once in a while some goat or other would finagle her way out of her stall and out of the barn, especially in winter when snow fell off the barn roof, making a mound the goats could climb over. They would walk across the crusty snow to nibble the bark from the pear tree. But mostly, we all—Ruth and I, the goats, and the chickens—settled comfortably into our designated spaces. As we continued to expand our animal pasture and vegetable gardens, create an orchard, and trim away at the dense green wall of forest that once pressed so tightly against our house, more stone walls would appear, with their gray, well-fitted stones, arching off into the woods, running beside the driveway and along the property boundary by the road. Together with the page-wire fence, the stone walls helped create a sturdy, pleasant, and comforting enclosure that embraced our gardens, pasture, and barn.

While this settling into place on our rural Maine farmstead felt right, it also felt strange. I was reluctant at first to buy a home, much less eighty acres of land. It's not as if I was a drifter who could never settle down. I'd previously owned a home with my ex-husband, a rambling, late-nineteenth-century money pit in Saint Paul, Minnesota, in the West End near the breweries. The entire five years of our marriage we spent tearing down lath and plaster, replacing walls and ceilings, insulating, rewiring, replumbing, scraping up ancient linoleum, and sanding floors. After we divorced, he kept the house, which he called

his "albatross." Owning a home was a lot of work, and what if your re-
lationship, or your job, or your infatuation with the place didn't last?
But Ruth persisted. She wanted the groundedness a house provided.
She wanted a home. I was the one dragging my feet.

What finally made me believe this land and this home with Ruth
were right happened one evening in late summer. I had been teaching
all day and was overdressed for the unseasonably warm weather; the
heat made me cranky. We decided to go swimming at Egypt Pond in
Chesterville, a stone's throw from the big farmhouse we rented when
we first came to Maine. I left my clothes on the dock and jumped in.
The silky amber water folded itself around me as I paddled about and
swam a few real strokes toward the middle of the pond. Not far away
a loon family created a neat V-shaped wake in the water. The small,
rounded hills circling the pond were dense with summer green, with
a red or orange changeling here and there among them. In my swim
toward the far shore, I crossed over warm and cool spots that made
my skin prick with satisfying shivers. When I opened my eyes un-
derwater, I saw how the bubbles from my splashing and breathing
danced wildly in shafts of evening sun that turned the pond water
gold.

After my dip in the pond, I felt a profound physical sense of
well-being—cool, dry, rejuvenated. Ruth and I sat on a rustic wooden
bench in the woods and talked about our days. It came to me suddenly, inexplicably—a powerful *yes!* I could live in this place, in the
woods of rural Maine, for a long time. Maybe even forever. I tested
the feeling—pushed against it—like a goat testing a fence. I didn't have
to stay here, but I didn't necessarily want to leave. That seemed like
something new. Other places I'd inhabited, other lives I'd lived, didn't
feel quite right. I'd felt hemmed in by them, constrained; "trapped"
might be a better word. But this place, this landscape of woods and
pastures, dirt roads, barns, stone walls, ponds, and old mountains,

finally felt like it could be home. And so, when Ruth said she'd found us an almost perfect house, a house we could make perfect for us, I was willing to make a commitment. For better or worse, we felt as if we were ready—for each other, for the house, for the land, and for a farming, gardening, and foraging way of life. I had no idea in the beginning how that commitment would be tested.

The Three O'Clock Cat

When we first moved to rural Maine, like any newcomers, Ruth and I wanted to know things: where to buy groceries, how to get our internet hooked up, the best restaurants, where to shop for clothes and hardware, the hours for the local transfer station (the new name for the dump), recommendations for dentists and doctors, and, high on the list, where to see good films. There was a theater in our small town that showed family-oriented films and the latest blockbusters, but some of the other kinds of films we wanted to see were shown at an independent art theater in Waterville, forty-five minutes away. It was always a companionable adventure to head to Railroad Square Cinema, sometimes just Ruth and I, sometimes with friends, in the twilight of a summer evening, or in the snowy winter dark, navigating back roads and watching for deer. The theater, home to the annual Maine International Film Festival, also served as an art gallery, showing local amateur work, as well as that of professionals.

While we munched our popcorn and waited for the movie to start, we often spent time looking at the artwork. We didn't have much money to spare then, especially for art, but one show in the small gallery moved us so profoundly we could not resist. The paintings were by artists with mental disabilities who were participating in a course taught by a local painter. One artist had created a series of paintings of cats. Many of them seemed to be in prison. Some stared out at the viewer, their paws grasping black bars in front of them. One was dressed in an old-fashioned striped convict suit and hat. One orange cat reached a paw out from its cell to touch a butterfly flying outside the bars. One, a purple cat, sat perched on a counter beside a vase of daffodils, the clock in the background showing the big hand on twelve and the little hand on three. We learned later that the artist had kept dozens of cats in her home and recently had been "shut down" by social service agencies, the cats rehomed to new owners and shelters and the woman put in the care of an assisted-living center.

The way the artist expressed her desire for freedom of movement, her sense that life for her was now violently constrained, must have resonated with me, although I couldn't then articulate why. The paintings' whimsy juxtaposed with the poignancy of the woman's situation was also striking. And I loved cats. We bought the painting of the purple cat and hung it in our new home. Ruth named it the "Three O'Clock Cat." It was "primitive," with its bold, slightly sloppy brushstrokes and refreshing, unbalanced perspective, and there was a hint of heaviness in it too. We couldn't look at the painting without remembering its maker and how she had been moved from her home, losing her independence and having to leave her cats.

Some years into our farming life, we registered our farm with the Maine Organic Farmers and Gardeners Association. To register, we needed a name. We were at the kitchen table, brainstorming a list over morning coffee. We had all manner of good examples from friends who had given their lands honorable and elegant titles: Windy

Acres, Stoney End, Rustic Roots, Sugar Brook, Pine Top, Full Circle, Counterpoint, Wildflower Farm. Ruth glanced up at the painting. "How about the Three O'Clock Cat Farm?" she said.

And so, it stuck. Ruth would go on to make labels for our jams and jellies and pickles, our handmade soap, our bottled maple syrup, our homemade granola, our goat sausage, and our eggs, all of which we produced and often sold or gave away at holidays, all sporting the purple cat with the crooked smile and the clock striking three behind him. When the seed orders came to our roadside mailbox in the spring, from Johnny's or Fedco, in their small cardboard boxes and envelopes, I was always happy and proud to see them addressed to Three O'Clock Cat Farm, Jay, ME. It seemed one more sign to me of the solidness and reality of our life. We owned a home—we had an address. We had created a farm—it had a name. We were a couple—Ruth and Gretchen.

Acquainted with the Night

When we first moved to western Maine I was astonished by the thick dark. Ruth had been raised in the country, so it was no surprise to her. I was struck first by the moonlight. The contrast between the dark of the night and the light of the moon meant that on nights when the moon was full, or even only partly so, it was so bright you could read a novel outside. Bright enough to cast lifelike shadows with crisp edges—shadows of trees, their limbs reaching out like the delta of blue veins under the thin skin of a delicate wrist; shadows of blades of grass, intricate fronds of fern, the cupola and weather vane atop a barn roof, the neighbors' bulky trash cans set out for Friday pickup; shadows of the stone walls that ran along the edges of the roads and fields; shadows from the beanpoles, from the tomato plants. Nothing standing escaped the attentions of the moonlight. In that darkness, lit by moon, one could imagine all manner of dramas taking place—small bloody murders committed by night-roaming house cats upon voles, the banditry of the raccoons feasting on the garden's ripe corn.

On a trip once to Bailey Island, across the waters of Casco Bay from Portland, Maine, Ruth and I amused ourselves on the spacious wooden porch of the inn where we were staying, rocking back and forth in high-backed chairs with woven seats, gazing out into the gathering dark. We could see the city of Portland aglow on the horizon, and we could see the light of the ferryboat, the *Scotia Prince*, which carried passengers from the Portland docks north to Nova Scotia. The lights of the big boat bobbed and blinked in the distance. The night ocean was so close that the waves crashing against the rocks sent foam spraying over the porch railing and into our faces. Later Ruth and I went for a night walk along the road bordered by pink, fragrant beach roses and wild bayberry. A wedding reception was taking place in the inn's main lodge, and a slightly drunk man dressed in a cream-colored suit, his tie loosened at the neck, had come out for some air. He leaned against his car smoking a cigarette, his head craned so far back that his Adam's apple and neck exposed themselves in a vulnerable white arc. His mouth was agape. As we passed, he spoke to us breathlessly, like a child having just made a discovery. "There are so many stars!" he said. "You can't see them in New Jersey." We left him with his head tilted back, gazing upward, his cigarette tip glowing orange in the dark.

Maine is a dark place on the map of the United States. It is mostly trees, rocks, water, wild creatures, hills, and sky. The land's eastern and southeastern edges are cut by ocean waves and foam. Rolling blueberry and potato fields, swamps, lakes, ponds, and great swaths of forest cover the interior. Only 1.2 million people live in Maine— forty-one persons for every square mile of land. The state's population ranks tenth from the bottom nationwide. A look at the Maine map shows a moderately peopled coastline and a somewhat lesser-peopled southern and western interior fading slowly into wilderness in the north—to Mount Katahdin, to the Allagash, to millions of acres of logging land owned predominantly by paper companies. At night Maine is as dark as the Rockies, as dark as the Great Lakes, as dark as the deserts of the West. The greater Portland area, with just over half a million residents, is the state's biggest metropolis, home to more than 40 percent of its residents, and, so far, the only city large enough to disturb this darkness.

Ruth and I lived in woods so dense that if we had not launched a project to cut down some of the trees around us and use them for firewood, we'd have no sunshine for our weedy lawn, full of wild strawberries, dandelions, and wildflowers; no sun for our perennial flower beds or our vegetable gardens. Our houseplants would suffer even in the windows. We were surrounded by a small log- and stump-filled "meadow" where our goats grazed and, beyond that, a still-thick forest of maple, oak, birch, beech, hop hornbeam, and ash. The house was a small Cape, with a steep roof, a door in the middle, and a window on each side. You reached it via a curving stone pathway. It was the kind of house you might expect a child to draw at school, on a big sheet of white paper with crayons, a curl of smoke snaking up from a red brick chimney in the roof's center, a nuclear family holding hands off to the side.

There was a porch light to the left of the granite steps as you approached the house, but we almost always left it off in the summer, as it attracted moths, mosquitoes, june bugs, and other insects to the door, and when we entered they slipped inside to flutter and bump against the lampshades and whine annoyingly in our ears as we tried to sleep. On summer nights we approached the house in the dark. We parked the car on the dirt and gravel pad at the end of the driveway, and as the light inside the car faded, we were left in near total blackness. As our eyes adjusted, the house came into view, with only the faint glow of the light from the bulb above the stove shining through from the back of the house to the front windows. The large, full-topped beech tree to the left of the walkway came into hulking shape, as did the barn at the end of the yard. The gray pathway stones emerged. We walked slowly to the door, carrying an empty bowl, say, from a potluck with friends, or groceries picked up late on the way home, and as we stepped carefully along the uneven stones, we looked up at the sky to see a milky litter of stars unknown to us but also some that were our familiar friends—Ursa Major and Ursa Minor, Polaris, Draco, Cassiopeia, and Cygnus the giant swan.

One June a friend from New Delhi, India, visited us. He had been staying for almost a week already, delighting in helping me till the vegetable garden, plant beans, mow the lawn, drive our pickup truck recklessly in small circles on the grass in front of the barn, collect fresh milk from the farm down the road and from it make delicious, creamy Indian rice pudding with cardamom and raisins. He often took pleasure in teasing us about being vitamin-fed Americans with all the attendant arrogance and privilege of our nationality, race, and class, but in time he softened a bit when he saw how hard we worked at growing our own food organically; recycling our paper, cans, and bottles; saving kitchen scraps and lawn clippings for the compost pile. With the farm down the road and the garden in the yard, the life we led had more in common than he had imagined with the lives of others who lived in less well-developed places in the world. One night Sudip and I returned to the house from dinner at a restaurant in nearby Wilton. As we made our way up the dark walk, he stopped for a moment and looked around, stretching out his hands as if to feel the night. "The night is so black," he said, finally. "So black. This could actually be my boyhood village in Bihar." Years later he confessed that when I had left him alone in the house for a few nights, he wasn't so much frightened by the far-off calls of owls and coyotes as he was of the dark silence.

Darkness brought a sense of danger, yet it also brought brilliance and joy. In late summer the tall fields of grass surrounding our house and the home of our good friends in nearby Chesterville hummed and buzzed with insects all day long. The fields were home to milkweed, fern, black-eyed Susan, daisies, sweet pea, clover, and all manner of other tall, waving plants, whose seeds and nectar would be harvested by birds, bees, and butterflies until fall, when the owner of the land would have his hired man come with a tractor and cut the fields so they would not become grown over with saplings and blackberry bushes. On the edge of the mown lawn, where the tall grass began, our friends had built a sauna from an old corn crib. We regularly spent evenings there, in winter and summer, bathing companionably and, depending on the season, leaping into the fresh snow or washing off under a portable shower hung on a nail outside the door. Afterward we went into the house for supper and stayed, usually, well into the night, talking of the news of the day.

On one such night our friend Doug, who had taken the dogs out before they bedded down for the night, called to us urgently: "Everybody outside. Hurry up. Now!" We all jumped to our feet, afraid that part of the house was on fire or that there had been an accident at the intersection down past their mailbox. Silently, he beckoned us to the front of the house, and then he gestured for us to look into the nearby field. What we saw against the dark background of the trees on the far edge of the meadow took our breath away. There were thousands of tiny lights. So thick were the clouds of fireflies that they seemed like illuminated raindrops filling the sky. They flickered on and off, diving and rising, settling on blades of grass and taking off again, creating great, gentle curlicues of light. The whole field, as far as we could see, all the way back to the stone walls, was glittering, sparkling, shimmering, twinkling. It was enough to make one believe in fairies, or help one imagine why fairies have been believed in. The dancing lights. The unexplained luminescence.

The second spring we spent in our house in the woods was the spring of the foxes. We discovered them first when we saw the small fuzzy fox kits sunning themselves on a gray boulder beside the road near the end of our steep driveway. We would drive by, the car window down, staring foolishly, and the kits would stare back, their eyes sleepy and lazy and their bodies limp from the warmth of the sun. Once I went to investigate the boulder more closely and found a deep, cool, dark hole dug beneath one end of the rock, a great pile of loose dirt and small bones at the mouth, the inside smelling of roots and earth and wild animal. Later, as the foxes began to wander farther from home, we would encounter the kits, bigger now and even more delightfully fluffy and red, playing in the driveway—tumbling in the dirt, rolling over one another, biting each other's ears and necks. In the mornings we found little piles of fox scat on the stone pathway leading to the house and even on the granite steps at the front door. It excited us, and slightly unnerved us, to think of the foxes out at night, exploring our yard, peering into our windows.

Fox kits in
the driveway

One night before bed, as I was about to shut off the last of the lights and take my tea up to read, I saw a small fur-rimmed face in the glass beside the door. The face was lit by the lights from the room, but beyond that all was dark. I saw perfectly shaped triangle ears still slightly soft around the edges, a black nose at the end of a rounded, puppyish snout, whiskers, and clear eyes in which the last lamplight of the house shone back. I called for Ruth to come and see, but at the sound of my voice the little fox ran away.

Later that night, after we had both fallen deeply asleep, we were awoken by a terrifying scream. We sat bolt upright in our beds. Again it came. And again, louder each time. We stepped quickly to the open window thinking we were witness to a murder. We were so frightened by the noise that I grabbed the baseball bat that stood in a corner beside the bed. The screams began at the back of a throat and gurgled and rose as if caught up in a flow of blood. A friend told us later that the cry was most likely from a fisher—well known, apparently, for its blood-curdling call; either that or a fox marking its territory. There was one final scream that night, and then the sound of shuffling leaves, the slight breaking of branches, and whatever unseen thing it was, was gone.

Woodsqueer II

We didn't generate much garbage at the Three O'Clock Cat Farm. Everything from waxed milk cartons to bacon grease seemed to have a second life in our world, so it was not often that I hauled the trash to the bottom of the steep driveway for pickup by the town of Jay. When I did, I'd put the big blue plastic bin in the garden cart and wheel it down, leaning back hard on the handles so the cart would not get away from me and careen down the driveway onto East Jay Road. I'd park it off to the side of the drive where in the winter it would be out of the way of the plow, and where in early summer lupine and wild daisies bloomed on the hill. I never worried about the cart being stolen. I left it with the bin in it until I was ready to push it back up the drive and set the empty bin back in its place in a corner of the barn.

One day when I went to retrieve the cart and empty bin I noticed strange drawings on its side. I had walked across the road to grab the mail from our large rural delivery box, the kind with the red flag that you lift to let the mail carrier know you have letters to send, and I noticed similar drawings on the mailbox and its wooden post. Upon closer inspection, I discovered them to be erect cartoon penises with sets of hairy testicles attached, scrawled in thick marker. Some had little squirts of sperm popping out of their heads.

I could have been amused, I could have been angry, but instead I was afraid. This was during the last time Maine went through a statewide vote on whether to allow same-sex couples to marry, the second since we'd moved to the state in 2000. Maine first prohibited discrimination based on sexual orientation in its Human Rights Act in 2005, and efforts to take it out of the act were immediate but failed. Maine first allowed domestic partnerships between same-sex couples in 2009, but the law was overturned in a people's veto referendum before it even took effect. The measure went on the state ballot again in 2012 and passed with 52 percent of votes. So, for the time being anyway, queer Mainers had civil rights protections and the right to wed, although there always seemed to be someone who wanted to make us illegal.

Ruth and I had supported the first effort by volunteer phone canvassing. The second time around we had a sign at the end of the driveway supporting marriage equality that read "Vote Yes on One." We had debated putting the sign out, afraid it would draw negative attention, but we decided to do it anyway. Such a small thing and yet, because we were lesbians in rural Maine, we felt trepidation. I won't say we were courageous to put a sign out, but it did entail a certain amount of reckoning with possible consequences. It occurred to me that the penises on the garbage bin and mailbox might have been a response to our sign. Our neighbors at the end of the road, whom we considered our friends, had a sign in their yard that urged voters in the opposite direction from ours: "Marriage is between one man and one woman." Their sign made us feel, at best, unwelcome and a little betrayed.

"They know we're lesbians, right?" I asked Ruth.

"I'm sure they do," she said.

How could anyone know us and not want us to have the right to get married, I innocently thought. *We're so nice. And so normal.*

"Do you think they put their sign out because we put our sign out? Whose sign was first?" I asked Ruth, in what was the beginning of a long discussion about the efficacy and ethics of political signs. Were

signs meant to advertise personal political opinions, to change people's minds, or to engage in ideological warfare with your neighbors?

In the context of what was going on in the state, the graffiti on
the garbage can and mailbox felt threatening. I thought I knew who
had done it. One of our neighbor's boys was a bit of a rascal. But, of
course, I couldn't be sure, and I didn't know where it might lead if I
approached his parents. I took pictures of the drawings and decided
to ask our lesbian and gay friends for advice. Their reactions ranged
from calling the police to doing nothing.

Our gay pediatrician friend, who practiced at the local hospital,
convinced me to wait and see what might happen next. "Boys get in
that stage where they just need to draw penises on things," he said.
He advised me to save the pictures I took, to scrub off the drawings,
and not to call the cops or to talk to the parents of the presumed
ringleader. I followed his advice. I rubbed off what I could of the
drawings, leaving a faint, stubborn trace behind. Nothing more came
of it, but it was a taste, a rare one thankfully, of what it felt like to be
singled out, otherized, noticed, harassed for being different, for being
queer.

Mostly, Ruth and I enjoyed an incredible amount of safety and
privilege in our rural community. We didn't experience racial prejudice; we were white in a state that tied with Vermont as the whitest
in the nation, and we had not personally been the target of Maine's
infamous historical prejudice against French Canadians. We were in
good physical and mental health, well insured, and well employed in
a state that ranks among the fifteen poorest in the nation. A broad
circle of friends and acquaintances had our back. We also did a good
job blending in fashion-wise; we tended toward jeans, flannel shirts,
fleece vests, and work boots, which was, as one friend joked, the way
just about every person in rural Maine dressed. Most of the time we
went about being who we were, but occasionally we were reminded

that we were different—we were lesbians in a heteronormative world. The political signs and the graffiti on the trash bin brought back, for both of us, all the old cultural messages—that gays and lesbians and other people who don't fit into our heterosexual norm are weird, wrong, bad, sinful, crazy, sick, threatening, and predatory. At times like this, despite all the years of good work and good living, my own internalized homophobia would come creeping back out of the shadows, and then I would feel a little sick and a little afraid, like maybe there was something wrong with me after all and I didn't deserve what "normal" people had.

When we first moved to rural Maine we lived in a big, hundred-plus-year-old farmhouse that we rented for a year from a couple who lived in Boston. Before we signed the contract, at Ruth's urging, I told our soon-to-be landlord on the phone, "We just wanted you to know we're a lesbian couple and hope you don't have any concerns about that." Before I'd even finished the sentence, she said, "Oh my, no. Some of my best friends are gay." Later one of my new colleagues told me that she'd gotten a call from the landlord asking what kind of lesbians we were. What were her worries? That we would show up on our Harleys with our Dykes on Bikes gang? Walk around naked, our hairy legs and armpits exposed? Host women's music festivals in the back field?

It didn't take us long to find the lesbian and gay community in Farmington once we moved there. Shopping in town during the first two weeks after our move, I found a flyer stuck behind the windshield wiper of our Subaru advertising an upcoming queer "Out to Dinner" potluck. We'd been part of the lesbian feminist potluck sing-along scene in Anchorage, where we spent the first two years of our relationship, and we were delighted to be welcomed into another gay community. That first evening we met at the home of D. and J., a longtime gay couple. Talk that night was partly about that earlier marriage equality referendum. After that first potluck we attended many others, where we could relax in the company of people who "got us," around whom we could kiss, hold hands, talk about our relationship, and listen to stories of other gay and lesbian, queer and trans lives.

Another scene Ruth and I enjoyed in Anchorage was a monthly dance organized by a friend who loved to two-step. Katie rented a meeting hall with a smooth wooden floor, bought cases of sparkling water and soda, set up a sound system and twinkly lights, and created playlists of the latest country-western line dance and two-step music. Those of us who liked to dance, or who just wanted some lesbian community, put on our cowgirl boots and dancing shoes and headed to the meeting hall, dropped ten dollars in the basket at the top of the stairs to cover the cost of rent, a buck each for a soft drink, and

Potluck summer table

danced the night away. Wanting to re-create that sense of community in Maine, Ruth organized a dance to celebrate my birthday. It was November. We put up signs around town and passed information by word of mouth. When the night came, we expected a small crowd and were completely shocked by all the queer folk who literally came out of the woods. A favorite that night was "YMCA" by the Village People. A new friend and faculty member at the university led the well-known routine of movements that go with the song. We discovered that at least three lesbian couples who came to the dance lived on our road or nearby.

The potluck and the dances waned and were replaced in part by weekly gatherings at a restaurant and annual gatherings at friends' houses, including "Lesbian Thanksgiving," always hosted by the same dear friend at her house in the woods. We brought our favorite seasonal dishes and shared them family-style at a long table made of several tables pushed together, covered with a tablecloth and dotted with candles. Sometimes these events included special queer-friendly allies, but mostly the gatherings were just for our small community of woodsqueers.

Another annual gathering that we celebrated with our rural queer community was a summer affair where our gang met at a local inn for cocktails on the rustic deck followed by delicious food at our own very long table on the screened porch overlooking the lake, the pine-scented breeze blowing through. There was also the Left Bank of the Sandy River Lesbian and Gay Cultural Salon, which was a fancy term for reading group. The group moved from house to house every other month or so. We'd gather to eat good food, enjoy a glass of wine or a beer, and discuss a film or book or issue that was on the top of our minds. We watched classic lesbian films like *I Heard the Mermaid Singing, Entre Nous, Desert of the Heart,* and *Carol.* We read classic works of lesbian literature: Djuna Barnes's *Nightwood,* Patricia

Highsmith's *The Price of Salt*, Alma Routsong's *Patience and Sarah*, Tove Jansson's *Fair Play*, and Radclyffe Hall's *The Well of Loneliness*. For the Radclyffe Hall event our host asked us to dress in the male or female drag of Hall's era—late Victorian, early Edwardian. One friend came in a floor-length mink coat with strings of pearls and a period hat. Ruth's clothes and makeup were so convincing, and her physique already so masculine, that our host wasn't sure who I had brought with me. Ruth, with her muscled body and thin hips and sweet boyish face, had always been able to pass, while my softness and roundness gave me away, despite my tweed sport coat, bow tie, wingtip shoes, and twill trousers.

The playfulness of trying to pass has always intrigued me. I've reflected many times on this, wondering if there was a part of me that wanted to be male and whether being a lesbian really was, like they say, some kind of deep body dysphoria. I always came to the same conclusion: I felt female and liked being female. The only reason I ever wanted to "be a man" was so that I could be in love with women. When I was a girl, like so many other lesbian youth, I knew I was different but wasn't sure how. I tentatively explored the word "lesbian" in the dictionary, although who knows how I even knew to attach myself to that word at such a young age. What I found in there did not sound like me; I wasn't sick or deviant, as far as I knew. Since I wasn't *that*, I concluded that the only way I could live out my feelings of attraction for women was by being male. And since I wasn't *that* either, I was left to live in an uncomfortable liminal zone. Until I finally came out, in my thirties, I believed that all women felt as I did, pulled toward their own sex but acquiescing to the norms of heterosexuality and carrying on despite what was, at best, ambivalence. Later, after I came out, everything changed. I discovered there really was such a thing as a lesbian, that I was one, and that some other women were decidedly not. Once I realized that I could be a woman and love women romantically and sexually, my life began anew. I was not a failed heterosexual, but a lesbian. Now, of course, there are many more options for us all in terms of expressing our gender and our sexuality, although none of them are risk-free, and they are always under scrutiny by the self-proclaimed gatekeepers of morality.

Even with all the joy and camaraderie of our small queer community in rural Maine, even with our community-building efforts and our support for one another, there was fear. Most of us were out in our jobs and personal lives. We were out in the community, gathering weekly for years at a local restaurant where anyone paying any attention knew exactly who we were. But there was still a very real sense of vulnerability and a need to stay not quite hidden, but just under the radar. At one of our salons, excited about a memoir we'd discussed, I asked those gathered what they thought about putting together an anthology of stories from our group about what it was like to be queer in rural Maine. It would be so exciting and important, I went on, thrilled by my idea. We could all tell our stories!

Naïvely, I wasn't prepared for the negative response from my friends, who thought the idea too self-revealing and possibly dangerous. What was I thinking? Again, as with the penis graffiti on the garbage cans and mailbox, I became afraid, and again the internalized homophobia came crawling back out of the darkness, opportunistic, always looking for a way to slither into my consciousness and encourage me to be invisible.

While Ruth and I hauled and stacked and lifted and shoveled and pounded and hammered around our farm, rassling goats, mending fences, chainsawing trees, splitting wood, painting the windowsills and barn doors, making furniture, planting beans, cleaning the chicken coop, mowing the lawn, digging compost—doing what one friend (and my mother, too) called "man's work"—I often thought how marvelous it was for two women to be able to live like this, knowing that whatever needed doing, they could mostly manage. We didn't need men to have complete and full lives, but sometimes we did need an extra pair of hands or a big machine. When that was the case, we engaged our friend Jack the excavator or Darrell the wood-cutter and hay hauler and his goat-and-chicken-sitting daughters. Sometimes Amy came to help mow, or Mary came to help clean. Our neighbor with the snowplow, Gene, helped us out in the winter. Our friends Doug and Judy and Dave and Jen loaned us their chop saws and sanders and pitched in on building projects. Mark came once a season with a truckload of manure, and another neighbor with a big tractor tilled the manure into the soil.

Ruth and I had our own division of labor. I took care of most of the finances and things that had to do with talking on the phone to insurance companies or banks. I kept our social calendar and did most of the shopping. I made pies. Ruth made bread. I was the writer. She was the musician. We both worked in the garden, although me more than her. We both put food by at harvest time. We both cooked and cleaned, although I liked cleaning more than her and she was better at cooking meat than I was. Ruth was the fixer of things, our own home maintenance handyperson whose skills as an electrician, painter, carpenter, and mechanic saved us thousands of dollars over the years. Her sometimes tidy, sometimes chaotic work bench in the basement included tools she won for being Vermont's Electrical Apprentice of the Year way back when. We made a good team, the two of us in our home in the woods. It was a good queer life. And oh, by the way, the penises on the mailbox and trash bin eventually faded with time.

Lesbian Wedding I

Come live with me and be my love,
And we will all the pleasures prove
That Valleys, groves, hills, and fields,
Woods, or steepy mountain yields.

— Christopher Marlowe,
"The Passionate Shepherd to His Love"

We called it our boat anniversary. It was one of many anniversaries that we'd created to mark our journey together. The first was our "laying of eyes" anniversary, named for when we first encountered each other in the Heavy Shop at McMurdo Station in Antarctica on August 30. Then there was the "come live with me" anniversary, for when I asked Ruth to come live with me in Alaska, wooing her from aboard a scientific research vessel in the Ross Sea by reciting, from heart, the Christopher Marlowe poem "The Passionate Shepherd" on January 6.

The boat anniversary, though, marked the beginning of our commitment to each other. It was our first lesbian wedding. Each year we tried to spend our boat anniversary on or near water, because it was on an island in Green River Reservoir in Vermont that we built a shoebox-sized birchbark boat that ritually launched our relationship. The boat was glued together with pine pitch and carefully laden with moss and symbolic objects: wild leeks, a poem written on paper-thin birchbark, wildflowers, a candle, and a loon feather.

The night remains vivid in our imaginations. We'd been together only a little while at that point. We had met in Antarctica, at the bottom of the world, in the highest, driest, windiest, coldest place on the planet, where I had been a writer with the National Science Foundation Artists and Writers Program, and Ruth had been an electrician and fire alarm technician at McMurdo Station. When my fellowship ended and Ruth's job on the ice was over, we headed our separate ways but were drawn back together by what felt like a gravitational pull. I had asked her to come live with me in Alaska, where I was a university professor, and she had said yes. After the school year in Alaska was over, I flew out to meet Ruth in Vermont, and we began our epic journey across the United States in her red pickup truck to set up house together in Anchorage, where we would live for two years before moving to Maine, where Ruth could be closer to her family. Before we headed to Alaska though, Ruth wanted to show me Green River Reservoir and some of her other beloved Vermont haunts.

Our campsite on the island was one Ruth was familiar with. She'd camped there with friends and previous lesbian loves. She'd also spent an idyllic summer there alone once, sometimes topless, sometimes completely naked, feeding herself with fresh fish and the few supplies she'd brought. Ruth relayed these stories as we paddled out to the island, unpacked our gear, set up a roomy tent, unrolled our sleeping pads and bags, and laid out our camp cooking gear, working to make a cozy and efficient site for our several-day stay.

It was on our second afternoon that we decided to build the boat. We worked quietly and companionably, collecting birchbark and pine pitch, improvising a way to stitch the boat together with thin strips of wood and vine, lifting soft hunks of bright green moss from the forest floor to line the boat's interior, searching for ritual items to lay within it (a red candle, a loon feather, a wild leek, a small hemlock cone, an acorn), and composing our vows.

At nightfall, we paddled our canoe into the dark lake, lit the red candle, and set our tiny boat adrift. Back on shore, we sat beside our fire, ringed by candles of different colors arranged around us in a wide circle. Each candle symbolized an element of our relationship: yellow for optimism and joy, green for good luck, blue for tranquility, red for passion. Ruth played and sang on her guitar.

From our enchanted fireside, we watched the little boat we'd made through the trees. It moved back and forth on the water, in and out of our view. We covered our eyes when the candle flame seemed to fade, only to uncover them and glimpse the boat again, a small bright light in the pitch-dark. Miraculously the candle stayed lit. We fantasized that the boat made its way to the reservoir outlet and eventually all the way to the sea.

What promises did we make to each other on the edge of the lake in the deep forest in the night? The piece of birchbark upon which we wrote our vows has been misplaced. I can imagine that we were wary of being too traditional and were careful not to make promises we could not really keep. But we were carried away by our new love then. Our moss-lined birch boat held the best of our intentions—and also our crazy hopes and dreams. Its candle had not blown out, even as the little craft floated on the windy night lake. That had to be an omen, a good one, we thought.

After we had left Antarctica and before meeting again in the United States, Ruth and I traveled briefly in New Zealand, kayaking and hiking and enjoying the green, snowless warmth of that very un-Antarctic country. One of our forays took us by bus into the countryside. Ruth had fallen asleep on my shoulder, and when she woke, her face soft and flushed, her brown eyes alert and bright, she looked out the window at a steep-roofed cottage set back from the road, smoke curling up from its stone chimney. "We'll have a house like that someday," she said. "It'll be perfect." We smiled broadly at each other. Yes, we agreed. It would be perfect!

"Perfect" became our favorite exclamation for anything good. As it turned out, our home together on the farm in Maine did look an awful lot like that New Zealand cottage, with its center door, two front windows framed by old-fashioned shutters, its brick chimney and steeply pitched roof. And it did turn out to be perfect, which does not mean flawless or without trouble or effort.

As the night of our wild lesbian wedding went on, we continued to watch our homemade boat with its candle flicker in and out of sight as it sailed, blocked from our view at times by the dark shapes of the trees on the shore. Barred owls began to call loudly in the night woods, their weird and chilling call strangely domesticated by bird lovers who say it sounds like "who cooks, who cooks, who cooks for you?" And then we heard footsteps. In moments when the wind, the owls, and the crackling of the fire quieted, we heard soft but distinct footfalls on the leaves in the woods behind us. The footsteps were circling us and the fire. A cougar? A deer? A human? A spirit? Bravely, I went to check, turning on my headlamp and peering into the trees. "Hey!" I yelled. The footsteps stopped. Whatever it was, it gave us a chill and drew us closer together around the fire.

For many years that night was our fairy tale. There was beauty and magic, danger and mystery, and we felt protected by the powerful ring of light and fire that was our love.

WITH THE ANIMALS

The Barn at Midnight

If I conferred with our furry friends, man to animal,
Think of the amazing repartee
If I could walk with the animals, talk with the animals,
Grunt and squeak and squawk with the animals,
And they could squeak and squawk and speak and talk to me
What a lovely place the world would be.

— Rex Harrison in *Doctor Dolittle*

I've been known to sleep in the barn with my animals, especially on Christmas Eve. Sometimes I would lie down in a clean stable on a bed of fresh hay or sleep in the hayloft, my bedding and pillow laid comfortably across several big rectangular bales, a thermos of tea by my side. On those winter nights with the snow piled high in the pasture and the field, weighing down the rooftops, pressing firmly against the earth itself, the moon half aglow in the sky, the shadow-arms of the beech tree would reach across the pillowy lawn all the way to the dark edge of the woods. Inside, I would wait. What did the goats and their babies, the barn cats, the hens and rooster do in the barn when the clock struck twelve on that inspirited night, when a certain kind of goodness was said to have been born into this world? Did a sweet blanket of serenity and equanimity fall? Did some inexpressible joining occur? Was there magic? Did the animals talk?

From a young age I had a keen sense that something about this human life was only half-known, partly realized, just out of reach.

I told my mother that when I grew up I'd be either a world traveler with many lovers, or a nun, thinking these would be the best vocations for someone who wanted to thoroughly grasp both the physical world and the world of the spirit and the heart. I instinctively felt that animals could help me unravel the secrets to this thing called life, so who better to fall in love with and choose as my mentor than Dr. Dolittle, as played by Rex Harrison in the 1967 film?

Dr. Dolittle was a nice man. He was funny. He was an iconoclast. He didn't want to be a people doctor, so he became a doctor of animals, learning, with the help of his parrot friend Polynesia, five hundred animal languages from alligator to zebra. He cured a mouse with a crooked tail and a fox kit with flat feet, and he even made a pair of eyeglasses for a horse. Of course, few people in Puddleby-on-the-Marsh, the village where he lived in England, believed the doctor could really talk to animals. His special enemy was the narrow-minded mayor, who lacked all imagination and thought anyone who believed he could talk to animals must be insane, and so Dr. Dolittle was committed to an asylum. He was rescued, thanks to Polynesia, and off the doctor went on an ocean voyage to find and learn the language of the giant pink snail.

In our house, when I was a child, thanks to our father's research interests and our mother's tolerance for mess and chaos, we had many animals: a cat (sometimes with kittens), a small box turtle or two that would roam freely about the house, a fish tank full of guppies and fat goldfish, another tank full of baby turtles, a terrarium that was home to horny toads, small and large lizards and various snakes, a hamster in a cage in the back hall, and usually a larger tortoise or two clipped to a chain in the backyard. Inspired by Dr. Dolittle, I would put on one of my father's white lab coats, hang a stethoscope around my neck, and, with a clipboard and pencil, make daily rounds to feed and check the health of the animals. I thought then that I might grow up to be, if not a world traveler or a nun, a veterinarian like Dr. Dolittle, or that I might go into the jungle like Dian Fossey and Jane Goodall and make friends with gorillas and chimpanzees, or I'd be Marlin Perkins's field assistant on the TV show *Mutual of Omaha's Wild Kingdom*. I wanted a furry, trustworthy confidant like Lassie, like Gentle Ben, like Brighty, that devoted and courageous little donkey that I learned about through Marguerite Henry's *Brighty of the Grand Canyon*. I wanted to connect.

What was appealing about Dr. Dolittle, besides his love for animals and his gentleness, was his claim that humans and animals were more alike than different, something I sensed as a child and seem to have never outgrown. In court, defending himself against the charge of insanity, Dolittle sang, "Well, it's true. We do not live in a zoo, but man is an animal too." I also cherished the doctor for his unshakeable belief in things other people thought were ridiculous, things they could neither see nor hear. To a child with common sense and an active imagination, that humans could indeed talk to animals was a self-evident truth.

Now, on the other side of childhood, I no longer thought of *Doctor Dolittle* as a simple movie to indulge the imaginations of children. I saw it as a narrative about how desperately human beings long to make sense of the world and find their proper place in the family of things. Western culture, broadly speaking, regards animals, the body, nature, as just stuff that exists—just *matter*; it doesn't speak per se, or make knowledge, or represent itself. It just is. On the other hand, humans, by virtue of their capacity for language and logic, don't just exist; they know. If animals and other supposedly nonsentient beings were not just things but also knowers, if they could talk and we could understand them, what would they tell us? Would we learn that we are less alone than we think? Would we learn, as the doctor said, that we are animals too? Then what would happen? Practically everything we'd ever thought was true would have to be reconsidered.

Dr. Dolittle's detractors, even as they ridiculed and tormented him, probably longed for this connection between their knowing selves and their animal selves, though they would never admit to such a thing. There seemed to be something shameful about adults wanting to talk to animals, something shameful about admitting there is a hole inside your heart that longed to be filled by connection to other living things, be they flowers, trees, cats, parrots, chickens, goats, or giant pink snails.

As my favorite American philosopher, Henry David Thoreau, writes in "Walking," this unaddressed longing for connection to nature and the shame over wanting it has produced a people disconnected from themselves and the natural world, a people divorced from their own animalness, their own humanness. "Here," he writes, "is this vast, savage, howling mother of ours, Nature, lying all around, with such beauty, and such affection for her children, as the leopard; and yet we are so early weaned from her breast to society, to that culture which is exclusively an interaction of man on man—a sort of breeding in and in."

Thoreau extolls the virtues of spending time out of society, out of doors, in the company of trees, swamps, mountains, fields, and animals. This is where a different but equally true knowledge might lie, a knowledge that did not insist, like Dr. Dolittle's tormentors did, on what we call fact. Thoreau called this "Beautiful Knowledge," "wild and dusky knowledge," "mother-wit," "a knowledge useful in a higher sense," and advocated for its celebration in the creation of a Society for the Diffusion of Useful Ignorance. After all, he wrote, "a man's ignorance sometimes is not only useful, but beautiful—while his knowledge, so called, is oftentimes worse than useless, besides being ugly." Perhaps we should strive not for Knowledge with a capital *K*, Thoreau wrote, but for "Sympathy and Intelligence." Perhaps the highest knowledge is not Knowledge at all but an awareness of our own ignorance—our sudden surprise when we learn that "there are more things in heaven and earth than are dreamed of in [our] philosophy."

Polynesia, Dr. Dolittle's parrot, taught him early on that animals talk differently than humans. "Most animal languages are a mixture of sounds and movement," Polynesia told him, and "animals don't always speak with their mouths. They talk with their ears, with their feet, with their tails—with everything." Is the soft guttural murmuring of a goat as it nibbles its bowl of morning grain animal talk? The choral howling of coyotes in the dark? The snort of a large buck once it gets wind of human scent? The excited wagging tail of a pet dog when its owner comes home at the end of a day? The meow of the cat whose food bowl is empty? Is an animal ever not in its body?

Don't humans, too, want to talk with their whole bodies, as Polynesia said the animals do? How I envied the animals this, and how I regretted the splitting that happened to me, a girl-child growing up in a family, in a culture, where living in the head was preferable to inhabiting the body—unruly, needy, illogical, and loud as it was. Patches, one of mine and Ruth's goats, a strong and handsome wether, was a great teacher, his gift to me his muscular frame, his soft, glossy brown and black fur, his bright eyes, and his eagerness for the hay and grain I delivered each morning. *Yes!* he said as he reared up on his hind legs, pounding his hooves against the stall door, demanding and joyful. *Yes, yes, yes!*

Our relationship to animals brings up some of the most troubling questions we wrestle with as human beings. What makes a human a human and an animal an animal? Research on animal sentience is like Dr. Dolittle's Pushmi-Pullyu, an animal that looks like a llama with a head on each end. On the one end, learned animal behaviorists have evidence that animals communicate with humans and with one another, have predictable languages, lead complex emotional lives experiencing fear, hope, love, sadness, rage, compassion, and even aesthetic appreciation and a sense of justice. On the other end are scientists who claim that most of the research supporting animal sentience is anecdotal, that the researchers themselves suffer from a bad case of anthropomorphism—projecting human emotions and values onto animals. Animals, some behavioral scientists say, are just stimulus-response mechanisms; when they exhibit what looks to us like fear, it is not an emotion but a stimulus response—push button A, and B happens. According to this theory, a moose killed on the highway may moan and roll its eyes backward, but that does not mean it is giving voice to pain or fear.

The truth is scientists just don't know—yet. They can't say for sure whether an ape can tell a joke, something that requires learned language as opposed to mere communication. Do birdcalls, prairie dog squeaks, elephant trumpets, bee dances, whale clicks, and dolphin sonar constitute language, or are they simple instinctual vocalizations relaying the most basic information about food, sex, and survival? Every day researchers come up with new evidence that animal communication is more sophisticated than previously believed. It's suggested that human language is part of an evolutionary continuum; the link that would solve the puzzle of how animal communication became human language is still missing.

It was hard for me not to think of the gestures of animals, the noises they make, their habits, the tracks they leave in the mud and snow as language of a kind. The forest, after all, was full of animal messages that were as compelling and clear as any written text—signs of rabbit and grouse and wild turkey, deer prints and those of bobcat and coyote. The scent of fox was unmistakable. Neat little piles of pulled-apart pine cones meant a squirrel had a good meal atop a stump. A ruffled-up forest floor devoid of acorns meant flocks of turkeys had come and gone. Ragged holes in aging pines meant a woodpecker had been at work, pounding away in search of insects. In the fall I looked for raw scratches on forest saplings where male deer had rubbed their sharp antlers, marking territory, leaving messages for female deer, along with the accompanying bare patches in the ground where the bucks scraped away the leaves and forest debris and left their scent. The forest landscape was like a book that could be read.

So it was in the barnyard too. With their voices and their gestures, animals seemed easy to talk to, easy to understand. They communicated perfectly. There had been many a time when the change in tone of a goat's bleating voice alerted me to something unusual, and when I went to see what was wrong I found a new baby with its hoof wrapped in a stray piece of wire or discovered that another had gotten out of the stall and had its nose in the grain bin and the others were jealously ratting him out, or that one had its head caught in the page-wire fence. A goat who seemed agitated, who was wagging her tail back and forth and bleating in yet another, different tone, signaled that she was in heat and ready for breeding. There was also the language of the terrified, exhausted doe in the final push of labor, confused and in pain, and the voice that came later, after the baby was born—contented murmuring as she licked the little one dry of blood and birthing fluid.

I had always been suspicious of the term "anthropomorphism," especially when it was used as a pejorative to suggest that anyone who might attribute human characteristics or behavior to an animal was no better than a fool. But why not? Why not believe that the doe was agitated because her baby was being strangled by a piece of fencing wire? Why not believe that she knew, on some level, that if she made a certain kind of sound one of those humans would come running?

Why not believe that the cat was annoyed with me and was being petulant about its empty bowl? Why not believe that the chicken emerging from the laying box and setting up that raucous cackling was joyfully announcing to all the world, "I just laid an egg!"

Fantasies they might be, hopeful soarings of imagination, but this is what led me into the barn at midnight, where I hoped I might find at least a thread of that something I sensed missing in life even in my childhood. What did happen in the barn at midnight? Was there magic? Did the baby goats dream of the day they were born, diving head and front hooves first, launching themselves from a watery sac in their mother's belly into a sea of fresh hay, to be licked clean and dry, to find a long pink teat for the first time in their lives, to taste their mother's milk? Did the chickens, in their dreams, recall their preexistence inside the egg, their feathers wet and folded in upon themselves so as to fit it all—wings, feet, beak, head and breast, tiny black eyes—in that yolky, ovoid house? Did they remember what it was like to be tucked under their mother's wings, against her breast, and how comforting it was to know that, whatever startled them or attempted to harm them, she would be there to open her wings and gather them under herself? Did they remember their first blade of grass, their first ant, their first sip of water, their first breath of air?

In those unguarded hours when their bodies were at rest and undefended, the animals did talk, yes, and there was a joining. The goats and chickens spoke in their sleepy repositionings of limb and head and feather. The hay spoke with its fresh scent, and so did the goat hair and dung. The chill of the winter barn spoke, and so did the comfort of animal heat. Awake in the night, I turned in my sleeping bag, on my bed of hay. Moonshine spoke through the goat door. There were soft murmurings and chewings, mouse feet, a cat's rhythmic purr, the hiss of hot pee, a burp of digestion, and at dawn, the rooster's call.

With the Animals

I think I could turn and live with animals, they are so placid and self-contain'd,
I stand and look at them long and long...
Not one is dissatisfied, not one is demented with the mania of owning things,
Not one kneels to another, nor to his kind that lived thousands of years ago,
Not one is respectable or unhappy over the whole earth.
So they show their relations to me and I accept them,
They bring me tokens of myself, they evince them plainly in their possession.

— Walt Whitman, "Song of Myself"

First, I gathered supplies: the shiny, stainless-steel bucket, the old yogurt container of warm water, the sponge, the paper towels, peppermint oil, an aerosol can of blue antiseptic spray. I was already dressed for the barn in a pair of old jeans and a shirt selected from a tall, folded stack of clean work clothes in the bottom of the closet. As I went out the door, I pulled on rubber boots and my brown canvas barn coat. Balancing the warm water and sponge, the milking pail, the paper towels, and the oil, I walked a hundred yards across the yard to the barn.

It was a perfect late spring morning in western Maine. Yellow and purple crocuses, daffodils, and tulips pushed up through the black earth. The dense red buds of the rhubarb were bullying their way back into the garden. A wind in the pines and hemlocks carried the chatter of chickadees. From deeper in the greening woods came the flutelike call of the hermit thrush. In the budding pear tree, a rare visitor—an oriole—showed its bright self next to the half orange we'd hung there for it to eat.

As I neared the barn I heard the goats making noises in their stalls. They were rambunctious this time of year; they had spring fever. The bells around their necks clanked loudly as they butted heads, scraped their horns, and banged about. When I opened the door and let the sunshine in, they talked to me: *Bah, Bah-ha-ha, Bah-a-a-a, Ba-ha-hah, Bah-bah*. I put hay in their feeders, then filled each of their black rubber bowls with a handful or two of grain and slid the bowls into their pens, all except for the old doe, Dora. I fit her bowl into a rounded hole cut into the tray on her milking stand, sprinkling a little vitamin C atop the grain. I opened the doe's stall door and she ambled out, climbed onto her milking stand, lay her neck across the cradle, and started to eat her grain. I lowered the two-by-four that kept her head locked into the cradle and hooked it into place.

Goat milking stand

I dipped the sponge in the warm water and pressed the warmth against her udder, reaching my arm and hand underneath, between her legs and up under her tail. The warm water would help her milk come down. I lathered my hands with a drop of almond-scented cas-tile soap, then cupped and massaged each of her soft teats, curving around her bag, going under her belly where it was pink and cov-ered with a thin layer of white swirling hair. I rinsed and dried her, dried my own hands, then settled beside her on the milking stand

and reached for the far teat. I squirted the first few sprays of milk from each teat into a test cup covered with a strainer, to get rid of any bacteria that may have collected there since the last milking and to check for any irregularities or clots in the milk. I set the test cup beside me on the floor and waited for Stripe, one of our barn cats, to join me. Predictably, he came down from the hayloft and stuck his whiskered face into the cup, lapping up the milk. I then put the milking pail between Dora's legs and began in earnest, with a teat in each hand, the milk coming out in strong white sprays and hitting the bottom of the bucket. *Tsst, tsst, tsst, tsst.* My fingers closed around each teat, creating a small balloon. After the milk came out I relaxed my grip and the balloon filled up again with milk. I could feel it coming down from the bag, flowing under my hands. As the bucket filled, the sound changed—it was no longer liquid on metal but liquid on liquid. *Shuut, shuut, shuut, shuut.*

As I worked, the doe finished her grain and began to eat her hay. She looked back at me occasionally and shifted her weight. Mostly she was still. If she settled in and became content, she would chew her cud. This was how you could tell that a goat was feeling safe and calm—it would chew its cud, burping up the hay and grain in one stomach to give it another chew before it went into a second. When our veterinarian came to call, she would take a good look around to generally assess the health of the herd and comment, "Well, they're all chewing their cuds. Things must be fine." While the doe was on the milking stand, if I did something she didn't like she'd kick and dance. I tried to keep her calm by leaning my head into her soft, hairy, earthy side. She smelled like sunshine and hay and dust. I was so close that I could hear the noises of her stomach, her teeth grinding together as she chewed.

My back and side began to ache and my hands were going numb. I was seated on a piece of wood raised six inches off the ground, twisted at the waist and leaning forward with my arms out in front of me. If I did this all my life—like a real farmer—I would wear out fast. I already walked a bit like an old farmer with the wide, slow, side-to-side gait that comes from stiff hips. I shifted my position. The doe was getting impatient. *Squit. Squit. Squit. Squit. Squit. Squit.* My arms and back began to burn. I was in pain. It had been a hard year, a midlife crisis year that there had been scarcely anything good about, except for the animals.

About four years into my relationship with Ruth, four years after our fairy-tale candlelit ceremony on the shores of Green River Reservoir, I'd started an affair with a woman I'd known long before I met Ruth, drawn back into that old relationship, I thought, by fate, compelled by circumstances beyond my control. When you are in that kind of situation you sometimes feel like your other regular life is trying to fence you in, limit you, corral you, and that your new beloved is your ticket out of bondage. Part of the powerful pull of M., the woman I was having an affair with, was that she had been my first lesbian lover. I met her when I was in graduate school. She was married to a man. I was separated and going through a divorce. I was her first woman lover too. We acted like eighteen-year-olds, lying and sneaking around, taking stupid risks by having sex in places we were likely to be discovered by her husband. We broke up and made up so many times I lost count. In a group counseling session I participated in during that time, trying to sort through getting a divorce, coming out, and negotiating my first fiery relationship, a group member asked why I stayed with M. if she was so unpredictable and confusing and brought me so much torment. I said it was because of our powerful, special connection.

"You mean the sex?" she asked.

"Well, yeah," I said.

"You can have that connection with someone you meet on a street corner," she said. "That's not special. That's just hormones."

Whatever it was, I had been completely intoxicated. My world was new, and for the first time in my life I felt connected to my own body—its urges and desires and pleasures. After a short time, M. and I blazed out in a dramatic, passionate, exhausting end; I went on to have other lovers, and so did she. For ten years I heard nothing about or from M. as she pursued a life elsewhere. Then she appeared again, and fate seemed to drag us both through a remake of our first encounter.

The bucket was filling up with fresh white milk. *Splosh. Sploch. Splosh. Sploch. Splosh. Sploch.* The doe's teats were softening. I thought I was almost done, and then she let down more milk. I reached high on each teat and massaged her bag to help her let down even more. I took a deep breath and shifted; she did the same, emitting a sweet grass-scented belch.

My contract with the goats and chickens was simple; I helped provide them with a happy and healthy life, and they went on being themselves, producing eggs, milk, and meat. There was no need for language, although at times I fancied that I was talking to them. *Bawk bawk bawk bawk,* I'd say to the hens. *Er, er, er, errrrr!* (a more accurate version of the standard "cock-a-doodle-doo"), I answered the rooster. In this relationship, they and I were reduced to our most elemental selves. For the chickens: water, food, being let out to scratch in the earth and forage for grubs and bathe in the dirt under the lilac bush. For the goats: fresh water, a few flakes of hay, a dish of grain, a romp in the sunshine, a tree or two to nibble the bark off. For me, it was also about the body—the satisfaction of movement, the sensuality of labor—hauling, pitching, sweeping, sweating, milking, brushing, mending fence. It was also about nurturing—the simple act of taking care of another being without expecting anything in return.

Finally the doe's teats were empty. I stripped each one, gently flattening them between my fingers, pressing out the last drops of milk.

I set the milk pail on the steps to the hayloft, where it was safe, then put a few drops of peppermint oil on my palms and massaged the doe's bag, taking pleasure again in its perfect roundness and texture. I sprayed each teat with antiseptic, unlatched the board across her neck, and let her up. She paused for a moment, looked at me with her wide, brown watery eyes, as if to say, *well, that was that then,* and went back to her stall. I locked her stall door and took the milk into the house, where I strained it through paper milk filters into a glass jar that went into the refrigerator. Already I could see the cream thickening on the top. In a few days, once we'd collected a gallon or two of milk, Ruth and I would make chevre, a soft goat cheese. We'd heat, curdle, and strain the milk, salt it, add herbs, then press the thick, creamy cheese into pretty logs or small rounds.

After milking, I tended to the chickens and finished the remaining chores in the barn. The chickens had already been let into the yard and they ran after me, from the house to the barn, expecting a treat of last night's vegetable scraps. I had nothing today, so they trotted off into the woods to rustle among the leaves. In their coop, I filled the waterer and the hanging feeder. With a dustpan and a scraper, I cleaned off the dropping boards under their perches, depositing their droppings in a bucket that would be emptied into the compost pile. Then I checked the laying boxes, gently putting the cream- and brown-colored eggs into the pockets of my barn coat. Sometimes I reached beneath a nesting hen to take the eggs from under her, still warm, having just emerged from the bird, perfect, edible, magic.

Feeding the goats and chickens, cleaning their stalls and coop, collecting eggs, and milking were daily chores that, as I fell into the rhythm of being a keeper of animals, gave me great pleasure. I was doing something that benefited me but was not for me. Other chores came at weekly or monthly intervals. One of those was trimming goat hooves, which I did every three months on the solstice or equinox. In the beginning, my technique was to tackle the goat in a clean pile of hay and lie atop her, my legs braced around her belly. Even the small goats required all the muscle my body could muster. The goat would cry and buck at first and flail her hooves. I could feel her panicked breathing, her rib cage heaving. *Shh, shh, shh*, I would coo, whispering in her ear, and she would breathe one more heavy sigh then quiet down. As she lay under me, I took up each hoof and first scraped it clean of dirt and manure, then clipped the hard nail on each lobe of the two-lobed hoof. Last I trimmed the fleshy pink pad. After experimenting with clunky garden shears, I purchased an expensive thin-nosed pair of hoof cutters that made the job easier on both the goats and me. Inexpert at first, I often cut too deep and drew blood, which I wiped up with iodine and cotton. When the job was done, I would ease my body off the goat, which often would lie still for just a moment—dazed or comfortable, I'm not sure—before scrambling up and going back to her hay. Later I adopted a more civilized technique for trimming hooves: I locked the goat in the milking stand with a bowl of grain to munch, then moved around the stand taking up each hoof one by one, gently bending the goat's leg backward at the knee joint. The goats liked this method better, but I missed the old way. I missed handling those muscular, furry, hay-scented bodies, pressed close enough to smell the grassy breath, to feel the goat heart beating.

When I got the goats, I purposely knew nothing about them. I didn't know what they ate or how much, that wild cherry and rhododendron could make them sick enough to die. I didn't know how to trim hooves, how to milk, how to make cheese, where to buy hay. I knew nothing about grain and minerals and stomach worms and mange; nothing about when a goat goes into heat, how long it carries a kid, how to help a doe give birth if the baby is coming out backward; nothing about electric fences or goats' famous disregard for them. All the questions one might normally ask before launching into such an endeavor were irrelevant to me. I didn't want to become an expert, read a book, watch a video. I didn't know why I wanted goats. It didn't matter. It didn't matter that I'd never owned them before, or that they would cost me money, or that they might make it hard to go on vacation. I must have felt, intuitively, that they would reconnect me to some necessary part of myself. Perhaps this is also what I wanted when I began my affair with M.: a connection to my own body, a return to the new self I had been when I first met her so many years earlier. It was a connection to a part of myself devoted to pure pleasure, to instinct, to *what it wanted—now*. I had always been such a "good girl," so focused and responsible, so smart and in my head. But now I didn't want to think at all, much less consider consequences. I wanted to kiss and caress and grunt and moan and burst into loud, grateful orgasmic tears. I wanted to be beastlike. A note I passed to M. early in our affair read: *Bring me your animal self and I will bring you mine.* I wanted to be amazed by other bodies, and by my own.

Part of my pact with the animals was intimate and pleasant; other parts were less so, like treating the hens for lice. Unsavory as it may sound, I was the chickens' caretaker, and lice control came with the job. The first year Ruth and I owned chickens, they began to lose feathers in late winter. This sent me to the internet where I learned that they were probably just molting, losing their old

Giving a chicken
a bath

feathers to make way for new ones. But as their feathers dropped out and patches of skin began to show, my concern grew. Another source suggested it might be lice or mites. To find out, I had to pick up each chicken, turn it upside down, and rummage around in the fluffy feathers of its vent area. When I gazed upon our chickens, this was one of the prettiest spots—a poof of feathers delicate and fine, fluffing out underneath their hardy tail feathers. This was the vulnerable space I had to enter to assess the problem. If there were mites or lice I'd see them, the source assured me, and I did—tiny pinkish creatures swarming over the chickens' skin and patches of eggs stuck like plaster to the base of the feathers. Knowing then what I was looking for, I took up each chicken, tucking it head down under my arm so its wings were firmly pinned. After a moment of unease, it calmed its squawking and, arching its head slightly, gazed around with glassy amber eyes. *Shhhh, shhhhh, shhhhh, sweetheart*, I whispered. *It's all right.* If the chicken seemed especially agitated, I circled my finger around its beak until it was hypnotized. As I held it, separating its feathers in search of what was causing it misery, it let out soft *huffs* and *croaks* and *moans*. It felt fine and sweet, holding that warm, feathery bundle beneath my arm, that alive thing, that breathing, speaking animal.

Yes, they all had lice, I found after my intimate examination. Then what? Chickens, I learned, need to bathe. They bathed in the dirt, wiggling down into little kettles of dust they created by scratching away at the soil, rolling around boisterously, flipping dirt up over their backs, and fluffing it down into every feathery crevice. Our chickens had been cooped up all winter; even if they had wanted to go out, which they didn't, the snow covering the ground made dust baths impossible. One source I consulted suggested putting a box of wood ash or dirt in the chicken coop, which we did. I emptied the ash trap in the basement and hauled the fine gray dust out to the coop. A few weeks later the chickens seemed to have cured themselves of lice, and their feathers had grown back thick and full.

Sometimes, if I was reluctant to begin the business of the day with its lists and phones and computers, I stayed with the animals the whole morning. I brought my coffee to the yard and watched the chickens as they pecked and scratched in the compost pile, as they frothed in the dirt under the roses. I watched the little goats as they delighted in the discovery of their brand-new long legs, hopping and twisting, scrambling up and tumbling down a rock pile or a tree stump. Sometimes I picked them up and held them tight as they struggled in my arms; I did it to feel their energy, their bodies at work. I watched the big goats as they engaged in their own diversions: they would rear up on their hind legs, forelegs bent, ears pointed skyward, heads cocked, and then come crashing down, their bony foreheads meeting with an earth-shaking *thunk*. Bodies.

Woodlot

Beechwood fires are bright and clear
If the logs are kept a year, . . .
But ash new or ash old,
Is fit for a queen with crown of gold.

— Lady Celia Congreve, "The Firewood Poem"

A hundred years ago in New England, a farming family might, in addition to their fields and barnyard, maintain a woodlot—a small parcel of land to harvest firewood used for home heating and cooking as well as wood for fences, buildings, furniture, wagons, and repairs. The woodlot might also harbor a sugar bush—a stand of maple trees that would be tapped each spring for maple sap. The woodlot would also be a source of beechnuts, acorns, berries and edible plants, ash for making baskets, evergreen boughs for winter holiday decoration; a home for creatures large and small—birds, fox, skunk, rabbit, raccoon, porcupine, deer, and bear; and a place to walk and take picnics and contemplate the beauty of the world.

In Maine, those of us who still heat with wood might find the process of creating our woodpiles and tending our fires a joy, and we might also find it a nuisance and a physical burden that we must labor at all year round. But as long as I am able to handle the physical demands of wood, I think this is one of the ways I'd like to spend my allotted time on earth. What I learn from the trees, the axe, the chopping block, the woodpile, and the fire is close to the bone of life, thick into the marrow.

Before I moved to Maine, I had never heated a house with wood. My childhood home in suburban Salt Lake City was heated by forced electric hot air. The heat came from the furnace through registers in the floors, which could be opened or closed by way of lovely, beaded pull chains with tiny metal bells on the ends. As a girl I suffered from chronic urinary tract infections. Their frequency confounded my doctors, who eventually suggested to my parents that I might be making them up. Psychosomatic, they said. The term means something different now, but then, to my father, it meant not real. Ashamed and afraid to seek comfort from my parents, when I was sick at night I huddled over the register in the bathroom, the fanned air lifting my yellow hair in little puffs, the heat a soothing presence. The source of the heat was a rattling mysterious thing behind louvered doors in the basement that my father would curse once a year when he changed the filters. We had a shallow fireplace that was part of a decorative hearth, and a woodpile that was so seldom used that the one cord of wood we had delivered when I was a teenager was still partly there when we sold the house after my father's death, forty years later.

As a child I was enchanted by the notion of a fire inside the house, and I sometimes convinced our mother to let me and my siblings light one, which mostly smoldered and smoked up the living room. Now, a house without a working fireplace or woodstove seemed quite incomplete to me, sterile, lonely, lacking in some elemental essence. Although Ruth and I had an oil furnace that backed up our wood system for twenty-five-below-zero nights, we seldom used it, choosing instead to bundle up in wool sweaters, slippers, and hats, and cover our laps with blankets.

Learning how to heat with wood, like so much of rural life, had been an education for me, whereby the lessons came from my own mistakes and defeats. Perhaps this was the best way to learn—by doing rather than by reading or being told. To really learn something, after all, is to have it enter you so that it transforms you, like the heat from the wood fire.

To our delight, our little Cape was equipped with a Finnish or Russian fireplace, also known as a masonry heater. In a regular fireplace, heat from the fire radiates somewhat outward, but mostly the warm air and smoke go straight up the chimney. In a masonry heater a series of baffles creates nooks and crannies for the slow circulation of the fire-warmed air within the chimney structure, heating up the brick or stone mass, which radiates heat outward. Two short, hot fires with solid dry wood would keep our small home (minus the far corners) at between sixty and sixty-five degrees all day long on even below-zero days. Additions to these old-fashioned, fuel-efficient heaters (said to have come into use in northern Europe during a time of wood shortage) included copper piping on the inside that heated a copper water box attached to the side, from which boiling water could be drawn for tea, cooking, laundry, or bathing. When I visited village homes in Russia while I was teaching there for a semester, their masonry fireplaces had built-in shelves for setting kettles to stay warm or dough to rise, faucets to access hot water, and even sleeping platforms for granny and the cat!

At our house, every morning from September through late April, the chores included filling the woodbox and starting the first fire. I was drawn to the discipline such regular chores required and the way they grounded the day in the physical. But I also sometimes chafed at their relentlessness and the inescapable consequences they insisted upon—a missed or half-done chore one day made more work for the next day. It was mostly with good cheer, however, that I gathered wood by the armfuls from the neatly stacked logs in the woodshed and tossed them into the wheelbarrow and then into the great wooden box on the porch, piling them up until they risked spilling onto the porch floor. They made a musical tumble and clunk as I tossed them, each piece of wood alive with the energy of years of sun and water. The logs came into the house from the woodbox in a canvas sling with leather handles. I could carry fifteen pieces at a time. This many, stacked in a crisscross pattern three to a row, would fill the firebox in our Finnish fireplace. To the right side of the iron fireplace doors were an iron shovel, a poker, a small broom, and a bellows. Beside the tools was a ceramic crock of kindling—pieces of dried birchbark, pine cones, bits of wood left over from carpentry projects, old cedar shingles, and waxed paper milk cartons—anything for a match to catch.

After many seasons of heating with wood, we'd learned that the best kindling for a one-match fire is dried birchbark and a bit of shredded (not crumpled) dry paper, laid carefully in the spaces between layers of crisscrossed logs. Then the match is struck and the kindling set aflame, the fireplace doors are shut, the air hole is left open a crack, the fire draws in the air from below, and the flames soon blaze! As I moved from the morning task of the fire to the task of coffee, I would listen attentively to make sure I heard the telltale crackle and pop that meant the fire had really taken hold.

When the fire was lit and had warmed the mass of brick in the center of the house, it was as if we had welcomed a long-staying guest. We became three living there—Ruth and I and the fire. I'd come to think of the fireplace as a big bear, down on its haunches, meditative, friendly, having chosen our home for its half-hibernation. On cold days we leaned up next to it, our front sides to the brick, and stretched out our arms as if we were hugging an enormous radiant friend. In winter, the overstuffed living room chairs were turned to face the fire, and a small table was set between them to hold our mugs of coffee, our books, notebooks, and pens. In spring when it was time for our guest to leave, we often felt melancholy. The fireplace tools and crock of kindling were moved to the basement and the chairs were turned outward, their backs to the cool wall of brick. The sounds of the fire were gone: the thunk and clunk of wood being laid, the creak of the iron doors opening and closing, the scrape of the shovel as we pulled the cinders from the back of the firebox forward into the ash chute. But the change of season brought other sounds—birds, wind, goat bells in the pasture, the screen door slamming shut, ice cubes being broken from a tray. The windows opened and the breeze came in, scented first with daffodil, then lilac, then phlox and cut grass, and the sound of bumblebees and hummingbirds.

When you heat a home with wood, you are always getting ready. The wood year began with moving the previous year's pile of cured, dried wood from our artful round woodpile to the empty woodshed, from which we would have burned the last pieces around the end of April. There's a saying I've come to find comfort in: "Half your wood and half your hay by Candlemas day." This date, February 2, halfway between the winter solstice and the vernal equinox, was celebrated by many cultures, pagan, Christian, and otherwise, under many names including Midwinter, Groundhog Day, Imbolc, and the day the Virgin Mary presented her baby Jesus to God in the Temple. It was also the day I made an informal accounting of our wood supply, figuring we should have three more rows of logs to get us through, and we almost always did, give or take a half a row if the temperatures were colder or warmer than predicted. It pleased me to think that even if I didn't have depth of snow and a thermometer to give me clues, I could chart the chilliness of the winter by the contents of our woodshed.

Once the cured dry wood was in the shed, we began the process of creating another stash of three cords, not for the winter coming in six months but for the one after that. Conveniently, three cords were just the right amount for our small hand-me-down garden shed. A cord is a stack of wood that measures four feet wide by four feet tall by eight feet long. Thinking a year and a half ahead was what Darrell, our woodcutter, called "being in a rotation." Those who didn't get into a rotation set themselves up for woodpile horror stories, like our friends Doug and Judy who, in their first year of country living, were so busy with young children and house remodeling that they were climbing around on icy stacks in the dead of winter hacking out one log at a time.

The next task in the chain of tasks was to have Darrell mark and fell new trees. Those that were old or sick, leaning toward the house, had begun to shade the garden, or had been damaged by storms were the first candidates. He also looked for a good mix of species so we didn't end up with too much pine or popple—called "soft wood." He usually arrived early in the summer in his battered green pickup truck with his orange hard hat, face mask, and chainsaw. After felling a tree, he bucked it into sixteen-inch "stove lengths," then moved them by the tractor bucketful to a pile near where the previous year's pile used to be. We used wood as small as the circumference of our forearm, so the pile Darrell created for us was a mixture of logs too big to wrap our arms around and those we could bang together to make music or toss to a dog.

Next came splitting. Although I admired someone who could split a year's worth of wood with an axe, this was not a skill I was confident or strong enough to manage. We invested in a gas-driven hydraulic splitter. Splitting turned the huge logs into manageable pieces of wood and allowed it to dry faster. Although one person could run the splitter, it was safer to work together, one of us hoisting the logs to the bed and the other running the lever that drove a spear-shaped iron head into the heart of the wood to crack it open. Doing this task together allowed us to keep an eye on each other, remind each other to put on goggles, gloves, and ear protection, to slow down, take a rest, stop for lunch or a drink of water, or get our fingers out of the way. If we were organized and efficient, the splitting took place little by little over the course of the summer, ending in the fall when the air turned crisp and snow was around the corner. As we split, we began to carefully place the pieces one by one in the shape of a circle, building up the double walls of the circle until they were approximately four feet high. Then we filled the center with the remaining wood until we had what looked like a lovely, rounded, rustic cake, which we

Woodshed and chopping block

covered with a tarp to protect it from rain and snow, keeping it as dry as possible. This was the wood that would be next year's fire.

Henry David Thoreau's woodpile, which he is often quoted as having looked upon with a kind of affection, warmed him twice, he said—once when he took an axe to his trees, and once when he burned them. Unlike Thoreau's, our woodpile warmed us many more times than two. And, to tell the truth, I have not always looked upon our woodpile with affection. I've looked upon it more times with anxiety, disappointment, and dread. We had friends who had reduced the number of times they laid hands upon their wood to five, but our count still remained high. You handled the wood each time you felled a tree, bucked up the tree where it fell, hauled the bucked-up logs to a central pile, split the pieces by machine or hand, hauled the split pieces to your curing pile and stacked them, hauled the dried wood to the woodshed on your annual rotation, stacked the pieces in the woodshed, hauled the pieces into the house to burn, built your fire, and perhaps once again as you scraped the ashes into the ash chute, and one final time when you delivered the ashes to the compost pile. With Darrell doing the initial cutting, bucking, and hauling to the woodpile for splitting, this accounting had us handling our wood nine times—nine times it warmed us!

Those woodpiles I envied most were the woodpiles of retired people, or those who paid top dollar to get their wood "cut, split, and delivered," or sometimes "cut, split, delivered, and stacked." You could also pay extra to have your wood delivered already cured. We had resisted this luxury because, despite my complaining, we liked the hard work of splitting it ourselves, we liked handling all that wood all those times, putting our gloved palms and fingers around it, smelling it, feeling the heft of it in our hands. But there was also a price to be paid for our willingness to spend our energy and time that way; sometimes the wood did not get tended to in a timely fashion, and a nice clean pile of wood can go "gaumy" (as our pal Bob Kimber liked to say) if left sitting in your dooryard too long, distracted as you might be by putting in a new perennial flower garden, entertaining summer guests, or reading a book in a hammock in the shade. If we left the wood too long, it would be caked with dirt and alive with worms. If it was not good wood to begin with, it might be rotten and decorated with fungus. Half of it would go into the pile we used to boil our maple sap in the spring, and the wood that had gone beyond that got tossed over the side of the hill into our organic dump. If the pile remained untouched too long, other creatures moved in, such as snakes and mice.

One year we waited way too late to split our wood. In the midst of a snowstorm, I held the logs steady on the splitter's level backbone, while Ruth ran the lever that drove the iron cleaver through each piece of wood. Over the din of the machine's engine and through the noise-blocking earmuffs clamped around our heads, we heard dramatic screams. As the log on the splitter fell open, we found in the hollow center of it a mouse nest of popple fluff and straw, squirming with blind pink babies. I gently put the two halves of the log back in place and set the piece out of harm's way. We watched over the next half hour as the mother mouse moved her babies, picking up each one in her teeth and shuffling it off to a safer home. There had been snakes in the woodpile too, and voles, and the small nests of other creatures that moved out when they heard us coming. When we split the logs, we often found curled-up fat white grubs, spiders, termites, and ant colonies spilling over with pearly eggs. Each splitting was a surprise, a glimpse into a normally veiled world of air and water and years: a magical moment.

It was in the process of splitting the wood that I'd come to learn the most about the trees themselves and the gifts they offered us. I'd come to appreciate the ash, that hard, straight-grained tree used for pool cues, oars, garden tool handles, and baseball bats. It was a no-nonsense tree that would sometimes crack open at the touch of the wedge, but more often it would slowly pull apart, its stringy fibers tenaciously holding to themselves. It was the kind of wood that, perfectly dried, you would not mind splitting by hand—it would make you look good, the axe coming down and passing right through the wood to the chopping block. If you looked at the rings on the butt end of an ash log, you'd see they were regularly spaced. This was what made ash amenable for making baskets, as the layers of a pounded log would peel off in even sheets and could later be separated into thinner strips for weaving. The butt end of a maple log revealed rings not evenly spaced, but wavy and varied.

Maple was also a pleasure to split—when it opened, the grain could almost remind you of the shimmering, oblique symmetry of a Gustav Klimt painting. If the maple wasn't going into a woodshed, it might end up one day on the floor of a bowling alley or a basketball court. You could tell you'd picked a piece of oak from the pile when it felt as if you'd hefted a rock. Then there was the beech, with a grain so slight and tight it looked nearly blank, like a tanned piece of paper. There was popple, which came apart not with a crack or pop but almost silently, as if you were slicing butter. Occasionally we got a log or two of cherry with its red streaks, or wild apple with its distinctive fruity smell, or soft and fragrant cedar. By attending in this way I'd learned that each tree species had its own personality, its own excellence and utility.

I didn't understand much about wood until I met Ruth. One of her many previous careers was as a furniture refinisher. She worked for Dave, a man in Stowe, Vermont, who was a self-proclaimed "garbologist." On his regular trash route Dave picked up valuable items such as bedsteads, night tables, and broken rocking chairs. Ruth would repair these and refurnish them, and they'd be sold at Dave's used furniture and antique shop. Ruth introduced me to the idea of wood as a living thing, even cut down, sawed up, and made into a table or cabinet. She could make a maple bathroom cabinet feel as soft as the skin of a baby by working with it over and over with successively finer grades of sandpaper, and then finally with fine steel wool and a soft oiled cloth. The secret, she said, was time and patience. In between each sanding she'd wet the wood and allow its grain to rise. When she was done the wood would shine as if it had an inner light. It was from her I developed a fascination and love for the grains of particular woods, each having its own beauty, and developed a preference for sanding and oiling over painting. In our own house, no matter how terrible the piece of hand-me-down garage sale country auction furniture looked when it came to us, it could be transformed into something breathtaking, simply by taking off the paint and sanding it and oiling it—letting its God-given intelligence and individuality come through.

There was a noble aesthetic component to heating with wood, particularly around the best and most beautiful way to stack it. There was the traditional long stack, fortified at each end by towers of crisscrossed logs. There was the hammock stack, which was a long double-rowed stack set between two sturdy trees or posts. There was the Scandinavian-inspired Holz Hausen stack with its peaked top. And there was the stack, popular in New Brunswick, that looked like a tepee, with the wood stacked on end in a huge A-shaped mountain. Our chosen method for stacking wood for drying was a variation on the Scandinavian stack; we felt its hutlike appearance gave the impression that we had fairies or gnomes living behind the house.

When it came to moving the wood from the drying stack into orderly rows in the woodshed, different aesthetics applied. The general rule of thumb, according to Ruth's dad, the late Alfred Hill, was that the wood should be stacked loosely enough for a mouse to run

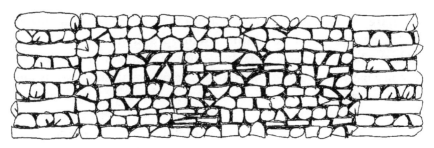

Traditional or tower stack

Teepee or New Brunswick stack

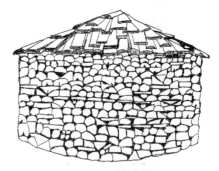

Holz Hausen stack

through but not the cat that was after her. I learned the hard way that Ruth was a better stacker than I was. She had an eye for angles that I just didn't have, and she would search for long minutes to find the perfect piece of wood to keep the pile tilted in just the right way. She would shimmy a log this way and that, sometimes even use a level to adjust a row.

I was forever asking Darrell if such and such a tree would make good wood for the fire, to which he might reply, "Anything will burn." You can get all fancy about Btu's (British thermal units), but when

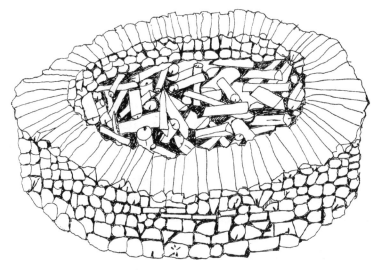

Modified round stack

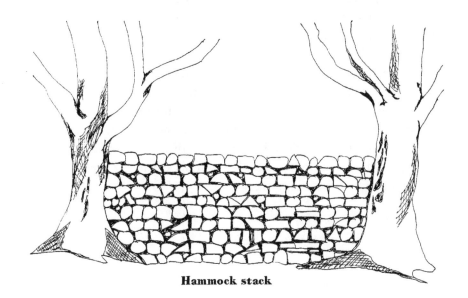

Hammock stack

you were cold and the wind was howling, it didn't much matter what you used to fuel the flame. It was true, however, that some woods burned hotter than others, and this I learned in my body first. One winter the fires we laid seemed not to be keeping up with the cold. When I hugged the brick bear in the center of the house, she was not quite as warm as I'd expected. The reason: our woodshed had an overabundance of pine, which burns quickly and doesn't give off much heat. The woods with the highest heating capacity, presuming they are properly dried, are elm, hickory, oak, beech, ash, and hop hornbeam. Apple is high on another list, along with balsam fir, birch, hemlock, maple, and willow. The hottest-burning woods in our lot tended to be maple, oak, beech, and ash. Our least efficient woods were popple, pine, hemlock, and birch. From then on, I was more careful to mix the woods as I stacked them. Now that I knew, from learning it in my bones, that not all wood was created equal in terms of heating power, Celia Congreve's 1930 "The Firewood Poem" made beautiful sense to me: "Birch and fir logs burn too fast / Blaze up bright and do not last, / . . . Oaken logs, if dry and old / keep away the winter's cold."

What a teacher the wood had been. What secrets it held. How satisfying to smell its different odors, run my hands across its many varied grains, watch it burn red and blue and green in the winter, hear the occasional log hiss and spit out the last of its watery breath. How peaceful it was to doze by the warm fire, doors open, and then to close them and let that brick, that gentle bear in the middle of the house, come alive for one more season.

Can of Stones

As I look back on it now, what is hardest for me to believe about the affair with M. is that I had the energy to keep it up—to keep meeting her in supposed secret, to keep lying to Ruth about it, to keep up an insane juggling act. I would meet M. in the morning at her apartment, then I'd shower before I met Ruth for a picnic lunch on a bench overlooking a small pond on campus. I'd invite M. to our house to practice salsa dancing, with Ruth in the kitchen not wanting to participate, the air thick with her knowing but not quite believing what was so obvious.

There was a hunger and foolishness in me then that belonged to someone who seemed to be a stranger. Mary Oliver's "Honey Tree," the poem that had been my erotic inspiration the first time around with M., surfaced again. "Joy does that, I'm told," the speaker says, about her crazy appetite. I wondered, though, whether it was joy that was propelling me, or something else. I was able to compartmentalize and pretend I wasn't doing anything that might hurt anyone else. After all, I still loved Ruth. What was wrong with me? Was I bored with Ruth, with our life, the life of our bodies? I didn't think so.

Ruth had never been boring, in bed or out of it. In fact, she was endowed with a silliness gene, shared by her three sisters, that helped me overcome my serious gene and got me to laugh and play in ways no one else in my life ever had. It was with Ruth that I rediscovered the joys of dressing up and goofing off for no reason. Over the years we'd amassed several suitcases and plastic tubs full of hats, shoes, feather boas, wigs, and masks that we brought out on special occasions, such as solstice and the equinox, to create ceremonial plays and processions with friends. One of Ruth's first musical ensembles was the all-woman band Too Much Rouge (too much for you is just enough for me!). Each member dressed in a different outlandish outfit and hat, faces thick with makeup, especially bright red lipstick. Their names were Avon, Marykay (rhymes with Parkay from the State of Confusion), and Maybelline. Avon played electric guitar and trombone and was drawn to funk and R&B. Marykay (Ruth) played acoustic guitar, banjo, and mandolin from a folk and bluegrass tradition. Maybelline had a background in classical piano and drums. She won the John Philip Sousa Award in her high school band for trumpet. Her musical tastes ran toward pop and rock and roll. The band did a mix of originals and cover tunes. Sometimes they were joined by cardboard cutouts. One night Babs Bush joined them on stage. They were known to be hilarious. One night Rosie O'Donnell, who happened to be in the audience, approached Maybelline and asked if she might consider moving to the big city to write for her show.

As a kid, one of Ruth's rural New Hampshire neighbors nicknamed her Goofy Roofy, the Hill from the Hill. In addition to dressing up in top hats and catsuits, orange yarn wigs and clown shoes (which both belonged to my mother, who had, for a short time, attended clown school), Ruth and I enjoyed speaking to one another in terribly rendered accents—one moment Italian, one moment Russian or Spanish or Norwegian or British or Irish—and making funny faces at each other to incite laughter. We kissed whenever possible, including in public, held hands, danced in the living room when we felt like it, and slept curled up next to each other in bed, where we often were joined by Blueberry, a small blue stuffed bear given to Ruth by one of her first, most important loves. Blueberry's prescient questions and wry commentary on the world of humans kept us both laughing.

Our early life as lovers was intense and delicious, sensual and romantic, nurturing and sweet. And then it began to wane. From everything I'd read, it happened to most couples, hetero and non. Life started to encroach on the romantic fantasy. You woke up with bedhead and bad breath; you let down your guard and flossed your teeth in front of each other; you revealed yourself at your most vulnerable when you got sick and had to be cared for. How did you maintain a passionate sex life in face of all that bodily reality? We joked about "lesbian death bed," which was actually "lesbian bed death," a clinical phenomenon known to therapists and thought to have something to do with the unusual closeness and familiarity in lesbian couples' relationships, combined with the lack of testosterone in the mix. That would never happen to us, we assured each other. Ever. And then, over time, of course, the intensity did wear off. So, was I abandoning everything Ruth and I had built together just for seemingly more exciting sex with someone else? Was that okay? Is that what people did? There had to be other solutions. I was full of questions.

I started going to therapy again to work through what was happening; it had thrown my life into a turmoil that was so much like the turmoil that was present in my life the first time M. and I had been lovers. The therapist encouraged me to engage in art projects. I made a plaster mask of my own face, with bolts at the temples and a string of twisted black and yellow thread trailing out of the mouth that looked like a wasp.

"Tell me about that," the therapist said.

"Well, I feel like a monster, like Frankenstein, and I feel like my head is being squeezed, and I feel like everything I say is poisonous."

I made great murals of black and gray swirls created with finger paint that I applied with wide, messy palm strokes, while I leaned over the huge expanses of paper, tears falling.

"Tell me about that," the therapist said.

"It all seems like shit to me," I said. "Inside me, I mean. Just swirls of shit."

I printed off copies of black-and-white family photographs, adding amendments such as a pistol and a martini glass to augment the truth of scenes they portrayed.

"What's going on there?" the therapist would ask.

"It always seemed as if something violent was about to happen when I was a kid," I said. "As if there was always a gun to my head."

I found an image of a girl who looked a lot like me when I was a little tomboy: long blonde braids, denim overalls. I made copies of the image and inserted her into different landscapes: jumping on a trampoline, standing amid a field of wildflowers. In each image I cut a small window over where her heart would be. When I presented my creation to the therapist, she gingerly opened each window to reveal what I'd written inside: "You Suck."

Then there was the collage of cats, which illustrated a recurring dream of mine. I loved cats, but in the dreams they kept coming, too many of them to take care of, and suddenly they were everywhere and they were dying, and they were mangy and smelled and were swarming with maggots, and they were eating each other.

"I feel totally out of control," I told the therapist.

And finally there was the can of stones. Taking a cue from the small stones I often saw in gift stores, imprinted with loving words like *Peace*, or *Smile*, or *Gentle*, I made my own signature collection. My smoothly worn river stones, which would fit nicely in a pocket or a palm, said things like *Worthless. Liar. Fuckup.*

"You know these are dangerous," the therapist said. "What are you going to do with them?"

"Throw them in the woods," I said.

"What if someone else finds one? Don't you think that could be devastating?"

It was the deep knowledge that the violence of these words might hurt someone else that woke me up to the perilousness of my own state of mind and the torment I was going through. This love affair was definitely not adding to my happiness. Quite the opposite.

There were many stages to the affair with M. Many times I promised myself and Ruth that it was over. One of those times was when I left the country to teach as part of a student and faculty exchange program my university had with the Komi Pedagogical Institute in Syktyvkar, the capital of the Komi Republic in Russia. I thought this break would be the end of the affair, but it wasn't long before I was sending M. erotic pictures of myself, and she to me. To call the affair an addiction, I think, might have been apt, because I felt I had very little control over what I was doing, and because of the way the sexual attraction fed some seemingly famished part of me. Again, there was a strange feeling that I was not one person but at least two, and that these different versions of me were pursuing lives quite independently of the other. While M. and I were exchanging titillating photographs and having transatlantic phone sex, another part of me was planning ahead for my return to Maine and my life with Ruth. I felt a bit like a puppet that some unseen power had control of, with a hollowed-out papier-mâché head and no will of my own.

Skinning the Beaver

April in Maine. The quiet white skin of winter folded back. Underneath lay the raw, expectant tenderness of spring. Wood frogs began their deep-throated quacking from the vernal pool in our pasture, joined by a chorus of spring peepers. Envelopes of seeds arrived in the mail. The long earthen humps of the garden beds emerged from the last thin covering of snow. The flycatchers returned to their nest under the eaves of the barn. Snowdrops nodded their heavy white heads in the warm belt of soil beside the granite slab out the back window. Daffodils pushed up through the matted beech leaves by the front steps. Our French Alpine does bulged with the bulk of baby goats eager to enter the world.

Along with all the other creatures, we too began to venture forth from our cocoons in front of the winter fire. One night in the first weeks of spring's cracking through, Ruth and I joined friends at the art theater in Waterville for a movie. Lost in thought in the passenger's seat on the hourlong drive home, I sleepily took notice as we crossed the green metal bridge over Wilson Stream on Route 156. The Sandy River curved to our right, cutting away at its bank. On the left was a farmer's field still stubbled with the previous year's cornstalks. Even with the windows closed we heard the meditative, pulsing song of the peepers, spring's heartbeat. Suddenly, Ruth braked and swerved.

"What was it?" I asked. She didn't know.

"Was it dead?" She wasn't sure.

"Let's go back," I said.

A pickup truck barreled down on us, its high beams glaring through the back window. Once the truck passed, Ruth turned the car around. Illuminated by our car's headlights was a beaver. We hadn't hit it; some other car had done that. It was newly dead, its body still soft and pliable. If I can, I usually stop for animals in the road, dead or alive. I've helped turtles cross highways, gotten out of the car to hustle a frog out of harm's way, paused to wait for a mouse to skittle to the other side. I've salvaged dead rattlesnakes and hawks, even made a meal out of freshly hit duck and grouse. At the very least, out of respect, I move the carcass off the road, which was what I did then with the beaver, leaving a bright red streak in its wake. Now its fur, flesh, bones, and guts would not be irretrievably plastered onto the blacktop. Now some fox or coyote could find it, whole and relatively fresh, and have a good meal.

"It was a beaver," I said, back in the car. "It was heavy, and its fur was thick and shiny." We drove on. Five minutes down the road I had second thoughts.

"Let's go back for it," I said. "It seems such a waste to leave it there."

Ruth asked me what I was going to do with it. "Maybe make a hat," I said.

She pointed out that I had never made a beaver hat before. I acknowledged that this was true but reminded her that I knew someone who could teach me how. And so we turned again and I lifted the beaver from the side of the road and set it on plastic bags in the trunk. As we continued the drive home, we both remarked at how the car immediately took on a not unpleasant fishy, watery, furry, musky smell.

The next day I called my friend Chris Knapp and took my dead beaver to his and his wife Ashirah's Main Local Living School in the nearby village of Temple. Chris was eager to share what he knew of skinning beavers. This furry little guy was a young male, he told me. He would have been born between May and June two years earlier, all snugged up in a beaver lodge on some nearby pond. He and his two-year-old beaver brothers were all in the same danger in springtime, as this was when they came of age and were evicted from their family groups. En masse, two-year-old male beavers set off from their home ponds in early spring in search of new communities.

"Beavers skin hard," Chris said. "It's not like a deer where the hide just peels away."

He lay the red-brown furry body on its back in the cold grass, stretching out the four paws and tail so the beaver was disturbingly spread-eagled, belly up. With a sharp knife he made a slit up the

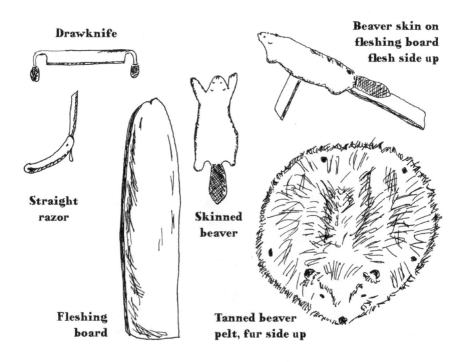

Drawknife

**Beaver skin on
fleshing board
flesh side up**

**Straight
razor**

**Skinned
beaver**

**Fleshing
board**

**Tanned beaver
pelt, fur side up**

middle of the belly. From his vest pocket he produced a skinning tool he had made from the legbone of a moose. One end of the bone was filed to a thin but not too sharp edge; the shaft was covered in a rough leather wrapping. The tool, a Cree design, was used to push the fat away from the skin without tearing or slicing the hide. Nothing he knew about skinning beavers was new, Chris explained, as he worked; it all came from the Cree. He left me to muscle and sweat my way through this first part of the process, then returned later to show me how to work delicately around the four paws, the eyes, and the nose.

Once the hide was off and I had rolled it up into a plastic bag to take home along with the tail (which Chris said he'd show me later how to transform into a skin purse), we were left with the skinless body. This particular beaver body was broken by its encounter with the car that hit it; internal bleeding had turned some of the meat dark, and some of its bones were scattered shards. Nevertheless, there was a body there—the red and pink flesh, the creamy fat, the white tendons and bone, the black eyes; a completely exposed, skinless body. Chris trimmed off the thin strips of meat from along the beaver's backbone, setting them aside for me. He'd take the rest of the somewhat questionable meat for a stew. "It seems like just the right time of year for a little beaver meat," he said with a smile. I wondered what to do with the carcass. "Ashirah and I usually try to return the bones to where they came from," he said. "If it's a deer, we put the bones in the woods. If it's a creature who lives in the water, we try to bring them back to a stream or a pond."

When I arrived at home, I showed off the fresh hide and the scaly, fleshy tail to Ruth, who admired the richness of the fur. Both the tail and hide would find a place in the basement freezer until I was ready to move on to the next step—tanning. Meanwhile, Ruth and I walked to Sugar Brook, which runs through a beaver-inhabited bog near our house. If ever there was a proper resting place for this beaver's flesh and bones, that would be it. We entered the bog just past a large culvert carrying spring's excess water under the road and spilling it into a deep, foaming amber pool. The water soon quieted and made its way from the pool through the bog among dense shrubbery and grasses. I found a place out of sight of the road and pulled the carcass from my backpack. If someone came along later and saw what we'd left there, the long, telltale beaver teeth would, upon close inspection, positively identify this unclothed creature, but on first glance, what I put there in the brown grass beside the stream could have been any small mammal stripped of its skin—any skull with patches of flesh still attached, any ridged backbone, any four limbs, any set of bare curved ribs. It looked eerily like a human baby. Beneath our hides, it seems, we and the beaver have much in common. I lay the multicolored viscera beside the body and, because I knew we would not be able to eat it, the meat Chris had sent home with me. The next day, curious, I returned to the same spot to find only a few drops of dried blood.

I had no sense of the violent or perverse as I set about tanning the hide, only a sense of respect and preservation. The beaver had been dead already. Now the skin was in my care, and I wanted to honor it. There was excitement, too, about participating in an act as ancient as preparing an animal hide for human use. Hides had clothed us from the start, created a second skin that kept us warm and shielded us from what might do us harm. Would it be going too far to say that

Scraping the flesh
off of the inside
of a beaver hide

the skins of animals might have also helped to create in humans a sense of self as separate from other, a sense of the integrity of the individual human body?

I began the tanning process by taking the small bundle of red-brown fur from the freezer, where it had lain among the pork chops and ground goat, and set it in a bucket of warm water. Once it had unfolded and defrosted, I wrung it out by hand like a hairy towel and set it upon a slanted piece of wood that became my fleshing board. No knife in our home was sharp enough to gracefully remove the small bits of meat, fat, and tissue that still clung fiercely to the hide, but I persevered, finally discovering that my grandfather's straight razor could suffice reasonably well. As I worked, I flicked the flesh and fat into a bucket and wiped the razor edge on the thigh of my workpants. The same fishy, waxy, pond-life odor I had smelled the night I found the beaver on the highway began to fill the basement.

I worked carefully around the beaver's silken snout and whiskers, around the tiny holes where the eyeballs used to be, down the center of the belly, and around the outer edges. Once I was satisfied that the hide was relatively clean (albeit with several small holes due to my lack of expertise), I put it in the washing machine. ("No beavers in the washing machine," Ruth had said before she left the house that day to run errands, only to come home to see it circling around in a sudsy rinse.)

Next, I mixed a solution of washing soda, salt, and aluminum sulfate, which fizzed alarmingly and threatened to overflow its bucket. The hide went into the bucket and stayed there, stirred twice a day with a stout stick, for two weeks. I rinsed it again to get the chemicals out, then it was time for stretching and drying.

Stretching the hide by hand to soften or "break" it required strenuous daily tug-of-wars with Ruth, rotating the edges of the hide between our hands and pulling backward with all our strength. This had to be done regularly until the hide was completely dry or it would become hard and brittle.

Finally, I rubbed the dry hide with mink oil and spread it out over a towel on our stair rail. Its dark furry length lent a feralness to the living room. As I passed it, going to and fro about the house, I ran my fingers through its luxuriously soft, thick fur, marveling at the subtle variations of color that emerged and faded into one another. The fur on the outer edges of the now flat oval of hide, where the belly of the beaver had been, was gray, soft, and dense. The fur down the middle of the hide, along the beaver's back, was longer, coarser, and redder. The fur on the tail end was strawberry blonde. When the light hit the hide just so, it shimmered amber.

What was I going to do with a beaver hide? I knew a woman in Alaska who sewed a teddy bear for her baby out of beaver hide. I owned a bona fide beaver fur hat with earflaps. Ruth modeled other possibilities for me, including a dramatic cone-shaped head covering and a beaver hide miniskirt. I could have made mittens. A bag. Slippers. A ruff for a parka hood. A throw pillow. While I pondered what to do with it, the pelt lay draped across the top of an upholstered ottoman in our living room. I rested my bare feet on it when I read. When I passed the ottoman, it sometimes startled me. Then I remembered: it wasn't alive, it was just the beaver *skin*. Amazing, though, that it still was so remarkably full of animal presence with its little leather ears, whiskers, and eyeholes intact. Eventually, Ruth and I gifted the skin to our friend Dave, a retired professor of English who worked at the same university my father had, and was also our summer rural Maine yard sale comrade, whose interests ran toward bizarre taxidermy (squirrels on skis). Dave received the beaver pelt with deep reverence and gratitude and draped it across the back of his favorite reading chair. When we visited him and his wife, Liz, at their camp in Chesterville, I was always struck anew by the skin's beauty and its power to remind me of the fragility and fraternity of our animal bodies; without our skin we, and by that I mean all creatures, are similarly elemental, like the beaver I returned to the bog—flesh and bone.

Tracks

One morning I woke to deer tracks crisscrossing the yard—delicate proofs in the snow, a step here, a step there, a chain of steps entwined with more chains of steps. They had come in the night, lit by stars and moon, when the woods and yard were still. They had come down from the ridge of pine and hemlock above the pasture and the barn. We had always known there were deer in our woods. I hunted them in the fall and knew some of their routes and resting places. But they had never before come so close to the house. I felt an excited delight and a strange chill—these creatures had been awake, circling the house, while we curled under our covers, dreaming, unguarded.

I put on my boots and followed the hoofprints in a circle around the arborvitae, then through the winter blackberry patch, catching my jacket on thorns. I found piles of dark pelleted deer droppings and yellow circles where the hot deer urine had made wells in the snow. I could tell the deer were relaxed and unafraid by how the tracks nonchalantly wove about and by the shape of each hoofprint, clearly visible where it had been carefully planted, its shape pressed firmly into the snow, and by how the snow in front of the track was slightly scuffed, as if this deer, like some lanky high school boy, had been lazily scuffling its feet, lifting each hoof just high enough, but not quite high enough, to top the next height of powder, and so it dragged just a bit and made its mark.

I continued to follow the tracks in their curly loops and figure-eights, stepping over the drooping chicken wire fence into the snow-covered empty vegetable garden, up to and around the plum tree, whose branch tips the deer had nibbled, then out of the garden again, and up to and around each of the three apple trees—the Wolf River, the McIntosh, and the Northern Spy—whose tiny buds they had also consumed. I went in a circle around the crab apple tree, still full with bright-red tiny fruits. Then, finally, the tracks led to three deer beds, the edges soft and fluted by deer hair, the bottoms melted away by their body heat all the way down to the dead orchard grass. Three beds, different sizes—three does, maybe, or two does and a fawn, perhaps a doe with two fawns. Probably not a buck at this time of year.

I found myself at the upstairs bedroom window after dark for many nights after that. I wanted to see the deer, dark gray against the snow, moving in the moonlight, unaware that I was watching. I could imagine their slow, graceful steps, how they might raise their heads and twitch an ear, alert for any sign of danger, then step again, put their dark noses to a blade of brown grass, their lips to the brittle dried bloom atop a stalk of Queen Anne's lace. I would check at 10 p.m. just before going to bed. I would glance out at midnight when I got up for the bathroom, and I would check again at 4 a.m., an hour I habitually stir. I thought I might keep vigil all night, with a cup of coffee and a book, but I didn't. I never saw the deer; they eluded me. With each new snow they came again, making tracks across the yard.

The day before, out walking on the country road that runs past our house, just across from our woodcutter neighbor's skidder and log pile, just in front of our dairy-farmer neighbor's wooden pasture fence, Ruth and I found four hypodermic needles scattered in the sandy gravel beside the blacktop. The orange caps over the needles and the plungers stood out in the monotone winter landscape of white, brown, and gray. Some of the syringes were uncapped, some not. I'd never seen that before. I'd heard of needles washed up on New York City beaches, but now, here they were, dropped beside the road so near our home.

The scattered syringes brought to mind the son of a neighbor who had nearly died of a heroin overdose. We had known him since he was a boy. He'd helped take care of our goats and chickens while we were away the year my mother was ill. His mother told me he'd gotten addicted to prescription painkillers after he'd been severely injured in a terrible car accident. When his refills ran out, the boy turned to heroin. After he was released from jail and started treatment, he asked his mother to take him to his appointments. "Mom," he said, "the dealers drive up and down the roads looking for guys like me." They'd track him down, he told her, and offer him the stuff for free to get him hooked again. They knew his routines, his hangout spots, the places he was likely to show up sooner or later. They'd wait for him down at the Citgo gas station, or at the Dutch Treat ice cream place, or at Rick's Market, where he might be buying a pizza or a hot Italian. It unsettles me—dealers in their pickup trucks, their ball caps low over their faces, their gloveboxes full of needles and drugs, cruising the back roads, circling around the farms and pastures and ponds and woods and houses. I waved at someone I didn't know the other day, that casual country wave, and he didn't wave back, not even two fingers raised off the wheel or a nod of his head. Could he have been one of them? I don't like feeling afraid. Do we need to start locking our doors?

Elsewhere, in other yards, friends tell me, the deer were wandering where they seldom did this time of year—closer to the houses, closer to the gardens and the orchards. Were they emboldened by hunger? Were they searching for beechnuts and acorns? Or were they just curious and able to move about more freely on account of this year's not-so-deep snow? Were they being driven out of the forests by snowmobiles or harassed by dogs or coyotes? What forces were at work that we could not see or did not yet understand? One friend told me there had been deer prints right up to his front steps. "They're big animals," he said, "yet they remain invisible, except for their tracks."

Maine, it turns out, is a perfect place to be a drug dealer. With the closures of the toothpick and clothespin and paper mills, the shoe and shirt factories, the sardine canneries, the job prospects in rural Maine dwindled. If you were young and jobless and could not afford college or were afraid to be the first person in your family to try, you might get bored. You might feel isolated up there in the country where they grew potatoes, and you might try any drug, just so you felt you were a part of something bigger than your Podunk little town in the middle of nowhere. Or maybe you just needed the money that selling drugs would bring. Or maybe that's not the story, maybe you worked at a mill, or in the woods, or you fished for lobster. You did hard, dangerous work with your body. You did okay, moneywise, until you got hurt. When you were out with a bad back, there was no money coming in. So, you took this wonderful painkiller that made it all okay. After a while your refills ran out, but you couldn't get out of bed without drugs. Your cousin said he could get you heroin; it was cheaper than the pills and easier to get. Poverty, joblessness, boredom, isolation, and a ready-made, already-addicted citizenry. No wonder drug dealers set up shop in rural Maine. Better for them that the profit margins were higher in bumfuck wherever. And besides, in those little towns stretched out across miles of winding roads and farms and fields and ponds and woods, there weren't enough cops to shake a stick at.

When I went out after that, across the yard to the barn for chores, into the woods for a ski, or for a stroll along the road, I was even more alert to tracks. I saw the wide, three-pronged tracks of wild turkey zigzagging through the snowy oak grove or in the sand beside the road. I saw the almost invisible tracks of mice, like beads on a string, so light that they barely compressed the snow's downy surface. Once in a while there were the prints of lynx, wide and softly furry. Galloping snowshoe hare made deep dents in the snow beneath the hemlock boughs. Fox prints daintily crossed the paths we'd made ourselves on our winter walks. The porcupine, lumbering along on its quite humanlike hands and feet, carved an extra track with its heavy tail. Sometimes I saw the wing prints of a hawk on the snow, showing where it had swooped down out of the sky and grabbed a small rodent. There were deer prints too, of course, and the cross-country ski tracks of our neighbors. Higher up, underneath the power line, was a densely packed road made by snowmobiles that was said to go all the way to the Canadian border. They were all out there, these tracks that branched and wove, like rivers, like veins in the thin underside of an arm; leading from who knows where, heading to somewhere else, they crossed one another, double crossed, creating knots and labyrinths.

I felt surrounded by invisible presences, some benign, even lovely, others malevolent. I thought it strange that I should find deer prints in my yard, that deer would come out of the woods and circle the house at night, just as I thought it curious that my path and my neighbor's son's path should intersect with the paths of opium poppy farmers from Central America, drug lords from Mexico, dealers who'd come from New York City to launch heroin startups. But perhaps I was being naïve. There must be no limit to the lives that exist unbeknownst to me and that connect with mine, no limit to the number of beings that go about their usual business while I am somewhere else, asleep, or not paying attention.

THE TYRANT
AND
THE APPLE TREE

Telling Her

"You did *what*?" M. said to me, incredulous. "You *told* her?" She hadn't wanted me to reveal the nonsecret secret of our secret affair to Ruth. She wanted to tell her lesbian partner first. But I couldn't wait.

It was winter when I finally told Ruth the truth. She and I had been in Portland at the mall, buying new wool coats. Mine was gray. Hers was black. They were expensive coats for us, and we were taking our time. Mine was a tailored combination of a peacoat and a car coat, with a double row of buttons in front and nice fitted seams in the back. The wool was elegant and thick, a deep charcoal gray. I kept thinking that my mother would approve. Ruth's coat was boxier, a hybrid of a peacoat and a cape, with large stylish lapels, deep pockets, and big funky buttons. She looked fabulous in it.

One of the perks of being a lesbian is that, if you are roughly the same size, as Ruth and I were, you could share clothes. And, when you were shopping, you could be in the same dressing room together. My style in clothes improved significantly after I met Ruth. No more uniform of khaki pants, desert boots, and a pressed white shirt. She had more stamina for shopping than I did and was more adventurous. She would encourage me to buy clothes I would normally never consider: a layered ensemble of a short dress with long sleeves worn under a sleeveless shift that was just an inch shorter than the dress, with a long scarf wound around my neck and halfway down my back, all made of thin blue-gray faux linen decorated with small sequins and lace. Ruth cared about bodies. She liked my body and wanted me to know how well-proportioned and attractive it was. "You have such a cute body," she'd say. "You should show it off." My new gray coat, she said, made me look snappy and urban, with a 1960s flare!

Portland, Maine's big city, was a two-and-a-half-hour drive from our farm in the Western Mountains. We didn't go there often. Why were we there that day? Was it the end of the semester, near Christmas? Could it have been that we had dropped M., the woman I was having an affair with, at the airport so she could go home to be with her partner for the holidays? I was still pretending that my infatuation with M. was a secret. We were just friends, I told Ruth, even though that was plainly not true. I talked with M. on the telephone for long stretches each evening, me all googly and spilling out over the floor, my back to a wall in my upstairs office, like an oblivious teenager, while Ruth made dinner in the kitchen.

The snow had started earlier in the evening. By the time Ruth and I began our drive north, the plows were out on the highway. I was driving. The dashboard lights floated in the darkness—green and red. The wipers flapped sloppily back and forth, creating piles of slush on either side of the windshield. The headlights illuminated what had by now become a curtain of fast-falling flakes. What did I say to her? And why then? Was I courageous or stupid? For the next two hours we'd be trapped together in this small space, forced to deal with whatever came up. It was this simple:

"Ruth."

She was staring out the window. Her face was marked by fatigue and worry but was still soft and at ease. "Yes."

"I'm having an affair with M."

"Have you had sex?"

"Yes."

"Since when?"

"Do you mean since when have we been having an affair, or since when have we been having sex?"

"Both."

"When she first got here, pretty much. But mostly since October."

"So you lied to me."

"Yes."

"What do you want to do?"

"I don't know."

"I love you."

"I love you too."

My telling Ruth would crack open new plots in the romantic drama. Once the truth had been revealed, the question became could we possibly just have an open relationship? Ruth considered it; she'd participated in open relationships before. They were not easy, especially for lesbians, she said. Everyone in a situation like that must trust everyone else and be trustworthy themselves; they have to be honest, and they have to be willing to share bodies and emotional allegiances and passions and not be jealous or covetous. It was difficult under the best of circumstances to make something like that work; all parties had to be extraordinarily attuned to their own psychologies. Under the circumstances we were in, Ruth said, it would be a disaster.

Why, I wanted to know, couldn't I have it all—both this reckless passion with someone I did not quite trust, and also abiding love with someone I would lay down my life for? Caught in endless conversations with myself, I mused that what made for passion might not make for true love. M. discounted the idea that over time in a relationship, sexual energy waned, and that something different and wonderful emerged in its place. Those people are fooling themselves, she said. Settling. She promised me a dream: if I stayed with her, we would have the kind of love Ruth and I had built, *and* we'd be ripping each other's clothes off every day.

Instead of breaking up, Ruth and I went to see a couples therapist, driving almost an hour to Brunswick. Mostly she helped us talk to each other and listen.

"Did you hear what Ruth just said, Gretchen?" she asked.

"Yes. She said she can't stay in our relationship if I keep seeing M."

Then it was Ruth's turn.

"Did you hear what Gretchen just said, Ruth?"

"Yes. She said she felt like she was reliving her sexual awakening."

What do you do when you've just been told the best, most raw truth someone can tell, the most accurate communication they can offer you? Sometimes all you can do is hold it.

North Woods Law

Leaves fall off the trees. A chill is in the air, and gunshots ring out across Maine. It's deer season, the most popular big-game hunting season in the state. For the game wardens of Maine, the woods are filled with danger. They save lives and fight crime.... It's the warden's job to make sure everyone follows the laws.

So begins "Deer Deception," episode eight of season two of *North Woods Law*, one of cable television's most popular reality shows, in which I played a small and decidedly unglamorous role.

I had been on my way to the barn to milk the goats and feed the chickens one frosty early November morning when a film crew in a black SUV pulled into the yard, followed by Maine game warden Kris MacCabe, whose black pickup truck bristled with antennae and emergency lights. I knew they were coming, I just didn't know when. I hadn't had time to alter my usual appearance and so was captured on national television in a black quilted winter Carhartt jacket with Ruth's name stitched in script across the upper right, an orange knitted hunting cap pulled down over my forehead (strands of unwashed, uncombed bed-head poking out beneath), and ripped, dirty black rain pants tucked into knee-high muck boots.

Since its initial airing, "Deer Deception" had been rerun multiple times, and years later I would still be surprised, and a little embarrassed, when in the grocery store or at the gas station I was greeted with, "Did I see you on TV? I knew it was you!" The clerks at the

Farmers Union where I got my chicken and goat feed, the tellers at Franklin Savings Bank, my faculty colleagues at the University of Maine at Farmington—even the guy who delivered our heating fuel—had seen me on-screen.

North Woods Law promoters pulled out all the stops when it came to hyping the show, taking full advantage of Maine's reputation as a place of wildness and adventure. Our case didn't involve peril, or risking life and limb, but it did involve wild animals, detective work, handsome game wardens, and those who, you might say, had strayed from their best behavior.

My encounter with the law and three minutes of stardom began on the first day of hunting season that fall, as I was wandering into the upper reaches of our land toward a long stone wall overlooking a gully. The wall was what remained of the hundred-year-old boundary line between our property and the next one over. On my way to my favorite hunting spot, I came across a circle of half-eaten red apples, scattered kernels of dried corn, a crumbled block of molasses, and a small mound of salt. All around the pile were signs of deer—prints, scrapes, and rubs. A scrape is a place where a male deer, a buck, has used his hooves to remove leaves and sticks, laying the rich forest ground bare; he then deposits a scent by urinating on the bare ground. A rub is a place where a buck has used his antlers to rub the bark off of a tree, leaving fresh scratches and cuts—another sign that the rut, or mating season, is in full swing. Footprints and scat around the pile also revealed that wild turkeys, blue jays, and squirrels had visited the site. Above me on the ridge behind the stone wall was a neatly camouflaged metal tree stand with a ladder leading up to it, hidden by netting and hemlock boughs. Even though I could clearly see what I was seeing, I was not sure what I was seeing. It was like walking into your own house, seeing glass on the floor inside the kitchen window, the TV gone, the living room trashed, and not realizing immediately that you have been robbed. I continued to the wall and sat down to wait. A flock of turkeys ambled through, noisy and heavy-footed as a herd of cows. Blue jays called loudly from tree branches around the site, dropping down to feast then fly away. Crows also came to visit, along with squirrels, but no deer.

Sometime later my hunting partner Tiffany arrived, looked at the pile of food, its sweet, yeasty odors stronger now that the sun had come out, and said: "You shouldn't be sitting there. This is a baiting site, and if a game warden came along right now you would be in big trouble." As I came down from the wall and joined her, we both noticed a game camera strapped to an oak tree about waist high near the pile. I had already unknowingly walked in front of the camera, but Tiff was careful to avoid being photographed. For good measure, she hiked to the top of the ridge to check whether the deer stand was marked, as required by law, with its owner's name, address, and telephone number. It wasn't.

It had taken all this time for the scene to come into focus. Someone unknown to me had set up an unmarked

Deer hunting stand camouflaged with netting and branches

Illegal bait of apples and corn

deer stand on the edge of our land, and in the gully below had baited the deer. On top of that, said person was using a game camera to monitor the comings and goings of the animals that had been lured in by the food. Use of the camera was legal, but the unmarked stand and the bait were not.

As soon as Tiff and I got back to the house, I called the Maine Game Warden service. Kris MacCabe, the warden in Franklin County, was at the house within an hour. Once we pointed him in the right direction, MacCabe took the lead, jogging the half mile or so up to the baiting site, Ruth and I struggling to keep pace with his long, youthful strides and wondering to ourselves how he knew where he was going. Evidently that pile of goodies in the woods had been luring in deer from quite a large radius, and their well-worn tracks were as obvious as painted lines on a highway to MacCabe. Once we arrived, MacCabe, red-cheeked and hardly out of breath, surveyed the surroundings. "This is a good one," he said excitedly. "This is really fresh. Oh, here, look, he came in on an ATV, so he lives nearby. This is a good one. We're gonna catch this cheater." Cheaters and liars. MacCabe disdained them both equally. The game was afoot.

The next morning as I was on my way to the barn, MacCabe returned with the film crew from *Animal Planet*. With a microphone in my face, I was a bit tongue-tied, but I managed to express what I sincerely felt about the necessity for respecting animals, not trying to trick them, not making hunting something you pursue solely for human amusement, and how offended we felt that one of our neighbors would plop down a pile of apples on our land, and a deer stand too, and not even ask us if it was okay.

What bothered me most about the baiter was the coldness of his tactics. Baiters, MacCabe told us, typically had two or three or more sites where they placed bait and game cameras so they could see which animals came to the site and exactly when. Deer, like most animals, are creatures of habit—if you've seen a buck arrive at a bait-ing site at 5 p.m. for five days in a row, you could expect he'd be there on the sixth day at the same time. Once the baiters download the footage from their game cameras, they have all the information they need to precisely time their arrival at their deer stands, and BANG! There would be no approaching quietly on foot before dawn, no lug-ging a backpack full of a day's provisions, no shivering in the cold, snow, or rain for hours upon hours, no suffering from hyperalertness alternating with excruciating boredom, no climbing down from your stand to pee and then climbing back up again, no praying that a deer would walk into your gunsights. None of that. You'd just get in, get your deer, and get out. MacCabe deduced that the baiter was still at work. It was not that no deer were coming to the site, he surmised; it was that the bucks weren't big enough. Our baiter wanted a trophy.

Not only was I disgusted by the idea of killing a living thing to have as a trophy, but the odds also seemed terribly lopsided, what with the bait and the game camera. The deer seemed not to be a respected and admired sentient being but merely an object of play; a thing to be shot at, maybe eaten, possibly stuffed or mounted, bragged about. Another conquest, a notch in a belt. Hunting this way seemed as sterile and disengaged as buying the perfect desired object from a mail-order catalog. The baiter's tactical approach seemed another example of the American penchant for accumulation and instant gratification.

Part of hunting for me has always been about the meat; I like venison. Part was about submission to time and chance—practice in letting go. I often thought that I had only a small bit of control over whether I shot a deer. Sometimes I imagined that the deer met me halfway. This may sound naïve and romantic, as in "the deer offers itself to be shot." But why not? I was willing to believe in things I didn't understand, such as the possibility of an intuitive relation-ship between hunters and animals. Deer meat in my freezer wasn't something I was entitled to; it was a gift, and hunting in any way that felt ungracious, greedy, or disrespectful dishonored that gift. As long as I hunted with a spirit of honesty, gratitude, and patience, I felt I was honoring the gift of the deer.

The film crew came every morning for a week, emerging from the late fall woods wet and shivering, their city clothes—blue jeans and cotton hoodies—soaked through. We invited them in for cookies and coffee and were regaled with stories about other *North Woods Law* adventures. The cameramen revealed that MacCabe was the most popular of the show's wardens, earning him the nickname Officer MacBabe, which made him blush.

After hiding behind trees for a day or two and failing to catch the perpetrator in the act, MacCabe put his own game camera in a tree overlooking the baiting site and caught the baiter on film refreshing the site with burlap bags of apples. "Got him!" MacCabe gleefully exclaimed. The culprit was a middle-aged, balding white male with a gray mustache. MacCabe's next step was to request driver's license photos of the mustachioed, fifty-something males in the neighborhood who had purchased hunting licenses that year, which yielded him three likely suspects. Finally, he went knocking on doors.

All the hubbub around the baiter set me to thinking about my personal hunting ethics. I admired Warden MacCabe's resoluteness in these matters. There was nothing wishy-washy about him. "I don't like cheaters or liars," MacCabe said the first day we met, "and poachers are cheaters and liars." His firm sense of fairness, of right and wrong, and his faith that being good and obeying laws were important, were all attractive to me. He also clearly believed in the power of conscience as a guide.

Aside from following the rules set out in current Maine law, what did I believe was right when it came to hunting? The Boone and Crockett Club, a sport hunting and conservation organization

launched by President Teddy Roosevelt in 1887, created a statement
of fair chase that has for more than a hundred years served as a guide
for hunter behavior, one that makes sense to me. "Fair chase," the organization says bluntly, "is what separates hunting from simply killing or shooting." The statement reads: "Fair chase, as defined by the
Boone and Crockett Club, is the ethical, sportsmanlike, and lawful
pursuit and taking of any free-ranging wild, native North American
big game animal in a manner that does not give the hunter an improper advantage over such animals."

The phrase "improper advantage" was where things got murky and
I started to wobble. While baiting and hunting over a baited site were
acts punishable as class E crimes, there were all kinds of other tricks
that could legally be employed to give hunters advantage over deer.
Old-timers advised that if you really wanted to get a deer, you had to
first be a keen hunter, have done your homework, and be hunting in
the right place. You had to know which way the wind was blowing
(deer have sensitive noses) and be patient. For those who thought
that approach was too old-fashioned and too much work, there were
lures and scents and gimmicks galore. There was 100 percent fresh
whitetail doe urine, with additional additives and preservatives. Such
concoctions sported brand names such as Hot-N-Ready XXX and
Fatal Obsession. Other tricks included covering your human smell by
spraying your hunting clothes with pine scent or, better yet, storing
them the night before the hunt in a big bag with fresh pine needles.
You could tie scent rags to your ankles so you smelled like a fox instead of a human, hang scent wicks on tree limbs, spray dominant
buck smell around your hunting spot, or pretend you were a buck
and make your own scrapes and rubs, sprinkling them with doe urine
and buck piss. "Think of a scrape like a sales pitch," read one hunting blog. "You are the car dealer and the buck is your customer." If
you made a mock scrape, you could hang over it a "licking branch,"

another way deer leave scent and communicate with one another. One such product went by the name Branch Magic. Another trick was to learn to use a deer call; you could make doe-in-heat calls or horny-buck calls.

Given all the schemes I could have legally employed to give myself an advantage over the deer I was stalking, what, I wondered, constituted improper advantage? According to the Boone and Crockett Club, improper advantage included hunting deer that could not get away from you (they were fenced in, caught in deep snow, or trapped), hunting animals by jacklights (freezing them in the glare of automobile headlights), driving deer, and using decoys or dogs—anything that "overwhelmed game species with human capabilities."

A modern hunting rifle could be regarded as an improper advantage, equipped as many are with powerful scopes, multibullet cartridges, and semiautomatic triggers. I owned a rifle called the Savage Lady Hunter, advertised as a gun for "the little lady." As problematic as the name was for me, on so many levels, it fit my small stature, was not too heavy to carry, and had a single-shot bolt action, which I was familiar with from my first days of hunting with my ex-husband when I was in my twenties. The process of shopping for my hunting rifle offered a doorway into a world of guns, bullets, and hunting paraphernalia that seemed far removed from my goals of harvesting food, spending time in the outdoors, and connecting with nature and animals. The spirit of this world was one of technology, dominance, violence, trickery, and human hubris.

The culture in the gun department of the major sporting goods store where I shopped over many weeks for my rifle was sexist and toxic. The most dispiriting thing I witnessed was the array of semiautomatic weapons and handguns on display, one a lavender pistol in a pink box, called the Lavender Lady. Bending down to look more closely at the product, I found myself head to head with a girl three feet high, her mother behind her. "Oh, look, honey," the mother said. "Go tell Daddy you want this one. It's your favorite color." Added to these disturbing gender dynamics was the presence of many dead trophy animals posed in taxidermic splendor amid sculpted sets of mountain peaks, stream sides, and woodlands. My shopping experience was, at best, deeply alienating. Really, all I wanted was some venison for my table.

As Ruth and I discussed the actions of the baiter on our land, she accused me of being uncharacteristically judgmental, to which I responded with some embarrassment at being called out. I do, after all, think of myself as one of the good guys.

"What does ethics have to do with it, if you are talking about taking the life of an animal?" she asked, in a spirit of debate. "If an animal is going to die at the hands of a hunter, who cares how it dies?"

"For God's sake," she added, "you hunt from a tree! Some people might find that appalling." She reminded me that she had long been suspicious of the supposed ethical superiority of catch-and-release fishing, which she argued tortured the fish for the sake of human entertainment. "Drawing up 'rules' makes it all seem like a game," she said, "and who are we to be playing games with the lives of animals?"

"Maybe you shouldn't be hunting deer at all," she offered, "unless you live a subsistence lifestyle and need the meat to survive." Perhaps, she suggested, setting up rules for killing animals, be they deer or fish, was a way for humans to let themselves off the hook, assuage their guilt, rationalize their violence.

Ruth was right, of course. Since deer are not used to predators that might approach them from the air, some might regard hunting from a tree stand as overwhelming the deer with human capabilities. And while the baiter's hunting tactics didn't feel right to me, mine might have seemed to him inept and careless. My method was to scout our woods several times in early fall before hunting season looking for scrapes and rubs. When I found a decent site, I looked for a tall, strong straight tree within shooting distance of the deer sign, where I placed my stand fifteen to twenty feet in the air. Then I waited. And waited. And waited. And waited. I never knew when a deer would appear. Sometimes I was taken by surprise and fumbled around and scared the deer, or I just plain missed the shot. Sometimes I wrote poems from my perch, or got on my cellphone, and the deer snuck by me; I'd hear a twig snap and see a white tail sailing away from me through the trees. Sometimes I just zoned out: listening to the wind and the songs that the crows offered back and forth to one another, watching leaves fall, admiring the birds, the squirrels. When I got too cold I climbed down and walked around, making lots of noise and scaring off any deer within half a mile.

"None of this is fair," Ruth reminded me. "You go out with a gun to kill an animal. You eat it. You do it for a purpose, but you don't need to eat deer. You can eat vegetables and peanut butter." And this presented another conundrum: If I didn't need to hunt in order to eat or clothe myself, was hunting, then, for people like me, just an elitist, sadistic pastime?

The visits from the *Animal Planet* film crew and word that we'd be featured on *North Woods Law* had our rural neighborhood abuzz. One neighbor was inspired to come by and apologize to us on behalf of the baiter. Come spring, after the show aired, the apologetic neighbor knocked on the door again to ask if we'd seen "our show." We had.

On the screen, we'd all seen MacCabe pulling into driveways in his dark truck, confidently striding onto our neighbors' porches, rapping on doorframes, asking, in disarmingly polite tones, questions designed to catch the men off guard and narrow the search: "Did you hunt this year? Do you wear glasses? Are these the clothes you hunt in? Do you wear glasses all the time, even when you hunt?" MacCabe's big break came when a neighbor flagged him down on the road and positively identified the "cheater": "Yep, that's him."

And so MacCabe approached the final door, knowing he had his man. "Any idea why I might be here?" he asked the baiter, who was at first incredulous that he had been caught on camera: "You *filmed* me?"

The baiter confessed. He did bait the site, but, he added defensively, "I haven't sat over it." It didn't matter, MacCabe explained. The two crimes were separate—baiting and hunting over a baited site.

"The sad part," MacCabe scolded the baiter, who sulked in the passenger seat of the warden's truck with his arms crossed over his chest, "is that they're large landowners over there and now they're gonna close their land to hunting because of what you did. Just think about all the other guys who want to hunt around the area. They just lost another chunk of land." In the end we did not close our land to hunting but posted it to permission only; anyone who wanted to hunt there would have to ask us first.

The baiter was issued two summonses and had to pay a three-hundred-dollar fine. Was that enough? MacCabe had remarked that the baiter, like all "cheaters and liars," like everyone who didn't follow the law, would have to live with the consequences of his actions; he'd have a karmic debt to pay. Even though I consider myself a law-abiding hunter, neither a cheater nor a liar, and find some succor in my good intentions toward the animals I kill, I still harbor the thought that I too owe amends.

A Chicken in Every Pot

I have sharpened my knives, I have
Put on the heavy apron.
Maybe you think life is chicken soup, served
In blue willow-pattern bowls.
I have put on my boots and opened
The kitchen door and stepped out
Into the sunshine. I have crossed the lawn,
I have entered
The hen house.

    — Mary Oliver, "Farm Country"

My grandmother, Anna Shoberg Johnson, was the matron of a Minnesota dairy farm with its fields and cows, tractors and teams of hired men, a barn and silos, its own huge vegetable gardens and a flock of hens. I never had the chance to follow my grandmother around the farmyard. She was bedridden by the time I was old enough to shadow her as she did her chores. But I do have a picture of her in a baggy white housedress and lopsided straw hat, her ample bosom and backside filling out the front and back of the dress, her flock of white hens gathered around her feet as she tossed them corn from a bucket. My mother told me once that Anna wore this same outfit every morning as she entered the hen yard to feed the birds or the coop to collect eggs; the hens would be upset by any alteration of the usual, and she didn't want to put them off their laying. The "egg money" Anna earned was a significant income; it helped send my mother to Saint Paul for voice lessons. To inaugurate my own chicken coop when it was brand new, a friend made me a collage incorporating this picture of my grandmother in her hen yard. The artwork adorned the door of my coop. When I looked at it each morning, I wondered if raising chickens might have been in my blood.

Ruth's and my chicken farming began with a flock of twenty birds, some little balls of fluff a few days old, some the mothers of those baby chicks, some well-established laying hens, and Big Red, our beloved rooster. The transition from fluffy cuteness to the realities of farm life was swift. When the chicks grew up, we counted seven roosters! Our yard was mayhem, the younger roosters honing their crowing skills with earsplitting warbles and screeches, and the older rooster fighting the young ones for control of the flock. There were roosters everywhere, crowing, strutting, stomping, puffing out their feathered breasts, and beating their wings in the air. When the roosters mounted the hens, they grabbed the girls by their necks and held on with their talons. The hens began to lose feathers and lose heart, their egg production falling off. We also found it disturbing to watch what looked like rape going on in our barnyard every five minutes.

We realized we'd have to cull the flock and began deciding which rooster to keep—we only needed one. We wanted a young one, we thought at first, and picked out a large, energetic, and beautiful red fellow with green-tinted tail feathers, a huge red comb, and stately bearing. Young Red would help create a new generation of strong and beautiful chicks, we reasoned. But then we began to watch how he acted in the yard. Turned out he was a bully; he'd race after the hens, tackling the girls to the ground. When Old Red intervened, Young Red would fly at the old guy with his talons stretched. In the end, we decided to keep Old Red, the original who came with the flock. The hens liked him. They ran to him when the younger roosters came after them. He was gentle and attentive, coming when the hens called, watching over them as they pecked at bugs in the grass, even alerting them to juicy morsels he'd found and wanted to share. Once he found a frog and brought it to the hens, calling them to circle around him, then dropping the frog in front of them on the grass. Big Red seemed as perfect a rooster as could be, so I set about butchering the other roosters.

Despite perhaps having inherited a penchant for chicken farming from my grandmother, the actual knowledge of how to manage a flock didn't automatically trickle down. Like most of the agricultural education I'd amassed, the information about how to raise and butcher my own chickens came from websites, articles, books, hearsay, the staff at the Farmers Union, other farmers, but mostly just plain experience. When I needed advice about butchering the roosters, for instance, Jack Mills, our excavator, recommended I lay the birds down on the chopping block in the yard and whack their heads off with a sharp axe. That's the way he did it when he was a kid. He'd joke then about how the chicken would rise up, flapping, and run around the yard spraying blood. *Just like a chicken with its head cut off.* I didn't see how I could lay the bird down and have it stay still enough for me to aim my axe. Besides, I was afraid I'd miss. If I wasn't comfortable with the "cold axe" method, Jack recommended the "hypnotism followed by the axe" method: lay the bird down on a chopping block, beak up, take a pencil and slowly circle the eraser end around the bird's face, then place the pencil beside the bird's head. According to Jack, the bird would follow the pencil and lie perfectly still with its eyes on the pencil while you raised the axe. I'd also learned another trick by watching a YouTube video: when you held a bird by its feet, head down, it was likely to be more docile, thus relaxing and quieting the bird before the axe.

I combined everything I'd gathered and created my own method, which I executed seven times over the course of a month. I would catch each rooster in the early morning while he was still in the coop, which eliminated sneaking up on him (you can't) or running after him (you'll never catch one) or trying to fool the bird to within grabbing distance with handfuls of grain (they're smarter than we give them credit for). I tucked the rooster under my arm until we got to my butchering station—a piece of baling twine knotted around the clothesline—whereupon I'd take the rooster's two feet in one hand and gently turn him, then tie his feet with the twine. There he'd hang in front of me, about chest height, his wings draped outward, blinking in the cool morning air. If he started to fuss, I'd circle my index finger slowly around his head—a version of Jack's pencil hypnotics.

Something wholesome and softhearted in me rightly rises up when it comes time to kill and butcher a chicken, but something in me that appreciates farm living and knowing the origin of my food keeps me dealing with the blood and guts and feathers nonetheless. The chicken soup that simmers on the back burner in the deep of winter doesn't, after all, originate in a can; it comes from somewhere else first. My grandmother Anna butchered her own fowl all the time. If she wanted to make her somewhat famous chicken stew, she'd begin by putting on her apron, sharpening her knife, and heading to the henhouse. Cooks all over the world do the same to this day; the fully feathered live chicken purchased at the stall in the village market is carried home in a box or basket and becomes dinner. Should I be able to escape the necessity, the givenness of killing, and still enjoy the privilege of a chicken in my pot or on my grill?

As I ponder this question, what comes to mind is a billboard advertisement I once saw for KFC, that American supplier of fast food chicken to the globe's hungry masses. The billboard featured a young woman whose face sported a naughty grin and the text "I ate the bones!" She only thought she ate the bones. Actually, there were no bones in the chicken thigh she just consumed. To meet the changing tastes of a population of young people who don't actually know where their chicken comes from and are kind of grossed out by the idea of a skeleton, KFC started serving its original chicken recipe without bones. I hold KFC's boneless chicken in my imagination next to the memory of a friend I met in Bhutan whose favorite dish was chicken necks with their hundreds of tiny bones, chopped into bites and simmered in mouth-puckeringly hot green chilies. It seems to me that if you are going to eat the chicken, you must honor the bones; the whole live sentient being.

I am satisfied that my ethics in relation to chicken raising and butchering are solid. I have the best of intentions. I have chosen a life that requires such tasks. But even so, on the days when I butchered the extra roosters, it took all I had to control my revulsion for the task. The worst moment was when I took the beautifully feathered neck in one hand and with the other sliced swiftly through it with a sharp knife. One quick movement and the rooster's head would be in my hand, his dangling body quivering and dripping blood from the neck. There was no squawking, hardly any flapping, only the rich red velvet of the rooster's blood silently pulsing down onto the grass.

The moment I end the life of a chicken is both a sacred and brutal moment; a flash of truth—a fleeting, exact second of blinding clarity. When the knife is at the throat and I resolve to press it deeper, a certain brutishness takes over. I don't believe there is any way, no matter how nice a person you are, to kill any living creature, from a fly to a human, without experiencing this spell of terrible ruthlessness. It's gruesome to slit a living creature's throat; that's all there is to it.

I had to do the butchering one bird at a time (one a day was quite enough), and each day that I killed a rooster had to be a right day. I waited for days when I felt unsentimental, but also strong, days when there wasn't any other emotional difficulty waiting in the wings, days when I loved each rooster, unconditionally, and could kill him without resentment or happiness, without being glad to get rid of him, or sad that he would be gone. On those days, as I reached for the handle on the chicken coop door, I crossed myself and took a deep breath. The act of crossing myself surprised me—this is not part of my religious heritage, but at this terrible crossroads ritual seemed called for. People for thousands of years have known this and practiced it. It isn't that I wanted to be forgiven for what I was about to do—after all, I was making food for myself and my partner and our friends. It was more that I wanted protection from the killer I was about to encounter within myself. *May I respect and honor this rooster and the food he will provide. May the thing in me that makes me able to kill the rooster stay where it belongs and not take on a life of its own. Protect me from the darkness that I approach when I get his blood on my hands.*

That was the beginning, one rooster at a time. After that, we moved on to raising up to as many as forty meat birds per year to fill our freezer and to sell or give to friends. We started our meat bird adventure raising Cornish Crosses—now the factory standard and a favorite of many family farmers. As they say in the business, the Cornish Cross "has a high feed-conversion ratio and low levels of activity," allowing one to raise a bird from a day-old puff of downy feather to a five- to seven-pound broiler in as few as nine weeks. Cornish Cross is what you buy in the grocery store. The birds are genetically engineered for meat alone, not eggs—in fact, they've been so lab-managed for fast growth and beefy thighs that they don't live long enough to reproduce naturally; they'd likely be long dead of heart or immune system failure by laying time.

The eight- to nine-week-long process of raising Cornish Crosses for meat has its distinct phases. The first step was Chick Day, a day we marked on the calendar well in advance, when we brought a cardboard box and our checkbook to Greaney's Turkey Farm in Mercer, Maine. The farmhouse kitchen at Greaney's on Chick Day was sweet with the smell of soft yellow feathers and chick poop. It was also noisy—a din of peeps. Everyone's face, as they left with a box of chicks, was goofy with elemental joy. This was the first step in the process of raising an animal to eat, and that bloody end wasn't in sight yet—just a sunny spring day and these newborn yellow puffs with their dark peppercorn eyes, impossibly perfect tiny feet and orange beaks, all of the animal weighing less than a clump of cotton balls in your hand. The world this baby bird had known up until that moment had been as far removed from "natural" as you could get: laid by a hen but then incubated in finely controlled machines that regulate temperature and humidity, hatched into a world of Styrofoam and metal, shipped off immediately in a cardboard box to destinations around the country, then home with a stranger; all that before it had even had a sip of water or a bite to eat.

Step two was raising the chicks to the point when their real feathers come in. Normally, this would be accomplished by a hen who would offer her warm breast and the cozy undersides of her ample wings to her chicks, who would duck in and out of her feathers, burrowing into their mother's heat. But these chicks had no mother. It was all up to us. Until they could keep themselves warm, the chicks needed close observation and temperature control. Upon the advice of Mr. Greaney, we added a small amount of sugar to the chicks' waterers on the first day, made sure to dip the beak of each chick into the water dish as we set them into their new home, and watched to make sure each chick understood what water was and how to drink. We put their food out in wide pans that they could easily get to and made sure to keep the dishes filled at all times. We used a simple plastic children's wading pool lined with wood shavings as a pen, keeping the chicks on the enclosed front porch, where we could keep an eye on them as we came and went from the house—watching to see if they were too warm or not warm enough, in need of more food or water, or, as was the case one year, stumbling around dehydrated and in need of Gatorade to replenish their electrolytes. When the chicks got their first soft feathers and could stand a little cold, we moved the wading pool to the barn, complete with the heat lamp, where they remained until fully feathered.

Once they were "adults," taking care of meat chickens was easy— they needed food, water, a clean pen, sunshine, and fresh air. We'd been advised that Cornish Cross were the "couch potatoes" of the chicken world and, even if let out to free range, would rather sit still and eat themselves silly on high-protein grain. Standard wisdom about Cornish Cross was that they needed about one square foot of space per bird. We learned that, in fact, our Cornish Crosses liked much more space than that. They liked to run and jump, leap for bugs, chase each other about, and preen in the sun. We locked them safely in a large covered outdoor pen at night, then during the day let them out to roam in a wide grassy area, protected by a portable electric fence. This way they could exercise their full chicken selves, running after butterflies and bees, scratching in the dirt, relaxing in the shade of a summer's day, pulling up worms. They got to ex-perience the pace of the day—the sun's slow rise and set, darkness, starlight, moonshine—simple things that every chicken, whether raised to provide us with meat or eggs, deserves. What we discovered delighted us and put to rest the lies we'd been told about these thor-oughly normal birds—when treated like real chickens, they acted like real chickens—and, by the way, tasted like real chickens. Their meat was firm and flavorful, with a hint of grass.

After nine weeks, it was time to "process" the birds—one of the many euphemisms for butchering. The same place where we bought the day-old chicks, Greaney's, where they used the word "slaughter" instead of "butcher," offered to quickly, humanely, and neatly do the job for $4.00 per bird, which significantly increased the cost of raising our own broilers. After having the processing done for us several years in a row, we decided to try it ourselves—it couldn't be *that* hard, after all, and would save us a tidy sum. At the end of a long, cold, exhausting day, we smelled like wet chicken feathers and fresh guts; our fingertips were nicked with knife pokes, our hands were red and raw. We had two garbage bags full of matted white feathers, another bag of feet, heads and offal, and a year's worth of hefty hens weighed and wrapped for the freezer. It was an invaluable exercise that taught us a lot about our relationship to labor and food, but one we never relished repeating.

In later years we would collaborate with a neighbor, Jonathan, who had created a small and lucrative business by helping friends butcher their barnyard fowl. His homemade whizbang plucker, a plastic tub fitted with rubber fingers spun by an old lawn mower engine, made quick work of the plucking. His general know-how was also useful. Among the things we learned from him was that optimal feather-loosening temperature of the water into which you dunk each bird prior to plucking should be 155°F—too hot and the skin breaks, too cold and the skin doesn't open to let out the feathers. We also learned that the quickest and most humane way to kill and bleed a chicken is to put it head first into an upside-down orange traffic cone, the tip of which you've cut off with a sharp knife.

These "killing cones" also come in a more professional stainless steel version. Once you pull the chicken's head out of the tip of the cone, you carefully make a quick slit on either side of the neck, severing major arteries, then allow the bird to bleed. Jonathan had reclaimed a stainless-steel countertop and sinks from a remodel at a local high school, which served as an excellent, expansive surface

Rubber fingers inside the spinning barrel remove all feathers

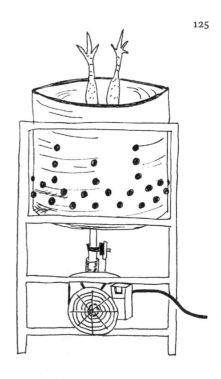

Chicken plucking machine

on which to gut and wash each bird. After that, each bird was placed upside down on a homemade drying rack (a circle of PVC piping with upright posts every six inches) and then put into a shrinkable freezer bag, which, when dipped in hot water, would conform neatly to the bird's shape, eliminating excess air and prohibiting freezer burn. During these marathon sessions, my job was to fetch the birds from their cages in the back of our truck, put them in the cones, and slit their throats. Ruth's job was to dip each bird in hot water and run the plucking machine, while Jonathan expertly gutted and washed each one. We had a hunch our "help" might actually have diminished Jonathan's efficiency somewhat, but it lowered the price of the processing to $2.50 per bird.

Our friend Leslie, who with her husband Ben and their sons ran a local CSA (community-supported agriculture) operation near us,

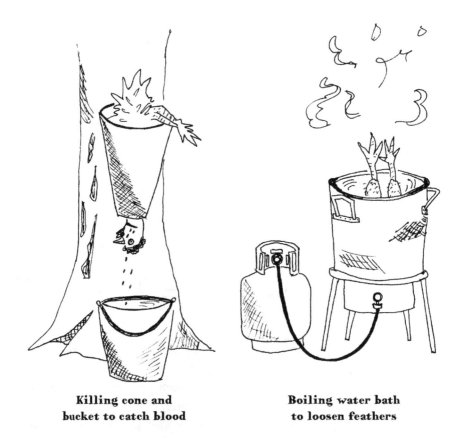

Killing cone and
bucket to catch blood

Boiling water bath
to loosen feathers

remarked once that farming is all about good recordkeeping. I have tried. My erratic records show that the average price of our home-grown birds had gone steadily down from a high of almost $5 per pound to $1.84 per pound, not counting our labor. The average weight of our birds had gone from a low of three pounds to a high of more than six pounds. One of our chickens weighed in at ten pounds—a bird the likes of which would not have fit my grandmother's soup pot, perhaps not even in her oven!

When I was small, I'd often watch attentively while my mother prepared our once-a-week chicken meal. I'd watch her use special kitchen scissors to cut through the meat and joints and trim away the fat. She'd then dredge each piece in flour. It seemed to me then a complicated technical exercise to cut up a chicken, but she made it look simple. She'd save the giblets, of course—the heart, liver, and gizzard—for fried chicken livers and onion (a favorite dish she made and ate by herself) and giblet gravy. The back and neck from the small whole broiler, which probably weighed three pounds or less, always went into the stockpot set into a well at the back of my mother's electric stove, a stove so formidable that it looked like the grille of a Chevy parked against the kitchen wall. I often wondered how she knew just where to cut to make all those legs and thighs, wings and breastbones. If I'd asked, I'm sure she would have told me cutting up a chicken was something she watched her mother do, just like kneading bread.

At the end of a summer of raising broilers, our freezer was full. Our sustenance was assured. We felt prosperous in the most old-fashioned of ways. And we had the entire fall and winter ahead to peruse our cookbooks for new ways to prepare these plump, delicious gifts—these gifts made of grass, sunlight, water, feather, bone, and our own labor. You'd think that once the thighs and breasts and wings and drumsticks were simmering in olives and rosemary on the stove we'd want to erase the previous phases of the chicken's life from our minds, but I found the opposite was true. Knowing where my chicken came from, how it grew, what it ate, that it had a personality, a voice, and a heart, provided me with a longer, deeper, more complex story about the relationship of living things to living things. Life is hard, even ugly, sometimes difficult, but full of delight and beauty too. It seemed a fitting tribute to remember as much as I could, to imagine as much as I could, about the life of that chicken, the one that was simmering in the pot—to remember the day it came to us, soft and yellow and so small it fit in the palm of my hand; and to remember the day I played a role in its transformation from a living creature into human food, how cold the day was, how wet, and how, as I lifted it from the back of the pickup truck, the bird beat its wings against my arms, marking me with bruises.

The Tyrant and the Apple Tree

The unyielding army will not win.
The rigid tree will be felled.
The rigid and big belong below.
The soft and weak belong above.

— Lao Tzu, *The Tao Te Ching*

The apple tree that hung over the driveway at our farm was a stunted, twisted, unhealthy thing that had been shaded for too many years by maple and ash. The sour green fruit it dropped onto the gravel at the end of the summer made food for squirrels and blue jays, but most of the apples never got eaten—we would find them in the spring, mushy and brown from the winter freeze and spring thaw, slippery and flattened by our car tires and the snowplow. One day, in the fall of the year when my mother had started dying, I decided to trim the tree back to health, an encounter that went horribly wrong and could have killed me. I escaped with my life.

It all started with our woodcutter, Darrell. In the process of culling some towering maple, beech, and ash that shaded a spot in the yard where we wanted to plant three new apple trees, a plum, and a pear, he had discovered several wild apples, remnants of the former owner's long-ago orchard. He cleared around them and trimmed their limbs so that, as he put it, "they looked nearly dead." He assured me that if they had any life in them at all, this drastic pruning, a near-death

experience for the trees, would jolt them back to life and into bloom
the next spring.

Darrell was in his early thirties, of medium height, with a wide-
open, friendly face, sweet eyes, a quick smile, a sturdy girth, and
thick, muscled arms. He dressed most often in loose, well-worn dirty
jeans, a raggedy sweat-stained T-shirt, a ball cap, or a hard hat with
a face mask and ear protection, and logging boots. Mosquitoes and
blackflies seemed not to bother him; he worked in short sleeves and
never used, as far as I saw, insect repellant. He made cutting down an
eighty-foot maple look easy, his fluid, sure movements reminiscent
of a tai chi practitioner. He worked hard from the moment he arrived
until the moment he left, which was often after dusk, stopping only
occasionally for a drink from a bottle of water he'd set under a shade
tree or, if pressed, a cold soda from our fridge. I never saw him stop
for lunch or a snack. At the end of the day he was always soaked with
sweat, rivulets of dirt trailing down his face and neck. He was strong
and had stamina and liked physical work. The day Darrell first helped
me move 150 bales of hay, he threw each rectangular fifty-pound
bale from the barn floor ten feet straight up to where I stood in the
hayloft, all the while keeping up a steady conversation with me about
weather, goat breeding, the antics of his daughters, and the price of
hay.

Having worked in the woods since high school, Darrell had a
good eye for trees. He found a few more problem trees for us—pines
and hemlocks leaning dangerously toward the house and hovering
menacingly over the barn. These he dispatched quickly, using several tools besides the chainsaw, including an aluminum ladder and
a come-along—a simple rope with one end tied to the tree and the
other attached to some other sturdy structure to gently encourage
the tree to fall in a desired direction. As I went about my own chores
while Darrell was working, I kept an eye on him, watching how he did

things, waiting for a break in the roar of the chainsaw to offer him a cold drink.

I admired the careful, slow way Darrell would assess a tree, looking it over from top to bottom, scanning the woods around it, the sky above it, looking to see how it intersected with the leaves and branches of the trees nearby, estimating its height, weight, the power and reach of its fall, even the number of two-by-fours one could expect from it after milling. Some trees he knew best to simply walk away from, such as the rotting rock maple at the end of our driveway, which dropped a branch or two across the road every winter. His advice was to let either nature or the town road crew take care of that one. Darrell's work seemed like effortless grace, or perhaps graceful effort—human physical power in near perfect balance with trees, bales of hay, with goats and oxen, with all manner of matter.

For my part, I have tended toward an unbalanced relationship with matter. I have been known to be what Ruth calls a "bull and jammer," someone who meets force with force rather than sensibly yielding. In other words, I break things, and though I feel heartily sorry for it afterward, in the fever that seizes me at the time of battle, I am dumb to consequences.

Searching for theories with which to illuminate my own stubbornness, I turn to my parents, who were the yin and yang of patience versus force. Theirs, however, was not that serene, black-and-white full circle of balanced female and male, hard and soft energy represented by the Taoist taijitu, but a perverted version of such—each supposedly mutually supportive quality somehow radically out of balance with the other. Being in my father's presence often felt as if you were the spoon in the trick where the magician directs all his psychic energy to bending the utensil into some contorted angle, only to prove the power of his mind. While he erred on the side of hardness and aggression, my mother erred on the side of passivity.

She met my father's mostly verbal blows and abuse by sinking into a soft cloud of daily drunkenness. While my father rubbed people the wrong way, my mother rubbed them the other. While his shaming and cajoling brought out either the best or the worst in those around him, she mostly just let people be. He made things happen. She let them happen. She was kind and generous and easy to be around; he was best avoided, and if that was impossible, quietly obeyed. He inspired anxiety and anger; she, calm and creativity. Perhaps their desperate, tragically imbalanced marriage was, after all, some sort of dysfunctional harmony.

For my father, nothing could ever be the result of chance, luck, or fate. If something bad happened to you, it was your own damn fault or someone else's. If you got sick, it was because you were dumb enough to be around someone spreading germs, or it was a character flaw. If you got a tenure-track position in a lousy academic job market after seven expensive years of graduate school, it was because you were a superior person and outcompeted your peers, not because you were in the right place at the right time. For my father, life was plannable, executable, preventable, and reflected directly on the efforts of the human individual. One of his favorite pieces of wisdom was, "If you want it done right, do it yourself." All these qualities, of course, are highly prized in America, while my mother's softness was often over-looked as a strength—even, sometimes, by me.

All Darrell's tree cutting got me excited. There was something energizing about the noise of the chainsaw, the smell of gasoline and oil, the magnificent sight and sound of a tree sailing toward the ground, falling, falling, falling, the blue sky looming behind the green crown, the surprisingly soft but earthshaking thump as the giant fan of leaves and branches hit the ground. One day, after Darrell had finished his work and gone home, I decided I would trim our old pear tree, preparing it for the wonderful life it would have because of our planting a new "mate" for it nearby. The pear tree in question had grown dramatically in the six years since we'd bought our house; the only problem was that it was nearly bare on one side. Darrell had taken down a gnarled pine that had been shading the old pear, and now the tree stood in full sun, looking strange and gawky.

I had promised Ruth that I would never use guns, large knives, or power tools, such as chainsaws, table saws, wood chippers, or wood splitters when I was alone, so I tackled the tree with a ladder and a tree-pruning saw—a sharp and deeply serrated curved saw at the end of a long pole. What I knew about tree pruning was not much, but I had these concepts under my belt: the limbs should spread open to the sun; the branches should not cross one another; suckers, or new growth shooting straight up from an established branch, should be trimmed; and, in general, a bird should be able to fly through the openings between the branches. The hand tools and the ladder proved sufficient for the pear tree, and after a rather severe pruning (remembering Darrell's comment about trimming the wild apples until they looked "almost dead"), I walked across the yard to survey my work from afar. The new tree looked open and shapely. In a year, I reasoned, it would, with the new and abundant light it would now receive, come fully into itself and, in companionship with its new mate, produce fruit for us. Emboldened, I turned to the apple tree over the driveway.

My parents could also reflect Joseph Campbell's mythic figures of the tyrant and the hero. While the hero submits to what is, the tyrant rages. "The inflated ego of the tyrant is a curse to himself and his world—no matter how his affairs seem to prosper," Campbell writes. The hero, on the other hand, is a person of "self-achieved submission." The hero submits to a kind of transformation. In a conversation with a group of Buddhists, I once mentioned that I'd spent most of my life trying to convince my mother to leave my father, for her good and for ours. Where was her strength? Where was her backbone? I told them the story of how during one of her last long hospital stays she asked me to come close; she had something to tell me, and she'd only say it once. I put my face next to hers, my hand steadying myself on the rail of her hospital bed. "I am not going to leave your father," she whispered, struggling past the still tender scar left from her tracheotomy. "He needs me."

"You should not have been trying to convince her to leave your father," my Buddhist friend scolded me, quite alarmed. "She was obviously a bodhisattva." To me she seemed a doormat, a punching bag. But what if she wasn't? What if giving in was really a strength?

Pruning the apple tree would require a chainsaw. Ruth's voice floated into my consciousness: "Remember that woman over in Mount Vernon who did everything right and still the tree kicked back and pinned her and she died?" The voice was loud enough for me to hear but not persuasive enough to stop me. I had already entered a tunnel of obsession, that tyrant's place of ego and desire; there would be no stopping me now.

After growing mostly upright for about five feet, the apple tree curved into a lazy S; it was trying to find light all those years in the shade. Despite my watching Darrell so closely, I had no idea how to cut a tree that was curved at a not quite ninety-degree angle—whether to cut up through the bottom of the curve, or down from the top, or from the side, or simply start much lower and avoid the curve altogether. I started the chainsaw and began cutting.

The smaller branches that came out from the main trunk were easy. As they crashed to the ground, I stepped off the ladder and stacked them, the butt ends facing one way so they could easily be fed into a wood chipper. I put the slightly larger ones aside to cut into arm-sized logs for the fire. Then came the main trunk. Whatever reason I applied to the problematic angle failed; the cut I made caused the limb to fall into itself. The two parts of the trunk that had wedged together did not yield to my pushing. They also did not yield to my makeshift come-along, one end of which I'd tied to a section of limb and one which I tied around a sturdy nearby tree.

By now, the place where the cut pieces of limb had wedged themselves together had become animate. It and I were in a test of wills, it hanging on stubbornly, and me pushing, yanking, swearing, and all the while wearing myself down in the heat, swatting at blackflies, until I decided to get the damned chainsaw and go at it again, for real this time, like I meant it. I was graceless. I began to hate the tree, hate all trees. I wanted to careen around the yard cutting down

**Old apple tree
and chainsaw**

trees, watching them fall, slicing them up with the chainsaw—*cut, cut, cut*—live branches turned into bits and pieces of mute firewood. Stupid with physical tiredness now, I set the ladder against the tree, climbed to the top step (the step that says NOT A STEP), and dug the chainsaw into the wedge. The blade squealed and smoked until CRACK! and I was on the ground.

I lay still for a moment, scanning my body, trying to assess where I'd been hurt. The chainsaw beside me had automatically shut off. I turned my head to come face-to-face with its still hot, oily motor. I examined my hands, then reached around to the back of my head, feeling for the sticky wetness of blood. There was no blood. Still in a pile of branches, flat on my back, I navigated a hand to the pain in my shoulder. There was no gash; the flesh was whole. I had suffered only a scratch.

What is most interesting to me, in hindsight, is not what happened, but why. Why did I need to prune the apple tree just then, when no one else was home? Why did I blithely ignore my agreement with Ruth? Why did I change my mind and decide not just to prune the tree but to cut the whole thing down? Why didn't I give up when it got too difficult, when it was clearly dangerous? Why did the danger seem, instead, to feed my crazy resolve? Why wasn't I wearing a hard hat, goggles, gloves, earplugs, and chaps? Why did I persist, even after the thick limb of the leaning apple had wedged tight against itself? Was there something wrong with my brain? Did I have a death wish?

A mania had taken hold of me. I wanted no tree where there had been one for seventy years. I wanted to see those smooth, raw, wet wounds in the wood. I wanted to see the limbs with their clean butt ends lying beside the driveway. I wanted what I wanted. I was in the tight, hot grip of what I'd heard mindfulness teachers call "the wanting mind." The tyrannical mind. It was pure selfishness mixed with anger at an inanimate object. It couldn't be dressed up as anything else. There was nothing ennobling about it.

"I see you got that apple trimmed," Darrell said to me the next time he came by. I said yes. He no doubt also saw the grotesque, mangled five-foot-tall stump I had left behind. I had imagined I'd return the next day to finish my job, but I wanted nothing more to do with that tree. It reminded me of my own failure and shame. I had gone into the project with the best of intentions, a rescuer of sorts, and I had become something else. "You can cut the rest down," I told Darrell, and he did. The thick, hard limbs I had managed to lop off were lying beside the driveway. I hadn't had the strength left to buck them up.

Those apple logs were split and dried and burned in the winter fire. Still, every time I passed where the tree used to be, as I drove into or out of the yard, carted the garbage down, or walked to check the mail, I was reminded of that day. I remembered how I tried to force the apple tree to do my bidding. I seemed to have been acting out some kind of rage, seeking a muscular release of my anger. And what was I angry about? My mother's death? My inability all those years to get her away from my father? What could I have done instead? I could have stopped. Simply stopped. I could have left that task undone. I could have gone into the house and had a tall, cool glass of water and turned my mind to paying the bills or reading the *New Yorker*. I was old enough to know better. I knew that every time impatience grabbed hold of me, its toxins were likely to involve me again in such a war of wills. I knew grasping and clinging led to misery, that letting go of desire was the pathway to grace, that the world was full of suffering. I knew that none of us can avoid loss and change, and that instead of force, being in the world requires flexibility, patience, compassion—none of which I could access during my bout with the apple tree. No, all of that wisdom was far, far out of my reach at that moment.

My mother's bodhisattva-ness presented itself in part during her stay in the ICU and later convalescence. From her hospital bed, ensnared by tubes and surrounded by machines, she wrote me funny notes, scribbled with big black marker on pieces of paper attached to a giant clipboard. One day she wrote, "I wonder if I will get better." I asked her if she was scared, and she shook her head no and wrote, "Nothing is the end."

If nothing is the end, then submission, that trait of the hero, becomes easier. If nothing is the end, then you have many lives to do whatever it is you think you need to do, so there is no hurry, no need to force anything, only time and time and time to yield to what is. I wonder if, as I age, I will become more like my mother, or even like Darrell, able to live in accordance—even imperfect, inelegant accordance—with what is, or whether to my dying day I will be more like my father, someone who seemed always at war with himself and the world.

Her Tenderness

Ruth could seem like a tough cookie. She was broad in the shoulders and thin in the hips, muscular, with a face that was both handsome and sweet. She'd worked in the trades much of her life, elbow to elbow with hard-hatted, tobacco-spitting men on worksites. She looked good in Carhartts, with a hammer and a measuring tape hanging from the loops on her canvas pants, a pencil tucked behind her ear. She was strong enough in body to carry whatever needed to be carried, swing a hammer and control a jackhammer, and strong enough in spirit and careful enough in word to handle harassment and earn the respect of her misogynist workmates, maybe even alter the perspectives of some of them. She once told me about a confrontation with a workmate who offered an unending string of grotesque expletives whenever he was around her. To amuse herself, she'd silently count how many times "fuck" was said in one sentence. Instead of telling her workmate that his speech was offensive to her, she asked, in a way that invited him to be candid, if there was some reason he was irritated by her presence. "Yeah," he said, "I like to have a place to go where I can just be who I am, where I can spit if I want to and wear the same dirty shirt all week, and having women on the worksite changes that." She told him she could totally understand where he was coming from. Their conversation didn't change his behavior all that much, but it created a sense of trust, she said.

Throughout the tumultuous course of my affair with M., Ruth had been a rock—honest, full of integrity, sometimes furious, but never blaming or insulting or shaming. Her equanimity and steadfastness shocked me, in fact. Even amid the turmoil, she was constant—she held a space for possibility. "I want to fight for this relationship," she said. "I want you, but I also want you to be happy and have what you need. You have to make up your mind. I've been where you are. I know how it can be." But she wasn't going to wait around much longer, she said; what I was doing was making her miserable, like a knife to her heart every day.

She always seemed so tough and resilient, so I was surprised to be reminded of what a soft and tender person she was, how easily wounded. Sometimes I would forget this and tell her things or show her things that were too hard for her, and it would make me feel cruel. It's not lost on me now that my lying to her, my having an affair with another woman, was also incredibly cruel, but I didn't understand that then.

We'd had trouble on the farm with creatures getting into our hen-house. It was hard to determine at first whether it was a weasel or a racoon. Over time, clues began to point to the latter. One morning I arrived to let the birds out and was greeted with a mess, the coop full of feathers and splattered blood, our rooster dazed, a few headless hens on the coop floor, the rest frantic to fly out into the yard. The coop door latch had been lifted. That suggested the nimble hands of a racoon. Our solution: put a plastic child lock on the door. During the next episode, a year later, the chicken wire on the coop door had been peeled back, torn away from the staples that secured it, and we found racoon fur on the wires. Our solution: put up another layer of chicken wire, with heavier staples, and close and lock the second set of glass doors on the coop each night. With those precautions, we were able to outsmart the racoon. We still lost an occasional hen to a fox, who would sneak under the pasture fence, grab a chicken, and drag it back under the fence, leaving feathers and blood as a sign. We felt friendlier toward the fox, which, after all, had babies to feed, as opposed to the racoon, who seemed to kill for the fun of it, leaving headless bodies in its wake.

It had been several years since we'd had a racoon incident, so perhaps my guard was down. We'd gotten a new batch of chicks, which arrived in a peeping box that we picked up at the post office in Jay early one morning in March. "We have a package for you," the postal worker said on the phone at 5 a.m. "And it's making a *lot* of noise!" We'd ordered them from the Murray McMurray catalog, choosing chicks that would grow into hens of a variety of colors and sizes and lay different colors of eggs. In the tiny box were a dozen fluffy chicks not much bigger than a few cotton balls. They would grow up to be Black Australorps, so big and dark they looked like ships sailing across the grass of the pasture; their big white counterpoints, the Cornish Rocks, with their pure white feathers; Light Brahmas with their elegant black-and-white neck capes and fluffy feet; stately and slim New Hampshire Reds; dazzling Silver and Golden Wyandottes; sturdy red and white Leghorns with their erect, bright red combs; Araucanas, which would lay beautiful pastel-colored eggs; and one surprise chick, a fuzzy-headed Polish, who would grow up to have a crazy Phyllis Diller hairdo.

Chicken tractor #1

After raising the new chicks indoors for a few weeks, it was time to move them to the outdoor chicken tractor, which Ruth had built and painted a bright white. It was A-shaped, with a steeply sided

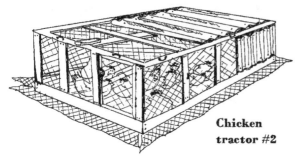

Chicken tractor #2

green tin roof over half of it and handles on the sides so two people could carry it around the yard, giving the birds access to fresh grass and taking advantage of the fertilizing qualities of chicken poop. It had a door at one end and one on the side, both with sturdy latches. Chicken wire extended outward for ten inches around the pen, forming a wire skirt that we'd pile rocks on for extra protection against weasels, racoons, and foxes. Inside there were several perches, a box where the chicks could huddle together for security and warmth, a hanging feeder, and ample water.

The morning after I put our new chicks into the tractor, I went out to greet the hens, enthusiastically throwing open the doors to the coop, welcoming the old girls into the spring day. I turned to similarly greet the chicks in their enclosure and was stunned by what I saw: a shallow hole dug beneath the enclosure, piles of bloody feathers and mangled bodies, most without heads, some with their throats torn out. A single White Rock was still alive, balanced on the perch.

I walked back to the house, feeling sick. "Ruth," I called. "Can you come to the barn?"

"What is it?" she said. She had just woken up.

"I can't tell you. Can you just come?"

She dressed quickly, and we walked across the yard together. "Why can't you tell me? What is it?"

"I just can't," I said. "You'll see."

I walked her through the gate into the hen yard, then to the edge of the chicken tractor. Still she didn't recognize what it was she was seeing. I reached in and picked up the little Polish with the crazy hair, limp in my hand. "They're all dead but one," I said, holding it out to her.

"Don't give me that," she cried, stepping away so that her back was to the barn wall, not disgusted by the dead bird but wounded by the vision of its ravaged body. She sobbed. "Why did you have to show me that? Why didn't you tell me?" She moaned as if she'd been injured. "Oh, this is too terrible to look at. I have to go inside."

Part of me felt, *Hey, I had to see this, why should you be spared?* Part of me felt, *I can handle it, why can't you?* Another part of me felt ashamed. I'd just compounded the violence of the scene by forcing Ruth to encounter it, just up from sleep, completely unprepared, utterly unprotected.

I had been warned, years earlier, by Susan, one of our beloved lesbian aunties. After meeting Ruth for the first time, she took me aside and, raising a finger to my face, said in a deadly serious tone, "She is a sensitive one. You had better be very careful with her." What she meant was, you had better *care for* her. And, of course, I did, or thought I did, until one of these moments occurred, like with the chicks, and I was forced to think again about what it meant to care for another person. Did caring for another person mean protecting them from things you knew would upset them? Should I have cleaned up the dead chicks before I went to tell Ruth, so she didn't have to see them? It would have been good to tell her right off: "A weasel killed the chicks." But I was in shock myself. I hadn't kept information from her on purpose; I just didn't have the words myself to describe the carnage. To care for and take care of Ruth in that instance would have required me to care for myself first. Perhaps I should have taken a moment to access my own terror and sorrow, my own tenderness, before I stumbled into the house asking her to come to the barn. Then we could have cared for each other and gotten through it together.

Wealthy

Word of mouth brought me to Francis Fenton's extraordinary orchard. There I encountered a universe of apples presided over by a spry, loquacious old man whose entire life, give or take a few years, had been devoted to these fabulous, mythic, and entirely ordinary fruits of the earth. I sensed during that first visit that I should get to know Francis a bit better and that I should bring my students to him as well, that he knew things we all should know. At Sandy River Apples in Mercer, Maine, we would walk among the trees, guided by Francis, and collect apples that we made into cider using an old-fashioned press. Francis is dead now; no person, like no apple tree, can live forever, but like Francis's spirit and wisdom, small branches can be grafted from one apple tree to another, and in that way some part of the life goes on and on and on.

It was an August afternoon many years after my first meeting with Francis that he came back to mind. I had decided to finally bottle the applejack that Ruth and I had begun eight months earlier. The cider-making process had begun on a sunny fall day in our front yard; overflowing bushel baskets of apples sat under the spreading branches of the beech tree, while nearby, upright on its wooden legs, was an old-fashioned cider press in which we crushed the apples and extracted their juice. The press, borrowed from neighbors, was as simple a machine as ever there was, all wood and sturdy iron and run by muscle—not far up the technological ladder from stomping grapes to make wine in long-ago Italy.

First the apples were tossed into a small box on the top of the press, which was fitted with a metal-toothed roller. One person turned a hand crank that spun the roller, which mashed the apples. The mash dropped into a cloth bag held by wooden staves beneath the box. The cloth and staves sat on a wooden tray with a hole drilled in it. When the barrel was full of pulp, another person turned an iron wheel on top of the press that slowly screwed a metal rod into a wooden plate, which pressed the apple pulp until the juice started to run like a golden waterfall into the tray and through the hole, into pitchers and bottles and cans and cartons. As the pulp was compressed, the machine creaked and moaned with the pressure, and then you knew you had gotten every last drop of juice from your beautiful apples and it was time to stop. The person turning the iron wheel would twist it the opposite way, letting up pressure on the wooden plate. The now dry apple pulp was hauled to the compost pile, the cider in bottles and cartons and pitchers was capped and moved to the shade, and the process started again.

As drops of juice and bits of pulp got scattered across the lawn in late fall, wasps and bees appeared, drawn by the yeasty sweetness. A bushel of apples would make about one gallon of juice. We pressed approximately ten gallons of juice that fall, enough to fill our new home-brew bucket plus a couple of gallons to put in the freezer to serve at Thanksgiving, make into mulled cider at Christmas, and otherwise enjoy in the deep of winter when apples, fresh on the tree, were a sweet memory.

Perhaps it wasn't fair to say the cider making started with the pressing. It actually began with the apples, which we collected in huge grain bags in Francis's orchard, him shaking the trees with a long hooked pole, the apples thudding to the ground, us ducking and dodging out of the way as they came raining like fantastic red and gold treasure from above. Francis, who inherited the orchard from his father, William Fenton, who inherited it from his father, Frank Fenton, who bought the farm from the first settlers in 1852, was one of western Maine's most respected and beloved apple men. Bucking the current market system that favored only a handful of shippable varieties of apples (McIntosh, Cortland, Granny Smith, and the like), Francis grew upward of 143 varieties, including at least one he invented himself—the Dolly Delicious, a yellow, thin-skinned apple that wasn't too tart, named after his late wife whose delicate constitution favored a sweeter, less acidic fruit.

On Francis's advice, Ruth and I mixed at least seven apple varieties for our cider, combining sweet with tart for ultimate flavor. If Francis was making fresh cider, not to be fermented like ours, he'd often throw in a bright red beet as well, turning the juice a golden-red and adding an earthy richness. The cider recipe Ruth and I chose was as old and simple as the apple press, as ancient as the making of alcohol itself. We invited wild yeasts to do the work of fermentation, just as Ruth's cider-drinking New England ancestors might have done.

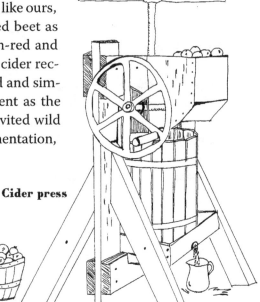

Cider press

One of the reasons bottling the cider rose to the top of my list that August day was that seasonal cues— cooler nights, the sight of green apples dangling from neighborhood trees, ripening winter squash, the chirp of crickets in the dry grass, fresh local corn for sale by the roadside—reminded me that apple season would soon be upon us again. Soon we would be visiting Francis again, collecting bulging bags of Romes and Cortlands, Macouns and Spys; soon it would all begin again, just like the year before. I wanted to pay the apples a certain respect

Cut apples for cider press

and complete the process we had begun—after all, so much had been invested, so much time and labor had gone into the cider already.

Visits to Francis's orchard always included a tour, where he named each tree as he loped along, dodging in and out of the grassy rows. As he passed a tree he'd impart some wisdom and opinion on the uses of its fruit (*Gotta eat that one before sundown. It'll rot on the tree*), some history of its growth (*Grafted that in '77*), and related (or not) observations about contemporary life (*Remember always go away from the table hungry. That's the trouble with American people. They eat like pigs*). In his mile-a-minute (perhaps he thought he had no time to lose), slightly slurred, spit-moistened speech, he'd tell his guests:

That's an old tree. My father planted that tree a hundred years ago. That tree is a hundred years old. A century old. That's a Wealthy. This was all Wealthys. My father cleared all this land and planted it to Wealthys a hundred years ago. But when I came back from the Navy, the pines, ya see, had taken over, see. All this out here was pines with apple trees growin' in 'em. So I cleared it again and planted all these different kinds. I got so many I don't remember 'em all.

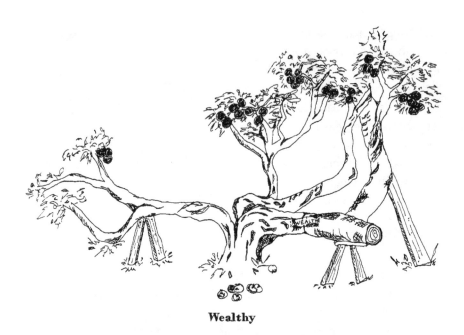

Wealthy

Apple trees typically live to be about 100 years, sometimes as old as 150. When I first met Francis, the Wealthys his father had planted were getting old, like Francis himself, who was then in his early nineties. The Wealthys in his orchard were easy to spot; they were the oldest and most elegant trees, bent, gnarled, propped up with weathered barn boards where their limbs sagged from so many years of bearing heavy fruit.

Francis grew up in the modest white house next to the white barn, with its huge, hand-hewn hemlock beams, which stood next to the long white apple shed with the big smiling, dancing apple painted on the side. *I was born in that house. I guess I'll die in it,* he'd say. Up until about 1940 life was okay for Francis out there in the woods and fields, *then things sort of went to pot. All the guys left. They went out west. After World War II everyone left. I even left myself.* He served in the Navy but returned in 1972 to take over the farm, which had been vacant for thirty years. He loved to regale guests with stories about the ship he sailed on during the war and the battles he fought. He wore his blue-and-gold commemorative ship's hat sometimes, other times a sweaty, stained baseball cap. He almost always dressed in a plaid shirt, long sleeves buttoned around strong, bony wrists, work boots, and khaki pants, all hanging off his thin frame. His eyes were deep blue and milky, his skin colored with age spots, his hands cragged, like the limbs of the trees. He shook. *A fact a life,* he'd say. *Ain't none of us get out of this world alive.*

A connoisseur of labor is what Francis was—someone who paid close attention to the ways physical effort produced things of value and the ways the ratio of effort to value changed over time. It took hard work, real labor, to replant the apple orchard after the pines had moved in—the kind of labor that is unfamiliar to many of us today—what you'd call backbreaking.

My age, see, is the machine age, but before that, back then, they made powerful men, powerful men, men who could eat a big bowl of cornmeal mush for breakfast then go out and work all day, cutting down trees, taking big chips out. I try that with an axe and it looks like a beaver had been at it.... In those days they'd work at it and a big chip would fly right out. Cornmeal mush for breakfast and another bowl at dinner and they'd go to bed and get up and do it all again. My father had either a spade handle or an axe handle in his hands all his life. Those men, those powerful men, they'd shave off the calluses with a jackknife. Those were some powerful men.

Each tree in Francis's orchard was labeled. Some tags were metal and had grown into the thick bark, while others were plastic bands with the apple variety recorded with fading black marker in Francis's arthritic scrawl. He didn't need the labels, of course; he knew his trees without their name tags. Black Oxford, McIntosh, Connell Red, Spy

(*Remember, Spy Pie, Spy Pie*), Idared, Dollie Delicious (*Now that was my wife's favorite apple, see. She's dead now. Hmm. I grafted that one and named it after her. That's the only apple she could eat. See. Nice and sweet, you know, without that acidity*), Haralson, Honey Gold, Jonathan, Macoun, Northern Greening, Sweet Sixteen, Tolman Sweet, Twenty Ounce, Wolf River, Golden Delicious, Fallawater, Baldwin (*Now that's a Maine apple, a keeper, good for midwinter*), Gala, Empire, Arkansas Black, Ben Davis (*Shipped those clear over to England back in the day*), Cortland, Halvorson, Cox Orange Pippin (*An old folks apple!*), New Delicious, Astrachan, Fireside, Russet (*Them's good winter apples, but I don't think much of 'em*), Rome, Sheep's Nose, Black Gilliflower, Spitzbergen (*That was Thomas Jefferson's favorite apple*), Blue Pearmain, Thompson, Snow, Honey Crisp, Yellow Delicious, Vista Belle, Wagener, Spencer, Red Cortland, Pewaukee, Paula Red, Milton, Rogers, Golden Russet, Tydeman, Hazen, Smokehouse, Winter Banana, Whitney, Wine Kist, Winesap, *Wealthy, Wealthy, Wealthy.*

If you visited Francis in the spring, his apple shed would be empty, the wooden crates stacked willy-nilly, the refrigerator clean, the bushel, half-bushel, and peck-sized green-and-white apple bags lying on the table, dust in the cool, still fruity-smelling air, a yellowed notepad with last year's penciled accountings on it. In the orchard pathways between the spreading trees would be bright green grass, pine needles, acorns, dandelions, blossoming clover, and strawberries in white flower. If you caught the week right and there'd been no early frost, the entire orchard would be pink and white with bloom and there would be the low hum of bees, their noses deep in the petals.

Everybody likes apples. Everybody likes apples. Bears, bees, chipmunks, deer. Every animal likes apples. Apples aren't native to here, ya see. They come from far away. All the way from Kazakhstan. The bugs like apples too, ya see. Back in the old days, there weren't as many bugs. You didn't have to spray. Now you gotta put poison right to 'em. The bugs are tougher than we are.

As we toured the orchard, we'd come across a few old oaks scattered among the fruit trees. *I should have planted all oaks,* Francis would say. *Could've made some real money.* He'd be the first to tell you: *There's no money in apples. Not anymore. Apples in Maine used to be big business. Big business.* The Ben Davis, a famously hard apple, was packed up and sent in huge barrels all the way to England. *Now you can't do that with a McIntosh!* These days, however, Francis told my carefully attentive students, no one wanted old-fashioned apples. *They're temperamental. No one wants temperamental apples. You gotta go with the market. That's farmin' for ya. Everything is shipped in now. You can go to the store and get strawberries and lettuce in the winter! Used to be we was all self-fecicient* (he stumbled over the word). *We used to wait until spring for fresh things—and we had fiddleheads and dandelion greens. Spring tonic. That's what we called it. Spring tonic. Other than that we had three meals a day of salt pork and potatoes.*

Those apples you buy in the store, he'd tell my students, *the ones in the big plastic bags, they come from China and they were picked a year ago!* One student asked why it was easier and less expensive to ship apples from China than to buy fresh ones from the orchard next door, and, more to the point, why weren't Francis's apples in the grocery store?

The answer would be sadly complex—it had to do with quantity of supply, agricultural politics, the cost of labor, demand, and food distribution systems. Francis, however, would make it simple—for him, it was all about labor: *No one wants to work anymore. There's no one to help me pick my apples. No one will take over this orchard. No one wants to work for nothing, like me.* Why didn't anyone but migrant laborers want to pick fruit and vegetables? Everyone had an answer, it seemed, but times change, was what Francis would say, with no hint of judgment. Change is inevitable. What one generation values, another one doesn't. With the gift of his old age, Francis could see into a past that my students would think of as ancient history but that he'd regard simply as his boyhood. Given his experience with the passage of time, the far future, too, seemed just as possible to him. Under his watch, we passed from the Age of Powerful Men into the Machine Age, and we were heading into another age he wasn't sure he could name.

People are in trouble now. In the Machine Age you had to know how things worked. Like that old Model T Ford over there. I took that engine and made a portable saw for logs. Just like that. All by myself. Today they make machines that are smarter than we are. Like that Toyota pedal.... I don't know what's comin' down for the next generation.... In the future your grandkids will be shooting around here with a jet on their backs. And all the numbers! How can anyone make sense of all the numbers you gotta have? Used to be only criminals were the ones who had numbers. Now everybody's got numbers.

In recent years, community members had solved the problem of Francis's lack of apple-picking labor by converging on the orchard each fall for a day or two of picking, cider pressing, picnicking, and merriment. The labor was happily supplied for free, and Francis would sell his many varieties from cases set up under a festive tent outside the apple shed, for so little money that, his daughter Carol said, he'd be lucky if he broke even. Clearly Francis was not in it for the money.

If Francis wasn't growing apples to make a buck, then why was he doing it? A hundred fifty years ago, a small orchard of fifteen trees could provide a rural New England family with enough fresh apples to last all year, plus make cider and feed livestock. The Wealthy, the apple tree Francis's father planted so many of, produced an all-purpose apple perfect for country life; it made for good eating, excellent pies and sauces and cider, and it was good for baking and freezing. An apple tree used to be an asset—like a house or a boat or a snowmobile or a retirement plan today. "As recently as the Great Depression of the 1930s, when many Americans were starving, many in Maine were doing rather well," Maine apple man John Bunker said, in a Common Ground Country Fair address. "They were cash poor by our standards but were well fed, clothed, and warm. These farming ancestors understood that wealth is not something you hold in the bank or the stock market. Rather, it is your land, your buildings, your livestock, your trees, your community."

What counts as wealth was something I had long puzzled over, as I tried to make sense out of what it meant to be an extremely privileged white, middle-class American college professor and homeowner with a 401K and two decent cars, on one hand, and on the other hand someone who owned eighty acres of forested land (from which the wood for heating the house came), who raised chickens and goats, and grew or collected most of the food she and her partner needed for the year. The job and salary and benefits, the cars, the health insurance, and the house were one marker of my wealth. The land, the small herd of goats, the well-stocked pantry, the sunny, fertile vegetable gardens, and the flock of chickens were another. In our topsy-turvy late capitalist economy, much of what one might think of as one's personal wealth is fleeting and diaphanous, like a dew-spangled cobweb, riches that come and go with the rise and fall of invisible forces. Yet there was another kind of wealth that I had no trouble understanding—a breakfast of eggs and vegetables brought to the table from the barn and garden, or a pile of dry hardwood for the winter fires.

In one tour of Francis's orchard, we came to a tree where he had created a fresh graft. There are many different styles of grafts: the whip graft, the side graft, the bridge graft, the saddle graft, the subtle

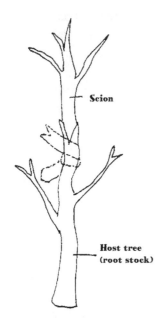

Wedge (cleft) graft

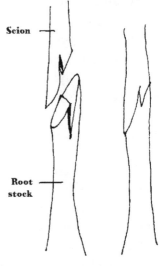

Whip-and-tongue graft

Apple tree grafting methods

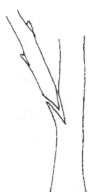

Side graft

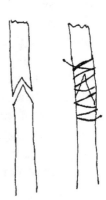

Saddle graft

graft, and the cleft graft, to name a few. Francis's method was simple. In the spring, just as the trees were beginning to bud, he'd take a small stem of first-year growth (called a scion) from a desired variety (say, a Dolly Delicious), insert it into a cut on a healthy host tree, and wrap the cut with tape or oiled cloth. If the graft took, the stem would grow into a branch that would bear fruit in the years to come. He showed us one tree that sported five different branches: a Wolf River next to a Spy next to a Yellow Delicious next to a Blue Pearmain next to a Cortland. It seemed like magic to me—like delightful fancy, akin to a lemonade spring or a rock candy mountain! It seemed impossible that the little grafted scion would ever hang low with fruit, but it would. It would take time, but it would happen eventually. *Apple trees are a young man's game*, Francis liked to say, again.

I think of the rural aphorism: "Walnuts and pears you plant for your heirs."

The same would be true of apples, no doubt. *They say in the paper you can get apples in three to four years.* Francis would pause, his comic timing impeccable. *I say that's right, you'll get three or four apples.* That particular year the apples blossomed on March 10. Warmer weather than usual forced them to open early, and then came an inevitable late frost. But that was okay by Francis. *Trees are smarter than we are. They don't work themselves to death. They'll take a break this year and then maybe double up the next.*

On the August day that I turned my attention back to our batch of fermenting cider, I spent ten hours reading about how to bottle our brew, comparing recipes, trying to decide whether to add sugar at the end (this would either create carbonation or blow my bottles open), learning about hydrometers, driving an hour into town and back to buy the proper dark-brown twelve-ounce bottles and caps from the home-brew store, and finally doing the bottling and capping. By the time I carted my cardboard box of twenty-four bottles of cider to the barn, where they'd wait for another two weeks, I could see the Big Dipper high in the night sky. If time was money and I was worth, say, twenty dollars an hour, then I had spent two hundred dollars on labor alone—on this one step in the cider-making process. Compared to buying a six-pack of hard cider from the refrigerated case at the store, my cider was outrageously expensive. A lot of work, a lot of money, and a lot of time—almost ten months from start to finish. And in the end, dear reader, it all turned to vinegar. Was my labor lost?

After my last visit with Francis, I brought him a pie as thanks—made from Wealthys I'd collected the year before and had peeled, sliced, and put in bags in the freezer, mixed with sugar, cinnamon, and lemon so I could easily dump the fruit into a crust and bake a fresh pie. I delivered this out-of-season treat to Francis one hot May afternoon while he was resting at the counter in his old farmhouse, eating his ice cream and applesauce. *Ice cream and applesauce. That's what I attribute my longevity to. Every day. Gotta have it.* As I handed him the pie, his eyes grew wide. *By golly, that's a big pie. I'll have to save that for when my daughter comes in September.*

I must have looked alarmed, knowing the pie fruit had already spent seven months in the freezer, and of course the pie wouldn't last until fall when his daughter traveled again from California to Maine to help with the apple harvest. But I was relieved when he added, *I'll put it in the freezer and save a piece for her. I can't eat that whole thing. That's a big pie, by golly. A full-sized pie.* As I left through the mudroom, closing the creaky screen door, he was still offering his thanks: *By golly. Such a big pie. My word. You can't buy a pie like that.*

VICTORY GARDEN

Death Comes for the Red Rooster

Big Red was our gorgeous, glossy, high-combed, mature New Hampshire Red rooster, the one we saved from the butcher block, our "man"—a glorious, lusty alarm clock, a showy presence in the grass, and a good "husband" to our hens.

All was well with Big Red until I was doing chores in the barn one day and heard a loud smash in the henhouse. I found Red standing in the doorway, head drooping, dazed and staggering. I moved him to his own pen and fed him sugar water with an eyedropper for several days. I called our friends in Virginia, the ones who had given us Red in the first place. Stephen said he had a low tolerance for the suffering of animals, and if he were me he'd put Big Red out of his misery right away, just slit his throat and be done with it. In response to my searching for a cause to Red's illness or injury (I was confident that if I knew the cause I could find a cure and save our rooster), all Stephen could say with any confidence was: "Sometimes they just die, Gretchen; sometimes there's nothing you can do."

After Big Red's fall, for that's what I assumed it had been, I went to the barn daily, hoping he had regained his strength overnight. I'd find his grain dish empty; at least he was eating, I thought hopefully. When the sun rose he still crowed but not as finely or loudly—instead, a low warbling. But his head was still bent. He still couldn't walk. Did he break his neck? Could I fix it with a splint? Ruth asked why I was so deeply invested in his recovery. It seemed to her, she said, that I wanted a miracle. That's exactly what I wanted.

The death of Big Red played out during the same period that my mother was swept into her many-years-long journey from the ICU to rehab to hospice to home to death. During that time my father just wanted, he said, to have things return to normal. He wanted my mother either to get better or to pass on. He hated seeing her in the hospital hooked up to tubes and machines. Should he authorize a tracheostomy? Would it help her heal? "I don't know what to do," he wept. "What should I do?" Like my father, I understand now, I wanted death to go away and leave me alone. I wanted Big Red to get better. I didn't want to stand idly by while he suffered, and most of all I didn't want to be the one to end his suffering by slitting his throat. I didn't want this responsibility. I didn't know what to do.

How was I to weigh my wish for Red's survival against the pain of his suffering? How was I to weigh my distaste for bringing about his death with the horribleness of his changed and unnatural life? How was I to weigh my needs against the rooster's? His quality of life was surely diminished. He was in a separate cage, not able to cruise around the yard with his hens, not even able to crow. He was barely able to stand, being fed by eyedropper. This was no rooster's life. But who was I to decide his fate?

In the end, death came for Big Red in the form of our sharpest kitchen knife. I gathered him from his cage and held his warm, red, feathery bulk in my arms for some time. I petted him, admiring his fleshy red comb, the heft of him. I took him to a corner of the barn where I'd spread fresh hay. I squatted, knees on the floor, and tucked him between my thighs, sitting lightly on him to keep him still. I took his magnificent head and pulled it up so his throat was taught. Then I drew the knife, deeper and deeper, until his head came off in my hand. I huddled over his body until it stopped moving, while the blood pumped out onto the hay. All was quiet. Big Red was dead. I collected his head, its sharp amber eye closed now under a fleshy yellow lid, the big comb limp, and I collected his still warm body, and I put them both into an empty grain bag, and since it was March and the ground was still frozen and covered with snow, making burial impossible, I put Red into the trash. That might have been what was most painful of all.

I am still not sure I did the right thing. I reasoned that it was pointless to make Big Red suffer any longer to satisfy my squeamishness and inability to act decisively; selfish, really, to prolong his life to assuage my own fear of having to really face death. I can say that I was glad when it was over. It meant I didn't have to worry any longer, didn't have to check on Red multiple times a day, feed him from an eyedropper, watch the dullness creep into his eyes. I felt light, in fact, even happy. Relieved. But doubt still lingers. A Buddhist friend was going through the death of her beloved dog during the same time Big Red was dying. She refused to have her sick dog euthanized because Buddhists vow not to kill. I judged her then: what good could it possibly do to watch the dog suffer, watch it die so slowly? It seemed deeply cruel, but she held fast to her belief and practice. Thinking about it now, I wonder if perhaps the logic behind

Little goat and big rooster

this Buddhist vow is partly that being present to another being's suffering teaches us not only about suffering but also about compassion, impermanence, and our own ultimate lack of control. The tendency we have to end misery with quicker death might be an emotional shortcut that doesn't do us any good at all.

The Gardener

What is it that we need when our mothers die? Places to begin again? Given my father's icy warning, *No ceremony*, I knew there was no hope of a family gathering to mark my mother's death. But my own need to mark her passing led me to plan a memorial service in Maine, a state my mother had never visited and where only three people, counting me, had ever met her in person. This didn't seem to raise concern among those who came to the service. "They're coming for your mother," Ruth explained, "but they are mostly coming for you." This service was for the living. Reverend Cathie Wallace, the pastor at Old South First Congregational Church in Farmington, where I had been attending for several years, agreed to officiate. Ruth would prepare deviled eggs. Our friend Juliana would bring a macaroni salad. I would make a photo display.

There it was—a life, her life, arranged on poster board and tacked to the kitchen wall. There *she* was, in black-and-white and color—from the age of four to seventy-eight: standing on the porch of her parent's farmhouse in Almelund, Minnesota, in fashionable high heels and a pretty dress, her auburn hair bobbed, her brother, Ray, beside her in his World War II uniform, his arm around her shoulder. With her father, outside the farmhouse, he in his World War I uniform and she in her majorette's outfit, holding her baton high, her tall white hat topped by a jaunty feather, dressed for a small-town parade. In her mortarboard and black gown, a college graduate in 1950, she and my bow-tied father grinning. At my father's parents' house in Massachusetts, him sitting on the edge of the sofa, leaning over her, his arm along the back of the couch, a cigarette in his hand, sporting a pencil-thin mustache and dressed in a nifty summer suit, a thin tie at his neck; her wearing an off-the-shoulder white blouse and a peasant skirt, her hair wavy and long, her eyebrows artfully arched. With her children after a parade in downtown Salt Lake, the four of us dressed in saddle shoes and baggy jeans with rolled-up cuffs, Ally, the littlest, with her finger in her nose, my mother squinting into the sun, her arms around us, her head covered by a scarf tied at the neck. On the front porch of the house we all grew up in, wearing striped form-fitting pedal pushers, waving goodbye to Austin, the oldest, as he trotted off to his first day of kindergarten, his shirt buttoned up at the collar, his head freshly buzzed, his pants cinched at the waist by a tight belt, me still in my pajamas, bagging from the diaper underneath. Walking with the four of us down a jungle path in Belize, where we lived in a trailer one summer while our father studied turtles, in the distance an ancient Mayan temple rising out of the forest, headed to Rockstone Pond for a bath, her wearing a jungle pith helmet, holding Ally's hand, Austin and Eddie a little in front scuffing up dust, staring at their feet, looking bony and alive. And here, looking very '70s, her hair long and parted in the middle, a cigarette in her mouth, wearing Jackie O sunglasses and examining a dried milkweed pod, which she no doubt took home, spray-painted gold, and added to her artful display of weeds. The spitting image of Sylvia Plath, in a crisp white oxford button-down shirt, an open book in her hands, her face relaxed, her skin sprayed with healthy freckles, her lips full, her eyes expressive and clear, my father taking the picture from his place across the table in our travel trailer and catching us kids in the background, outside the window behind my mother's head, the four of us, blurry unfocused figures, playing baseball, but me turning to look into the window at my parents. In her garden, stooping to pick a ripe tomato, in a turquoise tank top and baggy green gym shorts, her spindly white legs by now mapped with varicose veins, the skin on her arms dry and loose, her blue ball cap pulled down low, so she has to peek from under it, the small hump on her back caused by osteoporosis accentuated by her bending.

The pictures did not, of course, tell the whole story of her life. There was more. My mother didn't talk much. When she did talk about her childhood and early years, or about her heart, it was not in lavish tales. Like dropped seeds, she has left me with the barest facts and the smallest bits of story, leaving a trail I am still following. Here is some of what I know:

She was born in 1930. She had a good relationship with her father, she said. He was always there for her. She liked her mother, but they weren't close. She had a brother and a sister who were both older and left home long before she did. She did 4-H and won prizes with her cow, Trixie, at the fair. She went to a private Lutheran liberal arts college, Gustavus Adolphus, in St. Peter, Minnesota. She majored in English and acted in college theater. She got married when she should have to a decent man who had an interesting future. He was charming. He was a good kisser, she said. He haunted her. He came looking for her in Minneapolis where she worked as a secretary at a record company. "My adviser tells me if I go to graduate school I should have a wife," he said to her.

They moved to Kansas. She worked in a lab while he studied. They had parties and lots of friends. He was witty. She had a baby. Things started to change. She thought maybe he was jealous of his son. He got a job at a university in Utah. They moved west, driving all the way in an old station wagon during a hot summer with the baby and a cat. They bought a house. She thought the responsibility of a new job made him anxious. She had three more babies. At first he played with the babies after dinner—tickling and wrestling in a game they called "sleeping giant." She joined the PTA and helped with the Boy Scouts and Girl Scouts.

He spent most of his time at work. He had a temper. He'd call as he left the lab to let her know he was coming home. She made the kids send their friends away, shut off the TV, clean up their toys, and put on clean clothes. He only hit her once. Later he would fight with his son on the front lawn and chase one daughter out of the house. He kicked in his other daughter's bedroom door. They went on family camping vacations to the desert where his kids helped him collect lizards and snakes. They also went to the mountains where they backpacked and fished for trout. Sometimes they would take the trailer to a reservoir and he'd go out in the boat with one or more of the kids and they'd catch perch or trout.

She started going to brown bag lectures at the Women's Center. She bought books about how to take charge of her life. She developed stomach problems. Her doctor told her she was depressed and she should probably get a divorce.

He took many pictures of his beautiful family and sent them to his relatives. They traveled to Mexico and Belize and Panama and Australia for his research. When he threw wineglasses or saltshakers at the wall during dinner the kids sat in terrified silence. Sometimes she and the kids would run into his students at the gas station or the grocery store and the students would praise him: what a funny person, a genius, a great teacher. When he yelled at her and she cried, the kids hid in their rooms. The kids hated how he treated their mother. The kids wanted them to get a divorce. She knew that would probably make things worse—how would she support them, where would the kids live, what kind of a life would that be?

She made designer pillows for a while. She took up pottery, making big hand-built pots with carved patterns inspired by African and

Native American art. She had a show at a local gallery. Other artists admired her work. She got a job as a secretary, where she felt her skills and kindness and easygoing attitude were appreciated. The kids wondered why she stayed with this man. He was so mean. *Why was she so weak*, her grown-up daughters wanted to know. They thought she was pathetic, numbing herself with alcohol just so she could bear it. One daughter asked her much later why she didn't leave him. "It made me feel important to be married to him," she said. "It made my world bigger."

The kids left home or went off to college and didn't visit much. Now that the kids were gone, she could stop sleeping on the couch in the living room because her cough kept him awake. They could each have their own bedroom. Three of the kids went to graduate school. One of the daughters died by suicide. One of the daughters got married, then divorced, then came out as a lesbian. One son became an engineer, got married, and moved to Texas. The other one, the first son, also became an engineer, stayed around for many years, then got married and moved to Australia.

Sometimes she told the kids their father was proud of them and that he loved them. Sometimes she reminded them to go easy on him. They were both getting old. Aches and pains came. Small surgeries. New pills. He kept at her about her drinking, her body, how she talked, how she grocery shopped, how she cut her hair. The kids never called when he was home if they could help it.

They were doing well financially. They bought a cabin and some land in Montana. They also had a trailer parked on a ranch in southern Utah. She retired. He retired. They went to these places together, but he also often went by himself. He stopped going fishing with friends. His oldest son had been his best fishing companion. He still traveled all over the world for conferences and for a book he was working on. She was happy to have the time alone at home. She told her oldest daughter that he could not make her cry anymore—the tears were all gone. None of the children had children. Her kids liked to garden and read. When they called, this was what they talked about. She told the younger son one day that she had finally reconciled herself to being with their father for the rest of her life. She turned her attention to her books and to her garden. And then one night, she died in her sleep.

In the rain-soaked days preceding our service for my mother in Maine, Ruth and I did our best to shape a mound of muddy loam into a nuanced perennial bed, while our friend Jack Mills brought his excavator to haul giant slabs of granite from an old foundation site in the woods to add rusticity to the setting. We asked each person coming to the memorial to bring a perennial, which we'd plant in this new garden, in honor of my mother. On the day of the service, the ground was still a muddy mess and it was pouring rain, but our friends showed up in their blue and yellow slickers and set down their offerings in the soggy yard. Many of the plants had been freshly dug from our friends' own gardens. There was catmint and lady's mantle, foxglove, delphinium and daisies, iris, daylilies, forget-me-nots, corn-flower, lungwort, sedum, lupine, columbine, poppies, and lavender.

Reverend Wallace began the service with talk about "thin places"— the places where we make ourselves most vulnerable and are met with trust and honesty and delight in return. The thin places were the places that were most holy, the places where the light shone through. I had often felt that my relationship with my mother, built around plants, had a certain shallowness to it, a falseness—like a relationship built around talking about the weather, or collecting teacups—some-thing we grasped at just to have something. But I began to see that this something wasn't nothing. In fact, it was everything. The thin places for me and my mother centered around gardening—around iris and lilies, roses, tomatoes, and daffodils. What my mother knew about gardening was either already in her blood, or she learned it by reading and by doing. Gardening, like raising children, like sticking with my father all those years, took creativity, intelligence, imagination, physical effort, faith, patience, an eye for aesthetics, a willingness to open to joy.

What wisdom might the gardener have passed on to her eldest daughter? Conditions are not always optimal. Some things you simply can't explain or control. There is much joy and excitement among the drudgery, difficulty, and weariness of life. Whatever it is, it won't go on forever—everything changes in the end. You never know what might happen. It is good to keep trying.

At the end of the service, Reverend Wallace told the story of Jesus being mistaken for the gardener. There is a scene in the Gospel of John where Mary Magdalene stands weeping outside Jesus's tomb. Two angels ask her why she is weeping. "Because Jesus has been taken away and I don't know where they have put him," she says. Then she sees a man. She thinks he is the gardener. She says to him, "Sir, if you have carried him away, tell me where you have laid him and I will take him away." Jesus calls her name: "Mary." She recognizes him then. "Teacher," she says. He tells her not to hold him back, that he is ascending.

After she died, I never wanted to hold my mother back. I wanted her to ascend, to be free for whatever journey awaited her, unshackled in body and spirit from the confines of what, to me, seemed like a soul-killing marriage. I wanted her to fly away, not to hang around on my account, but I also needed some of her here on earth. Three of her wool jackets still hang in my closet, which my body slips neatly into now and then. I claimed a ring and a necklace or two from

Ginger jar

her jewelry box. Her massive hand-built ceramic ginger jar stands in a corner by my kitchen table. I have the perennial garden planted by well-wishers at her memorial service, but most important of all is that I have her roses, which have grown strong and wild in the barnyard from cuttings I brought from Utah to Maine.

Where has she gone? Her body to ashes, which our father spread somewhere, we don't know where or when. Her person commemorated with a marker in a cemetery within view of the Wasatch Mountains near a lovely stream, beside the markers for my sister and father. Deer make their home in this cemetery, grazing gracefully among the tombstones and the pines. What about the rest of her, that which was not body—where has that gone? To dreams, to roses, to voices I've more than once over the years heard calling my name. Near the eighth anniversary of her death, she came to me in a dream. She took my hands in her still-strong gardener's hands, looked me in the face with her milky blue eyes, the color of roadside chicory, and said with great tenderness, "Gretty, I did the very best I could."

"I know, Mom," I said. "It's okay."

The Sperm at the Door

I had never wanted children before, even when I was in a married heterosexual relationship with someone who already had three beloved daughters and wanted more kids with me. Craig's dream was of a house full of children, their laughter echoing from room to room. None of my siblings had kids, or wanted them, as far as I knew. One of my brothers told me once that he'd had insufficient role models for good parenting and was afraid he'd be a bad father.

Despite sharing my brother's fears, despite it being a turbulent time in mine and Ruth's life, despite being partnered with a woman and not being legally married, I decided I wanted to try to bear children. Ruth was not 100 percent enthusiastic about being a lesbian mom. As the third oldest of ten children, she'd been a mother already in her life to her infant siblings; she'd changed enough diapers, done enough feedings and laundry; she'd experienced the joy of being the first to watch her baby brother talk and walk. She agreed, though, to be my co-parent. I knew we could do a more than adequate job of raising a child. I knew that our playfulness, our love of nature, Ruth's musical talent and her fascination with tree houses and kites, and my love of books and stories and animals would all help provide a rich physical and imaginative life for a child. And maybe it would give us both a chance to rewrite parts of our own childhoods.

I had struggled for many years to come up with what I felt was a good enough reason for wanting to launch into pregnancy. I wasn't drawn like a magnet to babies, although I thought they were adorable and precious. I didn't particularly love working with young kids, although I enjoyed their company. Mostly I found babies and children fascinating, and when I was around them I'd watch them closely, like an anthropologist, which I am sure made some of them uncomfortable. I think in part I studied them to learn more about what it was like to be a child in the world—what alternatives to my own disquieting childhood might have looked like. I wasn't motivated by wanting a family, or children to carry on my legacy, such as it might be. I didn't feel like I had tremendous wisdom to pass on to a future generation. So what was it that made me finally decide in midlife to try to be a mother? After much discernment, my most authentic response to that question was this: I wanted to experience what it was like to be pregnant and give birth. When I shared this conclusion with Ruth, she considered me dubiously.

"Lots of people, including my own parents, never considered why they wanted kids," I said to her in my defense. "They just had them. My reason may sound selfish, but at least I'm being honest."

"But what about being a parent?" she asked.

"I think we both have enough love and patience and humor in us to make a good go of it," I said. I was confident that as parents we would, as the oath of those in the medical profession goes, do no harm.

Something about the timing of my desire to be pregnant might also have had to do with my affair. If the affair was about my connection to my own body, then wasn't being pregnant one of the most profound connections a woman might experience? And might it also be a way to renew mine and Ruth's partnership?

So we began the process of getting me pregnant. Ruth's former longtime partner had since married, and had successfully gotten pregnant twice. They proved to be excellent guides to the process. We used the same sperm bank they did and spent hours going over the dizzying array of sperm donors. I wanted whatever baby we had to look like Ruth, so we chose a donor with her geographical heritage (French Canadian, Irish, and British) and with dark eyes and dark hair. I began charting my cycle, creating a detailed spreadsheet of my temperature, vaginal moisture, menstruation time, mood, and libido. We'd try to time the sperm deliveries so they arrived on our doorstep within twelve to twenty-four hours of my fertility window—the time between ten and fifteen days into the cycle when conception is most likely. They arrived in a gleaming liquid nitrogen tank that looked ever so much like a tiny space capsule. At first we did the inseminations ourselves, thawing the milky sperm, pulling it into a small syringe, cuddling and kissing, and then having Ruth squirt the sperm inside me, my hips propped up on a pillow. The instructions in the kit said it would help to have an orgasm after insemination, so Ruth would put her mouth to my lips and folds and we would then rest together, imagining little swimmers urged along by my vaginal contractions meeting up with my eggs deep inside my rose wet cave.

After two years and many thousands of dollars, we gave up. We tried engaging the help of a health professional who did the inseminations on her exam table, but with no difference in the results. I even enrolled a dear old friend in the project, choosing the "old-fashioned" method instead of sperm in a vial, having sex with a man for the first time in almost thirty years. I was not so much devastated by not getting pregnant as I was simply surprised. My mother had four kids, all a year apart. Of course, she started when she was twenty-eight years old and I was in my midforties, but I still assumed, arrogantly, that I would have no problem. I had not seriously considered adopting a child, since my motivation, which I was still very clear about, was to feel what it was like to be pregnant and give birth. Ruth and I felt we'd given the project all we were capable of, and it was time to move on.

We discovered that there were many opportunities to mother and nurture in this world, to plant literal and metaphorical seeds and coax them to healthy and fruitful life. We had been invited to become godparents of the two granddaughters of dear friends and took on the role of Gaia Moms (the name their mother gave us) with enthusiasm. Not only were these human children in our lives, but there were the goat and the chicken babies, and later a pair of delightful kittens that would grow up to be our beloved barn cats. I got to experience, albeit not in my own body, pregnancy and failed pregnancy, birth and failed birth, death and love, and all the messy, compelling poignancy of being a nurturer of animals, children, and the earth.

Victory Garden

Get out and dig dig dig in the sunshine
You can make one garden grow
Every seed you buy will gladly multiply
Till we've overcome our foe.

— USDA Victory Garden campaign song

In 1942, when Eleanor Roosevelt peeled back the sod on the White House lawn and planted a victory garden, my mother would have been twelve. I wonder what she thought about Eleanor, what she thought about the idea of planting vegetables to win the war, what it was like to be a twelve-year-old girl living on a dairy farm in Minnesota during World War II. I can't be sure, but my guess is that like tens of millions of other Americans that year and in the ones fast following, she and her mother planted a victory garden too, a quarter-acre plot of vegetables to feed the family and help defeat Hitler.

World War II, the good war, was the war that framed my mother's childhood; "good" because it featured a tangible foe, an obviously tyrannical, insane bad guy; "good" because U.S. and Allied soldiers defeated fascism. It was also a war that galvanized many citizens in a "good" way on the home front: the call to "Dig for Victory" struck such a chord that in 1943 America's 20 million victory gardeners produced 10 million tons of vegetables—half the nation's annual consumption. "Sow the Seeds of Victory...plant and raise your own vegetables," read one victory garden campaign poster depicting a tall, big-boned woman dressed in an American flag, striding forward, her flag-dress billowing behind her as she flings her strong arm in a wide arc, sowing seeds by the handful. "Can All You Can: It's a Real War Job" read another poster encouraging women to put their own food by.

A 1943 report from the USDA Committee on Victory Gardens encouraged gardens not just on farms but anywhere there was sufficient open space with sunshine, access to water, and fertile ground. Golden Gate Park was transformed into victory garden plots, as were many other public spaces. For suburban gardeners, plot sizes of 30 x 50 feet were recommended, while a quarter of an acre was recommended for rural plots—enough ground to provide a year's worth of food for a family of four. "You *must* have a garden this summer," said secretary of agriculture Claude R. Wikard in his introduction to the 1942 pamphlet *The ABC's of Victory Gardens.* "You may not be able to carry a gun or drive a tank, but you can grow food for Victory!"

While World War II and its victory gardens shaped my mother's youth, Vietnam and its accompanying cultural upheavals shaped mine. Vietnam was the opposite of a "good" war, with its confusing cast of characters, nefarious Big Brotherish motivations, the rage it ignited and has kept simmering to this day, the lack of clarity about who was the enemy, the grotesque violations of human beings and environments that came to us in images of misty streamers of Agent Orange floating out of the bellies of low-flying aircraft, and burning, screaming napalm-drenched children. The antiwar movement, civil rights movement, and early feminist culture of the 1960s also seemed to be the flip side of the patriotic earnestness expressed in popular culture during World War II. I was born into an era of disobedience, of pulling back the curtain on authority; an era in which the youth of America had little interest in doing anything the government asked of them, least of all planting vegetables.

My first serious vegetable garden occupied the tiny backyard of the ramshackle nineteenth-century house my then-husband and I had bought in the historical working-class brewers and bricklayers neighborhood on the low bluffs of the Mississippi River, in the West End of Saint Paul, Minnesota.

By serious, I mean a garden meant to produce more than a few months of tidbits for summer salads. Craig had gardened before—big, farm-style gardens, fenced against raccoons, woodchucks, and deer, that provided enough food for an entire year: quarts of tomatoes and pickled beets, baskets of onions and leeks, pints of dilly beans, spaghetti sauce, sauerkraut, bread-and-butter pickles, dusky butternut squash, dry beans, corn, all put up in the freezer or the pantry. That was what I wanted—at least a beginner's version.

Dilly beans in canning jar

Being a novice, I followed Craig's lead, shoveled my share of soil to make our twelve-by-three-foot, double-dug French intensive garden beds, and kept up by reading the relevant chapters in the back-to-the-land book that was his garden bible, *How to Grow More Vegetables Than You Ever Thought Possible on Less Land Than You Can Imagine*, by John Jeavons. Once we had the beds prepared, Craig turned it over to me.

"What should I plant?" I asked.

"What do you like to eat?" he said.

What did I like to eat? I tipped my head to one side and furrowed my brow. The question was surprisingly challenging. Was it, *What* do you like to eat? Or, What *do* you like to eat? Maybe it was, What do *you* like to eat? Or perhaps, What do you *like* to eat? How about, What do you like to *eat*? First I'd have to get my mind around the "you," meaning me, I, and then "like," then "eat," and only then could I get to "what."

The planting of this first vegetable garden was during a period when Craig and I were seeing a marriage counselor because I was breaking chairs and smashing thermoses and crying all the time. I was pretty sure I was a lesbian and wanted a divorce, but I hadn't been able to articulate that to myself yet, let alone Craig. When the counselor asked me what I wanted in my life, I said, with complete earnestness and lack of awareness, "I want what other people want from me." I had very little idea of who I was and what I wanted in general, let alone from a garden.

In the intervening years I've discovered that not knowing what you want is completely normal—if, that is, as a young person you had little support for developing a sense of self. My siblings and I were brought up in a "children are to be seen and not heard" household, by a father who learned his parenting skills from an iron-willed German immigrant father and a strict, distant, and demanding Yankee mother. In our family, that tender, natural craving we all have to be noticed and loved exactly for who and what we are was, at best, thwarted— thwarted by discipline of the unruly, disobedient, wayward body.

At age twenty-seven, the year of that first vegetable garden, I didn't even know what I liked to eat! Nor did I trust that my feelings of desire for women might be real (or, for that matter, that any feelings I ever had were real) or that those feelings might be the best-ever clue that I was a lesbian. It took me until I was thirty to learn to say that my favorite candy was Callard & Bowser licorice toffee. It took me until I was thirty-two to fully claim my sexuality. Gaining the

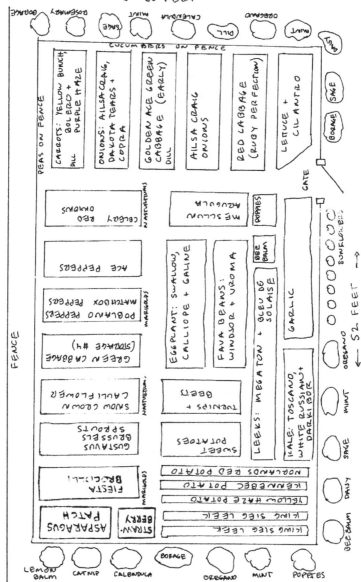

Front garden

confidence and self-knowledge to figure out what I liked to eat was probably inextricably linked to figuring out that I wanted to have sex with women—no doubt these hungers are intertwined.

It's hard to imagine a child more divorced from her own desires than I was, though my siblings were certainly in the same boat, and I shared a place in history with a whole generation of girl-children who suffered in similar ways. The 1960s were years of backlash against the restrictive mores of the 1950s, but they were still thick with the residue of isolation and containment—girdles, reinforced bras, and women like my mother who could not get a Sears charge card without her husband's permission. Suburban wastelands were full of college-educated, stay-at-home moms like mine with nothing more challenging to do than read *Woman's Day* magazine, watch soap operas, drink coffee, smoke, change diapers, cook meals, wash clothes, and dust and vacuum. Into the evening when the husband was still at work and the kids had been fed and read to and tucked into bed, there was a bottle of wine.

Our mother was certainly more attuned than our father to the embodiment of children. When we asked her to stop for ice cream at Snelgrove's in Salt Lake City, a ritual after visits to the dentist (our mother understood the healing power of sweet things), she'd say, "Sure, why not," or "Sorry, not this time." When we asked our father (we hardly ever asked him for anything, because we knew from experience he'd say something that would make us feel wretched), he'd say, "You don't want ice cream. Ice cream makes you fat." We thought we wanted ice cream. Were we wrong? If we didn't want ice cream, what did we want? These were the constant wrenches thrown into the machinery of our natural wanting. So it was a vegetable garden that presented me in adulthood with the terrifying ontological question, Who am I? If I am made of my desires and I don't know what they are, then am I not?

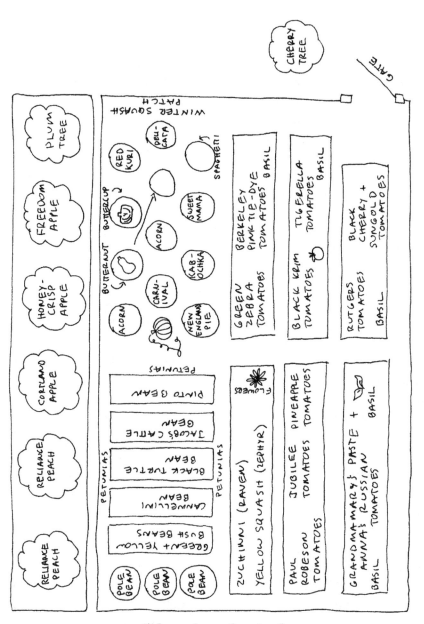

Side garden and orchard

Growing up on our home front, in that little suburban house in Salt Lake City, there was a war going on, an endlessly unfolding cloud of tension, confusion, silence, shame, and anger. If there was an enemy, he looked to me like my father, who was putting into practice his own strategy of containment, only it wasn't communism or Hitler that was being contained; it was us. It felt as if what he most wanted was for us to not be in the way, to not need anything, and to be, well, perfect, which took a lot of shoving down, a lot of bending, a lot of controlling.

I wasn't the only girl-child ever to be called fat, certainly. Not the only one ridiculed for being pudgy, round, or stocky, as they might say today. Not the only girl-child to be put on a diet, which started, for me, as early as third grade, when I was awoken late at night, my parents clearly having been arguing about me in the kitchen after I'd gone to bed. Still half asleep, I was led to the bathroom scale. My weight was reported to my father who, still occupying his place at the head of the kitchen table, gazed at me with a look of concern and disapproval. Then began my regimen of taking diet drinks to school. In place of a brown paper bag packed with a peanut butter and jelly sandwich and an apple, I toted the popular diet drink Metrecal, a canned protein shake in flavors including vanilla, chocolate, and butterscotch, which was widely regarded (I learned later) as being so terrible that many users were adding liquor to make it palatable. I imagine myself pulling that small can from my Snoopy lunchbox in the crowded cafeteria at Canyon Rim Elementary, where my mother was a member of the PTA, where our neighbor Betty Crocker (ironically an award-winning baker just like the famous cookbook icon) made and served wholesome hamburger and noodle dishes in her white dress and hairnet from behind the lunch line counter. I am sure this is where I developed an outer skin thick enough to save me from melting with shame as I drank my lunch from a can in front of my peers, all of whom were either eating the noodle hot dish or enjoying their baloney sandwich with a Hostess fruit pie for dessert.

Fat was the foe in our house. For my father, fat was synonymous with stupid and low-class. Fat people had no control over their desires. Fat people didn't know when to stop. Fat people were doomed to the lowest circle of hell. My father's children, least of all his daughters, would *not* be fat. Fat children were the fault of their stupid parents who fed their kids biscuits swimming in gravy with pie and ice cream for dessert. Such parents should have their children taken away and be sterilized so they couldn't produce more fat people. It was enough to make you want to starve yourself, to become entirely, cleanly, echoingly empty or, alternatively, to become full—to eat the entire universe and then throw it all up. What did I like to eat then? Everything! But it seemed every mouthful was forbidden.

My suppressed and disciplined hungers, of course, led to obsessions with food and a conflation of food and anger, food and sadness, food and despair, food and forbidden enjoyment. I started collecting candy in a German tin cookie chest. The chests, one for me and one for my sister, were given to us by our grandmother. Each was decorated with different scenes from medieval Deutschland—pilgrims astride horses high-stepping through fields of golden grain; peasant picnics amid piles of fruit, jugs of wine, and loaves of bread; shopkeepers at their fruit-laden stalls; maidens dashing after chickens; fat butchers with their axes over plump pigs on chopping blocks. In the cookie chest I had many colors of jelly beans, foil-wrapped chocolate eggs from Easter, candy bars, necklaces strung with sugar candy, Pez containers, candy corn from Halloween, candied raspberries and spun sugar ribbons from Christmas. In my mind, I likened my collection to pirate treasure, chests overflowing with sparkling jewels, gold coins, silver chalices. I felt rich, secure, delighted, and quite the connoisseur; this was my first attempt at being a collector.

I showed my mother my treasure one day. Her response became one of those moments that our adult minds cast back to that are so fleeting, so innocuous, so banal, but that leave their mark as distinctly as a brand that seems over time to burn deeper into the psyche. "You have no right to have a candy collection," she said.

Of course, her cruel dismissal didn't stop me from my obsessions. One day I rode my green bike with the high handlebars, the chrome "sissy bar," and the sparkly banana seat straight to the candy counter at the grocery store. The counter at Grand Central was the site of some of the happiest moments of my childhood. There, free from parental surveillance, my friends and siblings and I spent hard-earned quarters and dimes on Milky Ways, Three Musketeers, orange marshmallow circus peanuts, Look candy bars, Bit-O-Honeys, gummy bears, Red Vines, and any number of other now cool "vintage" candies. I especially was drawn to the bulk bins of Brach's caramels, nougats, and hard butterscotch and peppermint. I could plunge my whole hand into the bin (you could do that then) and drop the candy by the fistful into a pink-and-white-striped bag to be weighed at the counter. The candy counter also had a fancier side, which sold See's chocolates.

That day I knew what I wanted as soon as I left the house, my mouth watering for the whole mile-long ride: rum balls. Each rum ball was about the size of a golf ball, dusted with bitter chocolate and chocolate sprinkles. Once purchased, I took both of my rum balls outside to where I'd locked my bike and sat on the hot concrete curb near the garbage can. I gobbled down both of them in one or two bites, hardly tasting what I was putting in my mouth, and then, feeling deeply disgusted with myself, rode home.

This pattern would continue through my teens. If it wasn't rum balls, it was tilting stacks of buttered toast consumed when I got home from high school, before everyone else filtered through the door. I'd gorge on whatever I could find in the cupboards: Space Food Sticks, raisins, walnuts, potato chips, apples, bread, cereal, leftovers from dinner the night before, cold chicken and potato salad, whatever it took to fill me (this was after skipping breakfast and lunch in an effort to diet)—and then I'd fall asleep in an overstuffed stupor. When my sister woke me for dinner, I wasn't hungry and refused to come to the table. I told my parents I was studying. I knew this was the only acceptable excuse in a household where it was imperative that everyone be at the dinner table, every evening, on time, shirt and shoes and impeccable manners required.

There were other reasons to play hooky from the dinner table that might have played a role in my oppositional behavior. It was at the dinner table that our father's temper often flared (loosened by two or three before-dinner whiskeys), where we'd suffer through his bossing and belittling of our mother, his tirades against the idiocy of the rest of the world, and sometimes even a wineglass or saltshaker shattered against the wall.

I binged and dieted from grade school through high school, finally winning my father's approval (and, to be fair, my mother's as well—"Now that you are slimmer you can wear tighter clothes," she said) when somehow I'd gotten myself down from 136 pounds to 125. "You're looking kind of rangy," my father would say, looking me up and down as I leaned against the stove in the kitchen, my blue-jeaned legs crossed at my Frye boots. At this I felt a hot and confusing joy mixed with shame. In all the time a war was waged over my body, I had never weighed more than 140 pounds (I'm five feet, three inches tall). In fact, in all my life I have never weighed more than that (after quitting smoking) and never less than 120 (at the height of my smoking career, when I burned through two packs a day instead of eating). All of that misery, surveillance, control, and self-hatred over 20 pounds? What did I like to eat? At that time in my life I had convinced myself that my favorite foods were Tab diet cola, celery sticks, sugar-free gum, lettuce, and raisins.

In that St. Paul vegetable garden I planted zucchini and pattypan squash, tomatoes, cucumbers, peppers, eggplant, green and yellow beans, lettuce, sage, oregano, and parsley. There was a bed of cabbage and onions, broccoli, cauliflower, and basil. Because of that garden I learned to make dishes that are still my favorites: pesto sauce (Marcella Hazan's *Classic Italian Cookbook*), rich tomato sauce (my mother's recipe), ratatouille provençal (*Joy of Cooking*), zucchini relish, cabbage soup with caraway, minestrone, and gazpacho. This garden was my own victory garden—the real beginning of my garden education and the beginning of a new relationship with food.

The garden Ruth and I grew occupied a tenth of an acre all told— two plots about 36 x 50 feet each. In it were things that we liked to eat: fava beans, soybeans, leafy greens of all kinds (including kale, collards, and bok choy), fat white and red onions, five varieties of garlic, three kinds of potatoes, four kinds of eggplant, parsnips, leeks, half a dozen kinds and colors of dried beans (my favorite the True Vermont Cranberry Pole Bean, or perhaps it was the cannellini, simmered with sage and olive oil), three kinds of carrots (a summer, a keeper, and a rainbow), a couple of different kinds of beets, two kinds of parsley, and fancy yellow and green bush beans called haricots verts, which are excellent lightly steamed and tossed with toasted walnuts and blue cheese. There were, of course, rows of tomatoes in every size and color, including petite sweet Sungold, the deep red beefy New Girl, and the modest yellow Taxi.

Especially for Ruth we planted rows and rows of brussels sprouts, which when grown at home and left to ripen with a frost had an unexpected mustardy tang. For me, we planted winter squash, my favorites being blue Hubbard, butternut, buttercup, and red kuri. Winter squash, I could confidently say, was something I liked to eat. There was something deeply appealing about these vegetables: their dense, sweet dark-orange flesh, their blocky heft, their subtly differing textures and tastes, their shapes and colors and the designs of their thick outer skins. Treated properly at harvest, they kept well, providing us with food all the way into the following summer. Perhaps most appealing, though, was the way they refused to obey the boundaries of the rows and beds I'd prepared for them, cheekily spreading their vines wherever they wanted.

Almost three decades separated me from my first garden, years spent getting to know myself; coming to an understanding of my hungers and the things that shaped them. When I imagine myself in a garden now, I see myself squatting down next to a bed of radishes, or onions, strongly balanced on my haunches, barefoot, in early morning, a cup of coffee beside me in the dirt, feeling the pull of the

soil, confident and strong, thinking about what I will make for dinner. Every garden is a victory, but not like the victory gardens my mother grew up with—not a victory over a material foe, or a victory for the nation, or even a victory over the fear of hunger. A garden is a victory over the severing of the body from its home in the earth. A garden is a place of miracles: one takes a seed and produces something to eat; one encourages abundance out of something that looks like nothing; one produces a cornucopia of food to satisfy hunger, to delight the ear, the eye, the hand, the nose, the tongue, and the spirit. A garden poses the question *What do you like to eat?* and invites the answer out of the earth itself.

I Wish I Had Been the One to Sing to Him

My herpetologist father spent a good amount of time by himself, away from my three siblings and me and our mother, among his turtle bones and jars of formaldehyde at his laboratory at the university, off by himself collecting specimens in the jungles of Mexico, by himself early in the morning in his chair by the window at home with his cigarettes, coffee, orange juice, and the morning paper, by himself swimming endless laps in the university pool, by himself in his fly-tying room in the basement. What we didn't understand then, any of us, including him, it seems, was that this leaving home early and coming home late, this drinking himself into sleepiness every night in the living room before dinner, this going up to the university on weekends and holidays, might not have been because he didn't love us; it might have been the only way he knew to recalibrate his brain so he could live with any sense of ease. Perhaps he didn't enjoy being a mean son-of-a-bitch any more than we did.

In the last years of my father's life, Ruth and I visited him several times in Utah, accompanying him on errands to his lab at the university. Ruth and I were both astounded at the number of family pictures on display there among the skeletons and turtle skulls and snake and alligator skins. Lining the long hallways where he had his specimen cases, pinned to the cork bulletin boards on the walls of his office, taped to the windows of the vestibule off the stairway, magneted onto the door of the lab refrigerator, were pictures of my siblings and me at every stage of our lives, pictures my father took of us during backpacking trips, fishing trips, and vacations in our trailer. Me as a teenager, my hair in blond braids, posed among wildflowers in the Uinta mountains. Eddie, my sweet brown-eyed brother, at twelve, with a wicker creel full of shining trout. Ally, my late sister, snuggled next to my mother at a downtown Salt Lake City parade. Austin, the oldest, in his button-up Levi's with his BB gun, a hot desert vista shimmering behind him. My mother picking dried grasses and milkweed pods for an artful bouquet. Anyone visiting his lab would think this was a family guy, fully immersed in the intimate, boisterous, chaotic life of a big family. From my perspective, this could not be further from the truth. Pictures on the wall were exactly how my father wanted it—for him, family seemed most easily enjoyed two-dimensionally, photographically.

One of the pictures in that hallway was taken by my older brother, Austin, who traveled for extended periods of time with my father in the bush of Australia, where my father searched for turtles. The photograph showed my father in the foreground, both knees down on the cracked earth of a dried pond, holding a turtle. It looked as if he had just dug up the turtle from the dry earth at his knees. My father was wearing khaki shorts, leather boots, a green safari shirt, the sleeves roughly rolled to his biceps. He looked like Indiana Jones. A notebook and pencil poked out from the breast pocket of the shirt. He wore a bandana around his neck and a canvas brimmed sun hat. In front of him stood an aboriginal boy with a bare belly, dressed in loose baggy cotton shorts. My father was showing the turtle to the boy, holding it up for him to see. Look! Isn't it amazing? The child was smiling. My father was smiling. He had a brilliant smile. In the background, slightly out of focus, were a bank of eucalyptus trees

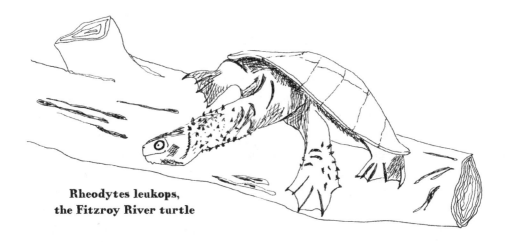

**Rheodytes leukops,
the Fitzroy River turtle**

and the child's mother, wearing a patterned sundress with her head turned slightly toward the camera, so that her eyes and round face were just visible.

After our father died, I asked my brother about the photo. They had been deep in the bush, Austin said. They'd asked the woman to show them where the turtles were under the dried bed of the pond, and she had walked directly to a spot in the dirt and pointed down, where our father dug one up. What brought me nearly to tears was that in the photo my father looked luminous, at home in his body, fully present to his task, fully present to the boy standing before him, present to and a part of the heat and dryness of the day, to the adventure of being out in the bush. My father looked happy. He didn't look angry or mean or irritated. I'd seen other pictures of him at work, surrounded by colleagues and assistants and students in the field, in Australia, in Mexico, in southern Utah, in Brazil. He looked happy in those images too. Part of it, I know, was that he felt at home in his role as a teacher, surrounded by graduate students, the center of attention. I often think that my father would have made an excellent bachelor professor, that he was never really meant for family life, especially life with daughters and a wife; that he just wasn't suited for fatherhood or husbandhood. He would have been much happier alone. Or perhaps not. Maybe he would have been miserable alone, but the fact is, he simply could not make his peace with people who needed something from him other than authority and expertise, something a wife and children might want, such as attention, gentleness, or love.

The insights I am gaining about myself as I age help me to better understand my father. I think he didn't like himself. I think he never thought he was good enough to please the only person he ever really wanted to please: his mother. To his dying day, he sought her love, love she was probably as incapable of giving him as he was incapable, in turn, of offering to us. Toward the end of his career he had the honor of having an endowed professorship in anatomy named after him at the university where he taught for fifty years. He didn't invite any of his family to the ceremony, and when I spoke with him on the phone about the event later, he wept and said, "I wish my mother could have been there to see me."

This was the grandmother I knew to drink her morning coffee in bed from dainty teacups; the grandmother who sternly enforced table manners, refused to hear us if we used improper grammar, and insisted when we visited her and my grandfather's spotless, well-appointed suburban Minneapolis home once every three or four years, that my mother cut our hair—we looked like a bunch of ragamuffins. She was thin and aloof and wore cat-eyed spectacles that dangled from a gold chain around her neck. She was not a climb-into-your-lap-help-make-cookies-in-the-kitchen kind of grandma. She was most likely not that kind of mother either. Two of her brothers, Marshall and Arthur Hertig, were the standard my father felt compared to all his life. Marshall was a Harvard entomologist who helped eliminate yellow fever in Panama and solved the riddle of the mysterious "belt of death" in the valleys of the Andes—night-stalking, blood-sucking sand flies. Arthur's groundbreaking work in embryology at Harvard Medical School eventually helped lead to the birth control pill. Perhaps my father felt that nothing less than "world famous" was necessary to get his mother's attention. It should not have surprised me, but after my father's death I learned from one of my cousins that her father had felt similarly measured and spurned by their shared mother, having to compete with not only these high-achieving uncles but also his own brother and sister for a chance at love.

My father told me many times about how, when he was a little boy, he believed that if he closed his eyes he would be invisible. He laughed about it. But now that he is dead and I am still trying to make sense of my relationship with him, it seems meaningful. I can imagine him, a cute three- or four-year-old with brown hair and hazel eyes, dressed, as was the custom in his family and at that time, in a blue-and-white sailor suit—short pants with suspenders, white socks, saddle shoes, a sailor's bow at the neck of the shirt, maybe even a little white hat. I imagine a crowd of adults, smoking, drinking their Tom Collins cocktails. He would have been instructed, as he repeatedly instructed us, to be seen but not heard. And so he shut his eyes in defiance. *I will not only be silent, I will also be invisible.* Or maybe he shut his eyes because it was too painful to feel ignored and disciplined, to be treated like an object, like a pet or a piece of furniture, instead of a boy. Maybe he disappeared himself to test whether anyone would realize he was missing, to see what they would do. I can imagine the questions at the center of his little boy heart—do they love me, will they miss me?

One of the ways he would dismiss and scold us when we cried or expressed any kind of strong emotion, even into our adulthood, was to say, "You're just trying to get attention." It seems as if he was doing exactly this in his own life: trying to get someone's—anyone's—attention. Was his professional work also a way to make himself visible?

There was so much of it—the one big final book at the end of his life, *The Turtles of Mexico*, along with all the monographs, the scientific discoveries, the generations of admiring students, the famous collection of turtle bones. Was it all so other people could see that he really was there?

His death took my siblings and me by surprise. Our relationship with our father was so distant that we had not even known he was in the hospital. He'd sworn his live-in caretaker to secrecy. After he had been in the hospital two weeks she left a message on my answering machine casually suggesting that I might want to call home. I did, and no one answered, which was not unusual; my father seldom answered the phone. The next day I received a phone call at two in the morning from a defeated-sounding doctor in the ICU where they'd been trying to shock my father's heart back into regular rhythm. They were not able to administer painkillers for some reason, and the shocks made him scream and writhe. They felt they were only torturing him. Someone, perhaps his favorite former student, whom he called his protégé and who was one of only two people my father allowed at his bedside, must have finally given the hospital my name and number. My brother Ed and I gave the doctors permission to stop their herculean efforts to keep him alive, but to their surprise he made it through the night. I decided to carry through with plans to spend a weekend with friends in Montreal before I flew to Salt Lake to be with my father, who assured me that since he was on the mend, there was no need for me to be at his bedside anyway. Two days later, sitting on the stairs of my friends' home in Montreal, I got a call from my brother telling me that our father had died.

The reason I'd been so angry with my father most of my life is actually rather transparently simple. It was not that I hated him. It was that I loved him. I loved him as a child cannot help but love a parent, and at every turn he had made himself unavailable to that love.

Not inviting us to his bedside in his last days was just one more injury, one more rejection. I'm sorry now that I didn't fly directly to his side; sorry that I was not with him when he passed. But I did get to see his body before he was cremated, and perhaps this was better than sharing a desperate, morphine-clouded last living moment.

Royal Wulff dry fly

My final glimpse of my father was at the mortuary, where Ruth and I had brought a box of belongings we thought would be suitable to include with his body when it was cremated. The box held his favorite clothes (khaki cargo pants, running shoes, ragg wool socks, a bush jacket), a selection of trout flies, his wedding ring, a tiny gold heart-shaped locket with a picture of him and my mother when they were college graduates, and other small objects. The undertaker settled the paperwork with us and then said he'd need me to identify the body. I had never seen a dead human body.

"I don't think I can do that," I said.

"I'll do it," Ruth said. Then she added, "Let's do it together."

As we climbed the stairs of the old mansion that was the funeral home, my mind was a buzzing fog. The steps creaked under my feet. Stained glass windows along the stairway sent rays of blue and red across the carpet, dust motes suspended in their light. Ruth was just ahead of me. She carefully pushed open the door to the room we'd been instructed to enter. The hinges squeaked lightly. There was a body on a raised bed, covered with a homemade quilt. The room was cold, like a refrigerator. Tall windows looked out on the street below, trees just coming into bud. There was an unused fireplace and a mantel with a small vase holding some pansies. I slowly approached the figure on the bed.

"Is it him?" I asked Ruth, thinking there had been a mistake. The man lying there, a crisp sheet pulled up to his chin, the soft contours of his seemingly small body laid over with the quilt, did not look like my father.

"It's him," Ruth reassured me.

This man's hair was silver-white and wavy, brushed back to reveal a high strong forehead, trimmed eyebrows, a handsome nose, a neat gray mustache and clipped goatee. This man's skin was smooth, flawless, glowing. His face was free of tension. His mouth relaxed and sensuous. The eyes rested lightly closed. I had expected that in death all my father's torments would be evident, that what I'd see on his face would be disappointment, sadness, rage, but instead the opposite was true. This was the face of a man who might pose as Santa Claus at the mall during Christmastime. You might imagine him swarmed by noisy loving grandchildren. He looked, Ruth would say later, like Pete Seeger, that holy troubadour of love and justice who sang America through the 1960s. Something had come to my father in death that I had never seen in him while he lived. I wept. I wished my brothers had been there to see him this way.

There was no formal ceremony to mark my father's passing. The world hardly blinked, in fact. While we cleaned out our parents' cabin in Montana, my brothers and I took time out to spread his ashes. After dividing the contents of the urn into three small containers, we each wandered off into the sagebrush and pines of their thirty-acre plot, sprinkling as we went. I don't know what my brothers thought or felt as they spread our father's remains, but I was strangely un-moved; there was no welling up of tears, no nostalgic ache. Ed and I met by a bench swing my father had built to face the sunset across the Madison River Valley, a place where he'd often go with a beer at the end of the day. Ed and I swung on the bench and each left a small handful of ashes at its base.

I had many dreams about my father in the years after his death, the first one terrible and violent. In the dream, set in the kitchen of my parents' house, the entire family was gathered to witness me mercilessly humiliate him, berating him for every fault, every failing, every flaw, until he was on his knees sobbing on the linoleum in front of the stove. When he was down, I may even have kicked him. If I didn't actually kick him, I certainly wanted to. It seems likely that this dream helped pave the way for the most recent one, which came to me in Montreal, in the same house where I'd heard news of his death three years earlier. In this dream he came to me quietly, his face open, his voice soft, and asked simply, "Will you forgive me?" I said, "I will."

Later I would receive a letter from the ICU nurse assigned to work with him the day he passed. "I thought you might like to know that I knew that you, like me, had a really, really tough relationship with your dad," the nurse wrote. "I did sing to him because I didn't know what else I could do (nothing we could do was working) and it seemed to help," she said. "I was able to treat him with dignity and compassion and professional caring and I thought of you and wished you well as I worked with him that day. I just didn't want to miss telling you those things." I was so glad she had been there at my father's side when he died—that someone had been there. And it made sense, given who he was, that it was not a member of his family but a stranger who was with him when he took his last breath. Still, I wish I had been the one to sing to him.

Foragers

The highbush cranberries red above the snow,
the sharpest, brightest flavor that I know,
a hint of bitter harmonized with sour,
and for this treat I beg you spare the flower
that decorates the woods in spring.
If you can learn to give each thing
your loving reverence, you will be able
to dine with me at mother nature's table.
We'll laugh at all the winter winds that blow
when highbush cranberries hang above the snow.

— Euell Gibbons, from the film *Stalking the Wild Cranberry*

Euell Gibbons, one of the world's most famous foragers, was one of my childhood superheroes. I was a kid starving for replacement father figures, and this one promised to educate me in a crucial skill—how to survive alone in the wild.

My first encounters with Gibbons were when my brothers and sister and I sat glued to the television screen on Saturday mornings. An icon of the 1960s back-to-nature movement, he is the man most of us know as the face of Post Grape-Nuts cereal, but more importantly, he is the author of many classic nature texts, the first of which was *Stalking the Wild Asparagus.*

The cereal commercials made an impression on me as a kid. Here was what seemed to be a fatherly fellow in a plaid shirt, out among the cattails, munching from a bowl of what looked like tiny pebbles. In one commercial Gibbons hangs out in an old flour mill in the Ozarks. In another he watches a Zuni elder pound corn. In another he's picking wild highbush cranberries in the winter to add to his cereal.

Stalking Gibbons as an adult, I learned that he, his siblings, and mother had been abandoned in their hardscrabble Dust Bowl–era New Mexico ranch in the early 1920s when their father left to find work. After the last chicken was killed and the family could not stomach another pinto bean (their sole food for quite some time), Gibbons headed into the mountains with a backpack and returned with piñon nuts, cactus fruit, and puffball mushrooms. Until their father returned, they lived on what he foraged.

"Wild food has meant different things to me at different times," writer John McPhee, Gibbons's de facto biographer, quoted him as saying in a *New Yorker* profile. "Right then it was a means of salvation, a way to keep from dying." Later, Gibbons said, foraging became more about relationships: "Man is part of the total ecology. He has a role to play, and he can't play it if he doesn't know what it is, or if he thinks he is conquering something." Like Gibbons, who uses the word "stalking" in the titles of his famous books—*Stalking the Wild Asparagus, Stalking the Blue-Eyed Scallop, Stalking the Good Life*—I, too, feel a little like Sherlock Holmes when I am on a foraging trip in the woods, stalking, looking for clues about who I am sharing the world with.

Ruth and I are both foragers; it's been one of the delights and cornerstones of our relationship. One day, slowing our car to a crawl in order to maneuver between the two huge granite boulders that squatted like friendly sentinels on either side of the rutted dirt road leading to our rustic one-room camp in Chesterville, Maine, I saw an odd shape attached to a tree. It was mid-June, early in the season for mushrooms, and there beside the road, attached in a voluptuous silver-white cascade to the trunk of a dead maple, were oyster mushrooms. Imagine soft, glimmering clamshells, one cream-colored, delicately gilled underside artfully overlapping the next velvet-smooth, cloud-tinted cap. When fresh, they smell sweetly of oyster, which is even more prominent when they are cooked. We had encountered oyster mushrooms before, but we were hesitant to try them. Finally, over years of encounters and research, we'd come to trust our knowledge of this fleshy, scalloped beauty, which we most often harvested from beech trees in the fall. I stopped the car, hopped out to collect a sample, and brought it home to identify. It turned out to be *Pleurotus populinus,* the late spring and early summer oyster. We sliced it up and included it in our next breakfast omelet, toasting across the table with our coffee cups, giving thanks to mother nature for this wild fruit of the forest.

**Boletes, oyster mushrooms, chanterelles,
and black trumpets on a cutting board**

On our own land we regularly make forays into the woods and yard to collect whatever might offer itself. We mark the transitions of the seasons by what we find. In spring there are dandelion greens, lamb's-quarter, fiddlehead ferns, coltsfoot, maple sap, wild asparagus, and new violets. In early summer sweet wild strawberries pop up in the lawn. Later, undomesticated thickets of blackberries and raspberries bear fruit. In late July and August we pick blueberries in an abandoned barren on a hill high above our house or from bushes that hang over the water on nearby ponds. Summer and early fall also bring out the bright-orange, low-growing lobster mushrooms, the boletes, chanterelles, the dusky black trumpets, the fall oysters, and the sweet tooths. As it grows colder we look for clusters of dark-purple wild grapes, bright-red highbush cranberries, and yellow, green, or red fruits of abandoned roadside apple trees. On the mountaintops we have picked and eaten alpine cranberries. At the ocean, the tide pools and beaches provide other fare, including sea greens and seaweed, snail-like periwinkles, clams, mussels, rose hips, and bay leaf. We have picked and eaten pigweed, chickweed, the leaves of the basswood tree, trout lily, and wild leeks.

In his writing about Gibbons, McPhee reveals a man who struggled with normal successes and failures, someone whose fear of not having enough, born in childhood, might have seduced him into compromising his values later in life and becoming someone he never intended to be. In becoming Mr. Grape-Nuts, some say he became a parody of himself, a laughingstock. His line, "Ever eat a pine tree? Many parts are edible," was perfect comic fodder. "He would live to be widely misassessed," McPhee wrote. At his best, he was "a man who advanced a special skill. He was a man who knew the wild in a way that no one else in his time has even marginally approached." He was never an evangelist for anything but getting to know the world around you.

I've never had to hunt-and-gather to live. With my father's professor income, a mother who liked to cook, our location in a middle-class suburb of Salt Lake City near food markets reachable by foot and by car, I had access to an embarrassing cornucopia of high-quality food—strawberries in the middle of the winter and all the other multitudinous luxuries that American grocery stores pull in from around the world. As an adult I've had large home gardens to supply me with all the seasonally fresh food I could eat.

I have always had more than enough food. Frustrated by my seeming inability to make peace with our family history, confused by the grudges I held on to so tightly, my mother said to me once, "You were provided for. We always had more than enough to eat. You had a roof over your heads. You had clothes." She was correct, but then, as now, it was not these material things that I hungered for.

Even as a child, self-sufficiency was more than an appealing fantasy. It was a psychological necessity: I needed to know I could run away and make it on my own without parents. My sister and I tried this more than once when we were little. Partly for fun, I think, and partly because we were scared by our father's temper, our mother's crying, and the knotted, bitter tension that seemed to course through the house. It would be a relief to get out of there—to go live in the neighbor's backyard, or up in the field, or down in the gully. I carried a tin children's toolbox full of sliced white bread, mayonnaise, peanut butter, and pickles. My sister had a few essential items stuffed into a bandana tied around a stick, hobo style. We would collect wild foods to supplement the meager diet tucked away in our luggage. Cattails, perhaps. Berries. Dandelion roots.

Euell Gibbons wasn't just teaching me how to survive in the metaphorical wilderness of life. His broad-chested, back-to-the-land

oneness with nature inspired trust, and while I sought self-sufficiency, on one hand, I also sought a relationship with someone who
could father me, mother me, teach me, gently, about connection,
love, safety, about how to feel at home in the world.

After my father died, Ruth and I traveled to Salt Lake City to begin
taking care of all the undoings that death demands. My mother had
died five years before my father, and while she'd left their finances in
good order, the house needed to be emptied and sold. My brothers
arrived from Texas and Australia to help excavate our parents' eighty
years of possessions and to supervise the transfer of our father's
research notes and specimens to an archive in Brazil. During those
weeks I reconnected with three beloved high school women friends.
We had decided to have a mini-reunion at Snowbird, a ski resort
in the mountains outside Salt Lake City, the town where we had all
grown up.

It was here, in these mountains, as a teenager, that I had started
what would become a practice of paying close attention to plants,
a stepping-stone on the way to a fascination with edible wild foods
and foraging. In midsummer the alpine meadows of Albion Basin
were a riotous sea of hundreds of different wildflowers: columbine,
lupine, Indian paintbrush, mountain bluebells, Jacob's ladder, daisies,
asters, yarrow. As a teenager I tried to get to know as many as I could,
learning their taxonomic classifications, their botanical structures,
memorizing their Latin and common names. They were, I think now,
my first attachment to something that truly made sense outside my
dysfunctional family—these wildflowers were breathtakingly beautiful and undeniably real. They offered a soothing antidote to the floaty
untetheredness I felt. They grounded me.

As my now-adult friends and I hiked through these same alpine
meadows, we talked—about children, siblings, partners, aging parents, recently deceased parents, our jobs, our sorrows and our joys.

And we named the flowers and the peaks, and from the tops of the peaks we named the lakes and the rivers and the dollhouse towns in the valleys that spread out below us. We were pleased to find that the qualities we had loved in each other's young selves were still present, only deepened and widened by age and life. We felt embraced in each other's still familiar company. We reminded each other of who we had been, and who we were now.

"You know," my friend Ann said, "I've always admired your curiosity about the world, and I think that must have come from your father." Her comment was a small, surprising revelation. I had never seriously considered that my scientist father had passed on to me, through genes and by example, one of the qualities that defines me to others and brings me the most joy.

In the same conversation, Ann and I spoke about the ways we were still reminded of our parents' failures to give us the childhoods we would have preferred. Our mothers were both alcoholics, our fathers both absent in different ways.

"We had to raise ourselves," she said.

Yes, that's it, I thought. I had to learn to fend for myself. Perhaps that's why I was so drawn to Euell Gibbons.

Like all children, I wanted to trust my parents, but I didn't. I also didn't trust myself. There were so many things I knew as a child, that I felt in my bones, that all of us knew, but that were denied or never spoken of. It seemed I was forever trying to figure out what was real. Were my feelings real? Was I real? Was anything at all real? It was the elephant in the living room story—no adult in our household would admit that my father was a violent, unpredictable man who was verbally battering my mother into depression, and no one would admit that my mother drank as a way to cope. Much of my adult life has been spent trying to verify my childhood experiences. If anyone could corroborate my felt sense of the past, it would be these three women—Lisa, Steph, and Ann. I decided then to ask Ann to tell me a truth about my father, if she could, a truth that would help me put a new, solid brick into a chink in my childhood.

"Did my father have an affair with one of his students, your sister's best friend?" I asked her. Part of what made me a forager was my ability to pay close attention, and it was likely that I learned this skill as a useful survival tactic in my family. What mood was our father in when he came home from the university? How many drinks had he had before dinner? When could an escape from the supper table be executed? One night I peeked through my nearly closed bedroom door to see my parents sitting on the hearth in the living room, my father with his head between his knees, chin propped up on his elbows, sobbing. "Why would she do that to me?" he wailed. My mother was rubbing his back, murmuring consolations.

Who was she, I wondered, and what had she done to my father? I immediately sensed it must have been something sexual, though I can't say why. That same week when I was visiting my friend Ann, her older sister came home from college with a friend in tow. Ann's sister paused in the doorway to the room Ann and I were in. She looked at me, then looked at her friend, and the friend looked at me, then looked at Ann's sister. A soft, gray web was woven from those exchanged glances. That was the "she," I thought. My father had had sex with her.

"Yes," Ann said, "he did have an affair with one of his students, but that's all I know."

So my intuition had been correct! I didn't feel righteous indignation at his behavior as much as I felt relieved to know I had been right, that I could trust my version of the past, that I could trust myself.

One of the many gifts of the therapeutic work I had so diligently pursued over many years had been, at last, a felt sense that truths can be complex; they didn't always come in the shape of either/or, black or white. "Hold that in one hand," the therapist would encourage me, when I labored over something utterly perplexing, a dichotomy that created painful tension in my psyche and body. "Hold the second thing in the other. Hold them both. One in each hand." And then what? "Wait to see what happens," she would say. "Wait to see what you learn."

In the one hand I held this: my father had cheated on my mother. He messed around with a student. Poor judgment. Lack of respect. Terrible boundaries. Abuse of power. And in the other hand I held this: he modeled for me a priceless skill that has enriched my life immeasurably—curiosity—a gift that Ruth has said drew her to me in the first place. "You weren't afraid to ask questions," she said. "You wanted to know everything!" It has been a gift that has drawn me into ever closer connection with the actual, solid, natural world, a gift that has saved my life. What am I left with, then? How do these two experiences of my father—my father the adulterer, my father the seeker of knowledge—make sense? For now, I only know that this shared experience of engaging in an extramarital affair is one more painful lesson in humility. This is not one of the ways I want to be like him.

Although the forager game continues to amuse me, I have come to a new understanding of self-sufficiency. While knowing how to fend for yourself is extremely useful, it can, if engaged in obsessively, be another way to make yourself lonely. "I will run away, I will take care of myself" is the child's way, the injured psyche's way of staying safe, but, ideally, only until a new home, a new community can be found.

I have found that community in many places—on a farm in western Maine, in relationship with Ruth, in the homes of dear friends, in the woods, in volunteering as a chaplain at our local hospital, in the offices of therapists and other healers, and in the pews at Old South Church in Farmington. Going to church opened a door to a deep longing that I continue to explore. In the beginning, one of the hardest things for me was communion. It took me years to gather the courage to join other parishioners as they walked forward down the aisle to the communion table, to lift a cube of bread or tear a piece off a fresh loaf, dip the bread into a cup of grape juice, and receive, from the pastor or an assisting deacon, a version of the following blessing: "The bread of life, for you, and the cup of blessings."

It's hard to articulate why I was so afraid to join in what I know now is a symbolic ritual meal, a sharing of love and food. I think my fear had to do with letting myself become a part of something bigger than me, a spirit of love. I was being offered an opportunity, at least metaphorically, to be a precious, invited guest at a table that everyone else was also welcome to sit at. We were all the same. No one had to prove he or she was worthy to sit at this table; no one was more or less welcome than any other. I was being invited to let go of my ego, to put down my burdens, and let someone or something else feed me. The simple hymn we sang while communion was in process often brought me to tears:

> Come to the table of grace,
> come to the table of grace.
> This is God's table,
> it's not yours or mine.
> Come to the table of grace.

The kindest, most generous words anyone had ever said to me were: "You are not alone. There is an end to your suffering, and you are not alone." The words weren't offered in a religious context, although that might be a familiar understanding for many of how God might be understood—as always being near so that we are never without comfort, never far from a loving presence. The words were offered instead in a psychotherapist's office, when I expressed a desperate feeling of loneliness and despair.

"You are not alone," she said.

"Do you mean I'm not alone because I have friends? Or because I have Ruth? Or because of God? Or because you are here right now?" I asked.

"All of that," she said.

All of that. Such a simple offering. The solid presence of another human being who is listening with attention and love. I trusted this person, as I trusted Euell Gibbons as a girl, as I trusted Ruth, as I trusted the plants that I found as I foraged in our yard, our woods, and the lakes and ponds, mountains and roadsides of my new home. I was never alone; I never had been alone. I know that now, in my bones. I swim in a sea of relations, with people dead and alive, with powerful forces I can't see or understand, and with every single living organism on this earth. I have come to the table—to mother nature's table, to the table of grace. What I forage for now is something both ineffable and real. I suppose you could call my foraging a hobby and be done with it, although the word "hobby" has a slightly pejorative whiff to it. I prefer to think of foraging as a spiritual calling. A way to practice gratitude. A way to become acquainted with the vast and intricate beauty of the world. A way to pray.

CONSIDER THE ACORN

God Gives Us Our Desires

The affair with M. ended when I finally reckoned with the mess I'd participated in and the wreckage it had created. Desperate in my confusion, I had gone to talk to my pastor, who sat with me, held my hand, and said, "Gretchen, God gives us our desires." She let that sit in the air for a moment and I was grateful. I felt seen by her and understood. It wasn't my fault that I was attracted to M. I wasn't a bad person. And if God gave me these desires, rather than inflicting them upon me, cursing me with them, that meant in some ways they were a gift. Why would God have given me such a gift? Was I meant to simply indulge in this gift or learn from it? If it was the latter, what was I supposed to learn?

After a moment, she continued, "And, Gretchen, Ruth *will* leave you if you don't stop seeing her." She said this in such a matter of fact and loving way that it felt like absolute truth, which it was.

Ruth did leave. For several months we lived apart. During those months she spent part of her time at HOWL, short for Huntington Open Women's Land, a lesbian-feminist intentional community in the woods of rural Vermont. She met someone there she was attracted to. Just as my affair awakened my erotic connection to myself and the world, so did Ruth's. She began taking pictures of snowstorms and cracked ice, marveling at their beauty and complexity. Why did erotic love do that—wake us up? And why do we so love to be awakened? Now I was looking at things from a different perspective, no longer able to luxuriate in my own confusion, but faced with the real possibility of Ruth choosing someone else.

There was that, and M.'s new partner sent me a strongly worded email: "If you don't leave M. alone, you will have to deal with me, personally." I realized then how truly crazy and dangerous it had all become. Not only was my personal life being shredded, but my professional life stood to be compromised.

It was true; it was hard for me to leave M. alone. I continued to contact her, drawn to her like a clichéd moth to flame, like a fly to honey, leaving ridiculous messages on her answering machine, hoping we could "be friends," have coffee, talk it out, agree that we'd both been idiots. In retrospect, her partner's aggressive notes were a gift of their own. I had thought that being with M. made me more of a whole person, that the sexual passion I experienced somehow completed me. After all the emotional turmoil and drama, when I finally understood that M. and I were not going to be together, ever, in any way, I felt as if I'd lost a part of myself. It was the part of myself that I found when I first came out as a lesbian. And now it was gone, I thought, this time forever. But I was wrong. In fact, I had lost nothing, only gained.

Whatever it is I felt was missing had nothing to do with M., or even with Ruth. It had to do with me. Rumi, the Sufi mystic poet from the thirteenth century, has called this missing thing "the beloved," which I understand as the divinity deep in the center of the self, a source of light within each of us. "Where do you find that kind of love?" I asked the therapist who had already helped me so much. After pausing, taking a deep breath, and looking me straight in the eye, she said, "I can't provide that love for you. Neither can any other person. Not even Ruth. What you are seeking is a different kind of relationship with yourself." In other words, whatever I thought was missing or incomplete in my life I had to seek within.

Another Sufi teacher, the twelfth-century Persian poet Farid ud-Din Attar, in his epic poem *The Conference of the Birds*, tells the tale of a group of birds who go on a long journey to find their king and savior, whom they call the Simorgh. At the end of their dangerous trek, which takes them through seven allegorical valleys, only thirty birds remain. When they find the Simorgh, a word that in Persian means "thirty birds," they realize that what they were seeking all along was not outside themselves, after all.

> Their life came from that close, insistent sun
> And in its vivid rays they shone as one
> There in the Simorgh's radiant face they saw,
> Themselves, the Simorgh of the world—with awe
> They gazed, and dared at last to comprehend
> They were the Simorgh and the journey's end.

Each bird in the tale represents a different and very human frailty. What they find, at the end of their quest, is not a savior or a king, but themselves, in all their beautiful, lustful, prideful, avaricious, ignorant, courageous, and strangely incomplete completeness.

Hunters

As I looked out the window on an early winter day, cup of coffee in hand, I saw one of our cats, starkly black and white against the winter grays and browns, prowling in the apple orchard, tail held high in a muscular curve, going after whatever moves there—mice, moles, voles. He was beautiful and sleek, powerfully built, agile and alert. A hunter. Both cats lived in the barn and under the house and woodshed. Ruth and I were both allergic to cats, so this was a necessary arrangement.

Mustache and Stripe, named for their facial markings—one with a white stripe down his nose, the other with a white mustache—came to us as kittens, a brother and sister, the unwanted progeny of someone else's barn cat. They may have lived outside, but they had none of that mangy, scabby dullness you might associate with working farm cats. They had bowls for food and water in the barn. They made annual trips to the vet. They met us when we came and went from the house, squirming over on their backs and offering their white bellies to be petted. They sat on the doorstep and printed their muddy paws against the glass-paned door. They meowed and purred and tangled themselves in our legs when we were in the garden or doing chores in the barn. They loved to be cuddled and squeezed, held upside down even, and enjoyed riding on our shoulders. Their bellies were always full; their eyes shining, emerald-green marbles. They were our pets and friends, our little white-mittened darlings.

They were also ferocious hunters, so much so that we removed our beloved bird feeders soon after the cats arrived, because they would sit under the feeders and jump up, one paw outstretched, to hook down a tiny chickadee or titmouse. The cats had certainly done the job we hoped they would do, which was to help us control rats in the barn, mice that invaded our home every fall, and the moles and voles that tunneled through our vegetable garden, destroying our onions, carrots, beets, and other root crops. As I looked out at the cat hunting in the winter orchard, I was full of admiration for these shapely, self-sufficient animals, their sense of purpose, their repose,

Cat hunting on a garden fence post

their joy for life, their effortless elegance and robust health, their seeming equanimity.

It had rained the night before, and the shim of ice on the road brought out the town maintenance trucks to spread sand and salt on the village streets and outlying country roads. Even with the sand and salt, as I slowly took a corner coming home from yoga class, the steering wheel of the Subaru seemed to float out of my hands, and it felt for a moment like the car and I were weightless, about to lift off from the wet dark pavement into the pines and naked maples and cattails beside the road. We settled back down, machine and I, and made it home. In the barn everything and everyone was safe and warm and dry, the chickens settled feathered-wing to feathered-wing in their coop, the goats resting in their bedding of dry fragrant hay, the cats perched on the stairs in the barn, their thick winter coats glossy and black and smelling of fresh summer from their cozy bed among the hay bales in the barn loft. In the house, Ruth had lit another fire in the woodstove before she left to spend the week alone in a small camp we had purchased on a pond just four miles away. The house held the signature of her consideration for me, her love—she had wanted me to have the pleasure of coming home to warmth and light, to coals in the woodstove still orange and glowing, ready for me to add more logs and renew the flame so I could sit in front of the fire, the stove doors open, and drink a glass of wine and eat some dinner, an omelet of eggs just collected from the chicken coop.

I was alone. Ruth was at the cottage on the pond, with its big windows looking out on the cedars and birch bending over the dark water with its own thin mirror of early winter ice. She was in her own warm place, and I in mine. We had been getting on each other's nerves, I guess you'd call it. We had just returned from five weeks traveling in Europe, a trip we both wildly enjoyed but one that had us in each other's company twenty-four hours a day, every day. It's a sad truth that such proximity can breed discontent even between people who love each other. Since our return I'd been finding fault in her at every turn. "You're wearing your shoes in the house again," I said, something that irritated me because she scolded me when I shifted furniture without lifting it, concerned that it might scratch our soft pine floor, and here she was tracking in grit that would leave little pockmarks in the wood. She often forgot where she left her phone or wallet or keys, and because of that we were sometimes late. "Why can't you just put your keys in the box near the door?" I would say to her.

When I began to behave this way I thought of my father, who was angry and impatient like that as far back as I can remember. Unlike him, however, I have been lucky enough to develop some skills that give me perspective on my emotions and allow me to say to Ruth, sometimes, during these periods of difficulty, "Sweetheart, I'm sorry. I think I just need some time by myself," which might lead to times like this, with me spending the week at home and Ruth spending the week at our camp.

During my week alone, I went to the woods for the last days of deer hunting season in Maine. I craved the physical strenuousness of walking in the woods with a rifle and a pack, the stillness and quiet of the forest, the opportunity to simply be still, and mostly the chance to be alone. I didn't want to talk to another person, negotiate competing desires or plans or expectations, be beholden to anyone else's needs.

I loved the bleak, elegant formalism of a late fall and early winter landscape, the harsh geometrics, the colors—brown, black, gray, tan, rust, a shock of red where there might be a bunch of winterberry on the tip of a naked twig. In late fall and early winter, without the confusion of greenery, it was easy to see what was real—how trees were built, how ground rolled and rippled, how rocks announced themselves. As I walked the woods on that hunting day, I noticed at my feet that the leaves of the wintergreen plant, which I loved to pick and chew in the summer for a blast of freshness in my mouth, had gone from glossy green to deep wine. The feathery princess pine, the moss and lichen (occasionally a shocking peach or bright orange-tipped specimen), made a dense dwarf forest that absorbed me as I walked. Eventually I came upon the place at the top of our

land where the stone walls meet in a tidy rock corner. What a sweet place that would be to settle into, I thought, lean my back against the stone, and be alone, maybe fall asleep into a peaceful nothingness, and best of all, no one would know where I was.

The beautiful, simple landscape of the late fall, early winter woods reminded me of the Ingmar Bergman films I watched as a college student. Even then, I felt an affinity for those outer landscapes of subdued colors, muted tones, and strong shapes.

Wintergreen

These were the outer landscapes that neatly complemented my own serious, complex interior landscape of melancholy. The geography of my thought was the same terrain Bergman explored in his films— death, illness, faith, betrayal, bleakness, and insanity. I wonder if it is true that some of us are hardwired to be melancholics, preoccupied with meandering about in the darkness.

I am not sure I am really a hunter, in the sense that I am after prey, like our barn cat patrolling the meadow. I think I hunt for something else. I crave most the exploration of the space between being ready for anything to happen (a deer could emerge from the tree line at any moment) and the need for patience, stillness, and grace. That clash of energies creates a strange liminal zone of perfect being in the moment. Something magical happens in that space of readiness and acceptance, a sense of ease, rightness, balance; a feeling of being in the right place at exactly the right time.

That first evening of hunting, I stood on a ridge about twenty minutes' walk from our front door, among the leafless beech and oak, overlooking a ravine. Deer walked down from the ridge into the ravine and up the other side over the hill to the old apple orchards on the neighbor's land. I listened to the small stream tinkle and gurgle below me, entranced by the black trail it made through the dusting of snow in the twilight. The moon rose. As I made my way out of the woods, its light turned from orange to white and reflected off the thin layer of snow on the ground, lighting my way.

On the last day of deer hunting season I sat up in a tree for five hours. I had come upon the stand by accident. I had been meandering through the woods, following deer tracks, when I looked up to see a metal ladder heading up to a wide cushioned seat set against a sturdy hemlock and draped with a camouflage blanket. A neighbor had fastened the stand to the tree but hadn't used it that season. It was on my land, I reasoned—I'd occupy it—and I climbed the fifteen feet up, rifle slung across my back, and settled in, arranging my lunch, my thermos, my notebook, extra mittens, and shawl to cover my legs if they got too cold. I wasn't hunting, after all, so much as waiting. I wasn't engaged in any kind of aggressive tracking or luring or baiting or outwitting; I would just sit there and see what happened.

Two nuthatches visited, doing their funny upside-down dance along the trunk of an oak nearby. A fat, bright blue jay came and went, came and went, came and went, making loud rustling noises in the dried leaves that lay two feet thick on the forest floor. It is amazing how vibrant, how startling, these small animal noises can be in the quiet studio of the woods. A chipmunk made a loud chirring sound as it hopped from log to log, branch to branch. A hawk began to circle above me, circle and circle and circle, ever wider, ever wider,

graceful, floating. I could hear the beat of its wings against the air. He or she, I thought, was hunting too. And so was the flock of wild turkeys, which came late in the day, shuffling through the leaves for acorns and beechnuts, finally lifting themselves on their massive dark wings into the treetops to roost for the night.

Suddenly the sky turned from a partly lit gray-blue to an opaque gray. Just as the light changed, the feeling in the woods changed. A hush fell. Some God-hand had laid a blanket over us all. Everything was still—wind, stream, squirrel, jay, turkey. It was as if the woods exhaled a deep breath, letting out all the tensions of the day. And then it began to snow, and the snow came down in icy flakes and as the flakes fell, each one, *each one*, made an individual tiny sound of connection on the leaves below. For a few moments, the sky was gray and full of snow and there was the music of snow falling on leaves—a soft *pat, pat, pat, pat, pat.* A gentle, natural, simple percussion, as simple as the pumping of a heart, the movement of breath, the beat of wings. I was enraptured, intoxicated, so happy to be alive in that moment. I was in that right place at exactly the right time.

My father was a hunter, just like the cat, the hawk, the jay and the nuthatch, the turkey, and the squirrel. My mother as well. My siblings. And me too, and Ruth and M. We all were. What were we all hunting for? Those basic necessities that propel us all through life—a mate, a meal, a safe place to live, a sense of belonging, the heart's content. Why was it all so hard to achieve, and why, in my life, had it taken so long to find even the faintest sliver of it? In that tree stand, with the snow falling down, all alone in the woods, just me and the rocks and trees and animals, I felt effortlessly full of the goodness I longed for and longed to share with all my beloveds. I felt complete, overflowing, and grateful. Joy does that, I'm told.

When it was finally too dark to see, I climbed out of my stand and headed toward the house. I could almost see the porch light through the naked trees. Ruth must have returned from her week at the camp. Halfway down the hill, she and our nephew Adam came to meet me, their orange hats and vests making them brilliantly visible in the fading light, and we walked the rest of the way home together.

Consider the Acorn

Consider the lilies of the field, how they grow;
they neither toil nor spin; yet I tell you,
even Solomon in all his glory was not arrayed like one of these.

— Matthew 6:25

Is there anything more perfect than an acorn with its jaunty beret, its burnished shell so much like the shape of a human face—wide at the forehead, tapering down to an excellent chin? What is more intricate and delicate than the designs on that clever hat—small triangles of hardened brown or green, layered over one another endlessly to create a design and texture of Fibonacci perfection, as appealing as any woven cloth? There are plenty of natural objects to match the acorn, of course: a silk-smooth, palm-sized, heart-shaped stone; a bit of bright-blue-speckled eggshell; a finely sculpted pine cone, its edges frosted with pungent sap; the tiny bleached skull of a mouse at the bottom of the woodpile; a brilliant pink shard of crab shell; an imaginative stick curved in the shape of a woman's dancing body; the husk of a spiky brown beechnut, splayed open like a tulip, the nut itself carted off to some squirrel's winter pantry; a tiny bird's nest woven of birchbark, pine needles, and blue baling twine; and, oh!—a bright red feather from the wing of a scarlet tanager. Yes, there are plenty of natural treasures to match the acorn, but none to outshine.

If you are a collector of such things you know what I'm talking about. You often find your pants and coat pockets, the zippered compartments of your daypack, the windowsills in your kitchen, bathroom, and bedroom, your desktop (at home and work), the edges of your bookshelves, and the corners of your porch stocked with stones, cones, nuts, feathers, dried leaves, and seedpods. You try to remember where they came from. When you decided to bring them home you promised you would never forget where you found them. You vowed that the object would serve as a memento of a certain place, a certain day, a certain slant of light, a felt sense, the person you were with. But you forgot. Never mind: these natural objects still ground you and speak to you of the joy of attending to the world's beautiful small things. Sometimes you wonder why that stone, why that flower, that leaf caught your eye. Sometimes it might occur to you that the supposedly inanimate object itself drew you to it, calling to you, *pick me up, bring me home.* Is it really so absurd to think such a thing? Japanese stone artists, after all, believe the key to their artistry is listening to the voice of the stone.

The next time you stroll to the mailbox, walk through a park or along a wooded trail, mosey beside the seashore, a lake, or a pond, imagine all those voices—pebbles, feathers, nuts and seedpods, bones, pine cones, shells, and leaves—clamoring for your attention, buzzing with the hum of life that flows through us all. What are they saying? *I am here.* Just that. The objects remind you that there is indeed something powerful and wondrous at work in a realm that you, despite your efforts and years, understand so little about. The natural objects you bring home to tuck into the nooks of your life are a direct line to something awesome and holy—call it nature.

Let us, just for a moment, consider the acorn. I pick a nut from the dish of paper clips on my desk. This particular acorn is the ruddy, burly fruit of the exquisite red oak. The perfect pattern of overlapping triangles that decorate this nut's tawny top defies any human crafts-man. A master knitter would be challenged to improve upon such a design. Could a painter create colors more artfully juxtaposed—the reddish-brown of the cap, the slightly duskier brown of the shell, the darker gray-brown of the tiny spike at the bottom, and the woody stem at the top? The acorn's textures are so sensuously varied—the bumpy but silky feel of the top, the slightly corrugated but smooth feel of the shell, the sharp prick of the spike at the bottom, the rough scratchiness of the nubbin on top. In this particular acorn there is a tiny hole, no doubt the entrance for a worm. What a smart worm; in-side the nut it found food and shelter. I snap off the beret and whack the nut open atop my desk with the heel of a shoe. Just as I thought! The worm has come and gone, leaving the contents of the shell re-duced to a medium-brown powder. This perfection, this beauty, this seed of a new tree, this food for a worm, was all made by nature, not by humans—by the oak itself, with the help of water, wind, soil, and sun.

Acorns, of course, are not only aesthetic marvels; they are also a vital part of the woodland food chain. In Maine, acorns are the main food for turkey, squirrel, deer, bear, blue jays, quail, and even waterfowl. As soup, gruel, mush, or baked cakes, acorns were daily sustenance for the first people who inhabited this landscape. A good part of their lives was spent harvesting, processing, and storing acorns. One historical source claims that the starving pilgrims at Plymouth stole baskets of acorns stored in the ground by their Native neighbors, thereby cheating death (and their Native neighbors) for yet another day.

Imagine all that good, sturdy natural food just lying around in the woods for the taking. Botanists say there are as many as six hundred different oaks in the world, with ninety species native to the United

States. Oaks divide themselves into the red oak group (*Quercus rubra*) and the white oak group (*Quercus alba*). Our lovely American oaks include the Arkansas oak, the Chapman oak, the Lacey oak of central Texas and northeastern Mexico, the chinquapin, the chestnut, the overcup, the swamp white oak, the turkey oak, the bear oak (aka scrub oak), the Oglethorpe, the blackjack, the Shumard, the Nuttall, the "live" evergreen oaks, and the most abundant oak in my neck of the woods: the northern red oak.

I am foolishly proud to say that this oak is the most important and widespread of the northern oaks. It likes sandy, loamy soils. It is prized for flooring, millwork, and furniture. Its name comes from the color of its autumn leaves, often a deep wine-red or orange at the peak of fall foliage in Maine. *Quercus rubra* grows well in cold climates. Its pests are numerous, including the gypsy moth. It is in the beech family and a close relative of the American chestnut. To modern biologists the oak is a keystone species, meaning it has a disproportionately large impact, relative to its abundance in any given woodland environment, on the health of the ecosystem of which it is part. Like the keystone in an arch, if the oak fails, the entire ecosystem collapses.

When I wander in the forest in the winter, on skis or snowshoes, following rabbit and deer tracks, for amusement I attempt to identify the trees by their bark alone. I often cheat, however, and look upward instead. In this way I can always tell the oaks from the maples and ash; unlike the others, the oaks cling to their dark-brown leaves even through the most turbulent of storms and snowfall. Under "lifestyle" in one of my reference books (*The Book of Forest and Thicket*), I learn that any oak with pointed, bristle-tipped leaf lobes belongs to the red oak group, and that all trees in this group produce acorns that take two years to mature. White oak group leaves, on the other hand, lack these telltale bristles, and their fruits mature in one year. Oak tree flowers, which I seem to have been oblivious to all these years, come in both male and female varieties. The male flowers hang in "slender, dangling catkins"; the greenish female flowers are "solitary and inconspicuous," growing out of the axils of new spring leaves. The male flowers dangle near the crown of the tree, the female flowers below. Wind carries what needs to be carried from one to the other.

Just as acorns are food for the body, they are also food for the human imagination. Oak leaves, acorns, the tree itself, have long been symbols of power, steadfastness, honor, aspiration. They are, as American philosopher Ralph Waldo Emerson would say, "natural facts" that are "symbols of particular spiritual facts." For strength, we look to the oak. Their wood is beautiful, hefty, and dense. Oak makes the finest furniture, the hottest fires. When Ruth and I prepare our three cords of firewood for the winter, we appreciate that our woodcutter includes plenty of oak in the pile of logs he cuts from our woodlot and leaves for us to split. The oak logs, with their deeply grained bark, are always the heaviest to hoist onto the bed of the log splitter. When the spear of the splitter first cracks the log in half, the long, dense, golden wood grain is unmistakable. In the fireplace in winter, nothing warms like a stack of oak logs burning down to all-night coals.

For fortitude and patience, we look to the oak. "Mighty oaks from little acorns grow" is a saying meant to prod everyone, from lazy children to lackluster management teams, into thinking big about the future. We even look to the oak for ideas about what might make a man or a warrior. The *corona civica*, a crown made of oak leaves, was the second highest military decoration awarded to citizens of the Roman Republic. Oak leaves still decorate military uniforms, and the song "Heart of Oak" is still the official parade march of the British Royal Navy, which, in days of yore, went to war in ships made of oak, like the Vikings before them. For perseverance and longevity, we look to the oak. In lists of the world's oldest trees, oaks abound; one list has South Carolina's Angel Oak in the middle of its second millennium. Oaks have character; among the ten most famous trees of the world is the Emancipation Oak, a southern live oak ninety-eight feet in diameter still flourishing on the campus of Virginia's Hampton University. The tree was the site of the first southern reading of the Emancipation Proclamation. Clearly we're amazed by oaks; over centuries the tree and its little nut have planted themselves firmly in our collective consciousness. As the sonorous voices of the authors of the *Textbook of Dendrology* put it, "the sturdy qualities and appearance of many of the oaks, together with their longevity in comparison with other hardwoods, have made them from very ancient times the objects of admiration and worship among the early people of the world."

Early people, ancient times: the Druids; the "oak knowers." Roman naturalist Pliny the Elder writes that Druids climbed to the tops of oak trees dressed in white robes and harvested the mistletoe growing there, using it to create a potion to encourage fertility. The ancient Greeks gave their god of sky and thunder, Zeus, the fiercest natural symbols they could imagine: the thunderbolt, the eagle, the bull— and the oak. When Saint Boniface converted the Germanic tribes to Christianity in the eighth century, he first cut down the revered tree at the heart of their sacred grove: an oak so large and powerful the pagans called it Thor's Oak. The fallen tree was milled and used to build a church. Imagine, a people defeated by the felling of a tree.

Rambles in our woods frequently bring me across stands of oak, the ground beneath the trees strewn with hand-sized leaves and green and brown acorns, the moist soil carrying the prints of deer and turkey. In these oak groves Ruth and I find not only autumn's acorns but, in the summer, delicious black trumpet mushrooms, their fleshy, fluted dark horns blossoming up from the forest floor. Maybe it's just me, but I often want to eat the things I love—small children, baby

Hen with chicks

chicks, newborn goats. There is a desire to consume these objects of admiration and desire, to gobble them up, take them in, fuse them with myself. Acorns have always looked to me like food. Good enough to eat! Woodland candy. A perfect shape and size to pop into your mouth like a gumball.

I had never collected acorns with the intent of doing anything except rolling them in my palms or putting them in my paperclip dish. But, I wondered, if deer and turkey could eat them, why couldn't I? And so I began researching how to process them for food. The snow had come by then, four feet thick, making it impossible to collect any acorns for my culinary experiments, so I logged onto the internet thinking that a click of the mouse would get me what I needed—a bag or two of acorns, or better yet, acorn flour. Incidentally, the snow doesn't stop the herds of wild turkeys from getting at the acorns. The woods and roadsides near our home are dotted with piles of scruffed-up dirty snow and leaves—a sure sign turkeys have been at work foraging even through the thick blanket of snow. In my own online foraging I came up empty-handed. In a world where one can seemingly buy anything at any time, why aren't acorns for sale in November? When I asked at the local health food store where I could buy acorn flour, I was told they'd never had it for sale.

"Okay then, how about acorns?" I asked.

"You can ask a squirrel," he said.

Disappointed, I vowed that the following fall I would comb the woods and collect my own stash. Then, on a wintry day when Ruth and I were lunching in the warm farmhouse kitchen of our friends Bob and Rita Kimber, who live in nearby Temple, I spied a cardboard box full of acorns next to their woodstove. Bob generously donated a pound or two and for information on processing suggested I seek the advice of my friend Chris Knapp, who regularly did acorn workshops at his and his wife's nearby local living school.

"I could tell you how to do it over the phone, but why don't you come out? It would be more fun to show you," Chris said when I called.

A few days later I parked my car on the muddy road and snowshoed my way across an icy stream and through the snowy woods to Chris and Ashirah's cabin, where he and I began my lesson in transforming the fruit of the oak into food.

First, the acorns have to be dry and capless; mine were. Before giving them to me, Bob had put them in his oven on low to suck out the moisture. Next, Chris instructed me to cover the bottom of a five-gallon bucket with a layer of acorns and smash them with a wooden mallet. *Pound, pound, pound.* It doesn't take long to crack the dry shells and free the nutmeats. Then we poured the smashed acorns into another five-gallon bucket that was three-quarters full of water. The nutmeats sank and the shells rose to the top to be skimmed off with a kitchen strainer. We repeated this process until all of my acorns were smashed and the nutmeats were separated from the shells. The acorn nutmeats were transferred to a clean five-gallon bucket with holes in the bottom. The holey bucket was placed in a nearby stream, with a piece of PVC pipe directing the stream flow into the bucket. The bucket was secured with rocks, with a clean dishtowel tied around the top to keep out curious creatures, sticks, and leaves. It would stay in the stream for at least two days, and the water would wash away the bitter tannins in the nutmeats. Then the acorns would be dried again, either in the sun or slowly in a low oven, and ground into flour.

Like an expert on a cooking show, Chris had on hand a batch of acorns that had already completed the forty-eight-hour soaking and redrying phase, so we could return to the cabin and begin the next step, grinding the acorns into flour. He fed handfuls of washed, dried nutmeats into a heavy metal grinder clamped to his and Ashirah's outdoor kitchen table, collecting the dark-brown, fragrant flour as it fell out the other side of the grinder. Inside, where the woodstove was on and Chris and Ashirah's son Owen slurped happily at a bowl of acorn mush and kimchi, Chris mixed the acorn flour with half buckwheat flour (you can mix in any kind of flour—whole wheat, white, rice, even cornmeal), added sugar, salt, baking soda, and water (you can also add an egg or two), and shaped the dough into patties, which he cooked in bear fat (any cooking oil will do) in a hot cast-iron frying pan atop the woodstove. The "cookies," as he called them, were dense and slightly bitter. But it was their color that was most appealing—a rich dark brown, as dark as dirt.

The philosopher Emerson believed that matter mattered, that we are grounded in the real things of nature, that these things give birth to language, that language creates meaning, and that meaning gives shape to human life. The acorn is matter. It is one of those still solid objects that fills our world, that reminds us that we are made, like the acorn, of air, of water, of sunlight. In each acorn lies the infinite rejuvenation of everything, even time. In the acorn lies the promise of another oak, another deer, another turkey, another squirrel, even possibly, if you eat acorns, another human. For me, the acorn cookies were a rare treat, but for this imaginative family they were—along with acorn porridge—a daily source of nourishment. I suppose you could say that my friends are made of acorn, made of oak. And because I have eaten acorn cookies too, so am I.

Lesbian Wedding II

Amid one of Maine's battles to establish marriage equality, the members of Old South Church had a lively discussion about the matter. One beloved member of the congregation, who enjoyed a long and strong marriage to a handsome, gracious, and witty woman, confessed that what he had with his wife of many years was special, and he was not sure at all that this kind of specialness should or could apply to same-sex couples. While I had compassion for his thinking, I was also deeply hurt. Was it inconceivable to some, I wondered, that two women, or two men, could love each other as deeply as members of a heterosexual couple and want to make a lasting commitment to each other?

Neither Ruth nor I particularly wanted to ever be married again. We each had been married to men—nice men, men we liked, and each for about the same amount of time. When she came out as a lesbian, Ruth gave up a connection to wealth and prestige that had her occasionally dressing in evening gowns, furs, and diamonds, attending the Boston Symphony, and practicing the finest of New England blueblood manners. She also gave up family connections to people who had become dear during her short marriage, including her husband's grandmother, who lived in Newfoundland. She'd taught Ruth to say the name of the province properly ("New Fen *Land*, understand?") and endeared herself to Ruth with her ways of making sense of the world. She knew it would be a nice enough day, she said, if there was enough blue sky among the clouds to "make a pair of pantses."

What I lost in my coming out was the company of a sensitive, creative, adventurous, and able friend I'd shared many outdoor adventures with, and a connection to his three wonderful daughters who are now grown with children of their own. My husband was a photographer with a special eye for the creatures of the natural world. With him, I'd learned to hunt for deer, collect wild mushrooms, and cultivate a home garden. What Ruth and I both gained when we left our marriages and came as out lesbians is what many queer folk feel, a sense of finally coming into right relationship with our individual selves, our bodies, and the world. The love songs on the radio suddenly began to make sense.

As it became possible for queer men and women to marry, some of our friends did so, traveling to other states and countries to tie the knot. Ruth and I often discussed becoming legally married but usually arrived back where we started—we were feminists and lesbians; we were more interested in discouraging people from supporting the institution of marriage than encouraging them into it. With our shared home, our shared bank accounts, our mortgage, and our long-term relationship, we qualified as domestic partners according to the University of Maine system, which was sufficient for allowing Ruth to share the health and retirement benefits granted to me through my employer. For us, that seemed good enough. We'd already had our commitment ceremony in the forests of Vermont on the shores of Green River Reservoir.

But then we changed our minds.

It was 2011. I had applied for a Fulbright fellowship to teach and do research in the Kingdom of Bhutan, a tiny, primarily Buddhist country the size of New Hampshire and Vermont combined, tucked between India and China in the lap of the Himalayan mountains.

The Bhutanese government would not allow Ruth to accompany me there unless we were legally married. We speculated that perhaps the Bhutanese didn't know we were both women. That might have been the case in the beginning, but later we heard through the grapevine that the government was proud of its first visas issued to a lesbian couple. Our departure date for Bhutan was nearing. There was no way Ruth was staying home in Maine while I traveled in Bhutan for a year. We had to get married, and we had to do it quickly.

"The State Department and the Bhutanese Government have a shotgun to our heads," our email invitation to friends and family read. One of my colleagues, who was born in China and wasn't familiar with the shotgun reference, asked another American-born colleague to explain it. "That's a saying used to describe having to get married in a hurry," she said, "usually when the woman is pregnant, and usually the shotgun is wielded by the woman's father to ensure the couple go through with it."

Our invitation continued: "Thank you for agreeing to be part of this madness. We know that no one has time to do anything related to this wedding except show up, so we will expect no gifts and no fanciness. We will all just be our authentic and unmade-up selves."

We concocted the plan for our wedding on the back of an envelope, giving ourselves and our friends exactly two days to prepare. The envelope read: "Leave home 7:30 a.m. Drive 4 hours to Montpelier, Vermont. Talk about vows on the way over. Get license at East Montpelier clerk's office. Bring license to Dave Grundy (Justice of the Peace). Shop for hors d'oeuvres and wine on the way. Ceremony at Rita's. 7:45 dinner at Sarducci's. Night at the Inn at Montpelier. La Brioche for breakfast."

Before the ceremony we had to obtain a marriage license at the East Montpelier town hall. That's when I felt the first twinge of fear.

"I'm afraid," I told Ruth.

"Of what?"

"What if they're mean to us?" I said. There had been stories of town clerks refusing to give marriage licenses to same-sex couples. On this day, of all days, I did not need to be ridiculed or dismissed.

We walked up the wooden stairs of the building holding hands and stepped up to the high desk where a clerk was busily filing papers.

"What can I do for you?" she asked.

"We'd like a marriage license," Ruth said. I held my breath for a beat, watching the clerk's face for any sign that we might not be welcome there.

She paused. "Absolutely! Congratulations," she said, smiling.

Afterward, she took a picture of us outside the town hall leaping joyously and holding up our newly acquired paperwork. After the town hall and the paper signing at the justice of the peace's office, where we had to present our license and where we were officially, legally married, Ruth and I both beamed big smiles when the JP said, "Congratulations. You may kiss!"

Whatever made it so—the speed with which we executed the wedding plans, resulting in minimal expectations, or the relief that we'd be able to travel together to Bhutan, or the amazing support of our friends who dropped everything to travel to Vermont on a summer weekday on such short notice—it was the best wedding ever, officiated by our dear friend and poet Doug Rawlings and witnessed by a handful of friends who stood (or crawled—there was one infant) in the lush, flowery rural backyard of our married lesbian friends Rita and Elyse and their sons and their menagerie of pets and farm animals.

Doug's words for our ceremony were quilted together from mine and Ruth's life—her songs, our travels, my writing, our love of the outdoors, my passion for opera, his own favorite poets, and our long friendship with Doug and his family, which began on our first day in

Maine, when we found a plate of cookies, a bouquet of flowers, and a note reading "Welcome to Chesterville" on top of the woodstove in our rented farmhouse, which happened to be across the road from their longtime home. In a crisp summer suit, against a background of massive black-and-white dairy cows (Rita and Elyse lived next door to an elite dairy cow breeding farm), Doug began: "Cellists pull their wistful bows across throbbing strings; divas launch forth in arias soaring down rows of wildflowers. Daffodils spring forth; fireflies dance in the night; barn swallows stitch together the evening air. The cuckoo warbles. Gretchen and Ruth have come to walk in sunshine, to drink the joyous wine of love."

Ruth read her vows to me: "Gretchen, within this circle of friendship and love, I, Ruth, offer this ring as a symbol of my love for you and my commitment to our shared life. I promise to honor and nurture you as an authentic individual, even your inner Norwegian, and I also promise to honor the mystery that brought us to each other and will HOLD us together thru' good times and hard times, for richer, and poorer, in sickness and in health, for as long as we both shall live." The vows for our second lesbian wedding still were full of hope, but they also reflected a certain maturity and confidence that came with having been sorely tested.

When it came my turn, I was barely able to get through my vows; I doubled over, laughing and sobbing incoherently through the words, overcome by unexpected emotion.

Doug concluded the ceremony: "And now, Gretchen and Ruth, as you head forth into a world of goat cheese, maple syrup, lamb's-quarters, apple cider, and chicken stew, into a world of your own making... I, with the power vested in me by the Great Gaia, pronounce you Beloved Free Sprits, a couple for life."

After Doug's benediction, Rita, Ruth's first long-term lesbian partner, stepped forward to speak. "Ruth and I were together once," she said, holding fast to the hand of her partner, Elyse. "I thought at one point that Ruth and I would be where she and Gretchen are now. But our lives turned out differently. My wish for Gretchen and Ruth is that they have as much happiness and love and luck as Elyse and I have, for as long as they both shall live."

At the Inn at Montpelier where we spent our wedding night, we continued the celebration on the wide front porch, sharing an elaborate fruit tart prepared by Rita, whose baking skills were renowned, and drinking champagne, one bottle courtesy of the inn, which gave us the honeymoon suite, and another gifted to us by friends who'd arranged to have the bottle waiting in a bucket of ice on our arrival. It had been an exhausting, surprising, and glorious day.

Buoyed by the joy of our wedding and our new status as married Americans, which would allow Ruth to join me in Bhutan, I flew to Washington, D.C., to attend orientation meetings for my Fulbright fellowship. During a discussion about how to arrange for our families to join us in our respective foreign postings, I asked how to arrange travel for my spouse and what her travel allowance would be.

"We have to talk about what we mean by 'spouse,'" the administrator said, looking nervously around the room.

"Who does qualify as spouse?" I asked.

"Not who you might want it to be," she answered. Afterward she took me aside and explained that, unfortunately, according to the federal government, Ruth and I weren't actually married.

It felt in some ways like we had compromised our integrity to conform to a system that promised us corresponding privileges as a result. We did it. We got married. But the privileges were still withheld.

We still are glad we did it; it changed us in ways both subtle and profound. Given our reluctance to be married again, our suspicions of the tradition itself based on our feminist and lesbian leanings, and the still-healing wounds from the years of turmoil caused by my affair, we were both bowled over by how powerfully moving the ceremony was, how joyous it felt, how deeply, emotionally gratifying. Something was triggered by the ritual in community that had not been there during our private forest ceremony so many years before. We felt recognized, celebrated, and held by a circle of friends and even strangers (the clerk, the justice of the peace, the Montpelier innkeeper) who understood and recognized in us what they also had felt and known.

Later Ruth would tell me that my affair had cured her, in a cruel but useful way, of her initial innocence about our relationship, about any relationship. And the same was true for me. The honeymoon and the fairy tale were over. "I know now that I can live without you," she said. "I know that I can do well on my own and have a full life. I know that anything can happen, and I can survive it and thrive. And I know that whatever does happen, we can work it out."

Perfect

It was a lovely fall day on our farm in Maine. The maple, beech, and oak leaves had turned, and the woods seemed deeper now, more alive and dimensional, with the contrast of yellow, orange, and red against the dark green of the hemlock and pine. It had been a long, unseasonably warm autumn. The garden's productive days had stretched out and out and out. There were still tomatoes on the vine and hearty lettuce producing leafy greens for dinner. We had not scrambled to cover our tomatoes, which we often did this time of year, surprised by predictions of killing frosts. Such warnings often sent us fumbling in the dark by the light of car headlights, draping the plants with bedsheets and old blankets. Most years, the garlic didn't get planted until the ground was spiked with ice, but this year the earth wasn't yet frozen, so we still had time to push the papery white cloves into the soil to gather their resources all winter under a bed of leaves and be first up in springtime. The mild weather had afforded us the leisure to harvest slowly and deliberately, putting up each crop as it came into the house—the cabbage turned to sauerkraut and preserved in glass jars, the onions pulled and laid in the sun to dry before being put in baskets in the basement, the winter squash hardened off and stored by the boxful in the cool spare bedroom upstairs, the beets and beans pickled, the eggplant cooked into savory dishes and frozen for later in the year. You could say, from a gardener's point of view, that this season had been perfect.

You could call this a perfect day, as well. My time had been my own, and I'd happily engaged in feeding the goats and chickens, harvesting potatoes and carrots, planting a late row of kale, eating my lunch in the sunshine, stopping whenever I wanted to rest, taking a long cold drink of water, even going into the house to make a third cup of coffee. The blackflies of spring were long gone. There were no more mosquitoes. The beagles in the kennel on the other side of the road were not barking. The sun was warm, but not too hot. I was physically tired from my labors, but not too tired. The harvest was in full swing, so I had a lot to do, but not too much. Everything seemed in balance.

I was sitting in a metal lawn chair on the gravel patio near our side door. The chair, in the style of 1950s motel furniture with bent metal legs and a back that looked like a fan or clam shell, had come from the local transfer station in the days when supervisors still looked the other way as Ruth or I climbed down into the bin of trash metal to fish out the good stuff—the stuff that was perfectly usable but had been discarded because it was bent, dented, scratched, or spotted with rust. "Can you believe someone threw this away?" Ruth would exclaim, balancing carefully on the edge of the bin, sometimes reaching in with a hooked pole she had designed at home especially for this purpose. "This [whatever] would cost hundreds of dollars new!" Handy as she was, Ruth made short work of the dents and rust in the chairs, and now we had a collection of vintage patio chairs, a little the worse for wear but perfectly functional.

Much of our stuff, come to think of it, was a little on the ragged side, picked up at yard sales, discount stores, and auctions, salvaged from the side of the road, or given to us by friends who had moved on to newer models. Sometimes these imperfect possessions—the battered suitcase, the worn wool coat, the scuffed pair of shoes, the rusted barbecue grill, the stained shirt with the frayed collar, the taped-together hairdryer, the chipped plates—felt like the right thing to do, making do, but other times it all felt overwhelmingly tawdry. Sometimes I wanted everything to be new and clean and bright. Sometimes I wanted to clear away this out-of-style, rundown, patched, and repaired junk and start over.

The impulse to perfect my environment, to purge and begin again, was strongest when I was leafing through the catalogs that arrived in our mailbox: catalogs for seeds and garden gizmos, clothing, furniture, linens, chickens, fencing, gloves, tools, outdoor gear, books, fruit! In Catalog Land everything was perfect; nothing was dirty or broken or dull. Catalog Land was full of dust-free bedrooms outfitted with crisp linens, the sun streaming in through clean windows. Groomed golden retrievers lounged on spotless dog beds in front of tidy fireplaces surrounded by people with trim waists and straight white teeth. None of *their* shirts were missing buttons. When I was under the spell of this yearning, it felt as if my smudged, dumpster-diver, rough-around-the-edges life was a grubby second-rate one, that there was something wrong with me and the choices I'd made that landed me in it.

In these moments a fearful anxiety overtook me; I made up all kinds of reasons to justify my wanting—my old thing was worn out, out of style, didn't fit, wasn't the right color anymore. The new thing was better, prettier, classier, more efficient, and besides, it was a good deal. This hedonic treadmill was a never-ending cycle of getting, spending, and wanting more. Like the poet Wordsworth, I felt out of sync in these torturous moments, out of orbit with what I knew to be more important than stuff. "The world is too much with us; late and soon," he wrote. "Getting and spending, we lay waste our powers; Little we see in Nature that is ours."

At this point in my life, of course, I knew that capitalism depended on advertising and that the central trick of advertising was to make me feel like I was a loser unless I had the latest, newest, shiniest, coolest, cleanest, crispest, fastest, most perfect thing. Psychologists studying what makes people happy have discovered that the perfect new thing doesn't raise the level of life satisfaction for long and, in fact, creates craving for more perfect new things. But none of this knowledge seemed to cure my malady for good and for all. What made it so hard for me to be happy with exactly what I had, flawed as it may have been?

But I digress. I didn't come to sit on the battered 1950s-style patio chair on this perfect fall day to get sucked into a rabbit hole of self-judgment or to rant about unsustainable consumption. I came to sort pears.

Between my feet was a bushel basket of pears, full to the brim. To my left was a bucket for the rotten ones, which would go to the chickens or into the compost pile, depending on their state of corruption. In front of me on a low table were two large bowls, one for whole perfect pears and another for parts that could be salvaged for preserves. The pears had come from our friends Doug and Judy, whose two huge pear trees bore fruit in abundant amounts every other year. Their back lawn during these bounteous years was thick with dropped fruit, most of it dented, bruised, slashed, half-eaten by squirrels, munched by porcupines and raccoons, pecked at by birds, and stepped on by humans and dogs. During these years of the rain of pears, Judy invited us to take some off her hands; we readily obliged, and she packed us a basket. Because I didn't do the picking, I never knew what was in the basket—which ones would we display in the fruit bowl on the counter to let ripen and then eat for snacks or dessert over the next few days? Which ones would we make into ginger-pear preserves? Would there be any to put up in glass jars with a little sugar syrup for later in the winter? And how much would there be for the chickens or the compost pile?

As I began my sorting, taking up each pear for examination, fruit flies swarmed up from the basket, tickling my nose. I reached for a pear that looked firm and displayed that ideal pear shape—narrowish at the top, curving gently out to rounded abundance at the bottom—with just a blush of pink blending with the pale yellow-green of its skin, and *ugh*, my fingers melted into the sticky mush that was concealed from me on the pear's other side. I sliced off the mush and let it fall into the compost bucket and placed what I thought might be useful for preserves or sauce into the parts bowl. This was not an easy task. It's said that pears ripen from the inside out, so even if the skin is perfect, the inside might already be spoiled. Again and again, I'm fooled by the pears. What looked perfect from where I was sitting—the pear slanted just so, leaning against the one next to it, with its rosy hue and lovely curves, tiny stem still intact—turned out to be marred by a puncture, a scab, a deep bruise, a slit, a scar.

"Perfect" was the word Ruth and I first used to imagine our future together. We would have a small home and garden like the fairy-tale

Bees in a squash blossom

cottage in the New Zealand countryside we had spied on one of our early adventures together. A fire would be in the hearth. We would be in love. It would be perfect. It was almost a mantra in the beginning. Perfect, I would say as she brought me coffee in bed. Perfect, I'd say as I finished folding the last towel in a stack of clean laundry. There were perfect roses and squash. Perfect trips to the dump. And then what had been perfect, or so we thought, started to crack.

I was halfway through my bushel basket of pears. The bowl of pear parts and the bucket for the chicken food and the compost were growing much faster than the bowl of whole, unblemished pears. My bar, after all, was set quite high. In my mind floated the image of the pears I sometimes bought at holiday time from the Harry & David catalog. Their Royal Riviera pears, wrapped in gold foil and nestled in a cushioned box, were guaranteed to arrive at your door exactly ripe and utterly without defect. I had never found their promises wanting. How on earth did they do it? Did they employ sorcerer gardeners like the ones in fairy tales? Did they grow the fruit in their own little Camelot, where by law the climate must be perfect all year? Oh, how unfair my expectations were! My simple, untended, organic country pears were no match for those pampered fruit. My pears were, by comparison, malformed, discolored, and motley. No two were anything alike in shape, size, or color. Some were hard as apples and grainy on my tongue, while others were on the verge of decay. Some were round as baseballs, others comically asymmetrical. Some of them even had worms!

I wondered, as I continued my triage on these wounded fruits, what happened to all the produce that didn't make it to the sanitized showcases of our grocery stores, our modern palaces of perfection where every apple, pear, orange, pepper, and cucumber, every squash, potato, onion, and radish, every tomato, lime, lemon, and cabbage, was vetted and shined and waxed and misted into paradisiacal splendor. If I didn't know better, the grocery store might lead me to believe that every fruit and every vegetable emerged from nature perfect.

When I was focused on a pleasant, repetitive, physical, and mental task, like sorting pears, I was less likely to be assaulted by anxieties about my own imperfect nature. Most of my life staying busy had been, besides a much-valued American habit, a wholesome and productive way to turn down the volume on the grim, judging voice in my head that tried to convince me of my basic unworthiness. I'd rather not listen to that voice carping about my supposed faults and deficiencies, going on and on about how I was not good enough the way I was or, worse, rotten at the core.

I'd begun to realize, however, that staying busy might not be so much a virtue as it was an evasion, a way to avoid finally coming to terms with that grim judging voice. For many years I had been a student of meditation and mindfulness practices and the client of a gifted and compassionate psychotherapist. By these means I'd come into valuable psychological cures and spiritual insights. It was comforting to learn that the voice badgering me about my imperfections was universal, part of what it was to be a human being. I was not alone, and I was not crazy. Almost everyone had a voice that reminded them occasionally, if not constantly, of their incompleteness. This voice might have originally, in my childhood, been trying to protect me. The psyche is clever that way. If I could be the first to persuade myself of my own uselessness, then I'd be immune to further harm.

But as years have gone by, the voice wasn't so helpful in that way, and its chidings and scoldings exhausted me, depressed me, made my heart race, and set me running fruitlessly on a treadmill toward something, anything, I thought would make me faster, thinner, richer, smarter, more admired, more efficient, more generous, more kind. It told me I should work harder, work longer, spend more time with friends, read more books, get student papers back sooner; I should exercise more, drink less, watch fewer movies, write more, publish more, win prizes, be on *Oprah*. In short, be someone else, someone more perfect. I'd learned not to ignore the voice (it clearly needed my attention) but also not to take it too seriously. It was, after all, a bit of a trickster; it was not telling me the truth about myself. The voice was a thought, a dream of its own, a reaction, a memory of snow that fell a long time ago—all those things, but not the truth.

The cut pears in the bowl were turning dark at the edges. I went into the house for a wedge of lemon to squeeze over them to prevent more browning. While I was gone, yellowjackets had come to feast on the juicy sweetness of the fruit. I shooed them away with a wave of my hand, unintentionally smacking one in midair. The wasp fell to the ground. I thought I had killed it, and for a split second I was heartsick. Who's to say why, but the sight of the wasp on the gravel brought an upwelling of tears and memories of recent deaths (my mother, my father, dear friends, animals), along with worries about future deaths (my oldest brother who had recently had heart surgery, friends who were in ill health or were simply growing old) and melancholy over long-ago deaths (my sister who died by suicide thirty years before). But in a moment, as long as it took for these thoughts to arise and begin to fade, the wasp moved; it was only dazed. I was glad. Now I sat with the web my imagination had woven between the wasp and the pears; *memento mori*, reminders of death, and *memento vivere*, reminders to live. In the face of death, my pursuit of perfection, any pursuit of perfection, was just one more useless vanity. Everything was impermanent, especially life; this law would never change. With a half-rotten pear in one hand, a knife in the other, I said aloud into the perfect, sunlit, wasp-inhabited fall afternoon, surprising and embarrassing myself a bit with the drama of it all, "I am going to die. Why spend one more moment of this precious life worrying about whether I am perfect or not, trying to be other than exactly what I am?"

What is perfect anyway? Should humans be perfect? Can they be? Can anything ever be? Aristotle deemed perfect that which was complete in all its requisite parts. Others have argued that real perfection requires incompleteness, since only when a thing is incomplete can it continue to improve. Some regard perfection as unpardonable hubris. Perhaps that is the impetus for the myth that every authentic Persian rug contains within its elaborate tapestry an intentional flaw. The poet and mystic Saint Teresa of Ávila, whose self-doubt and yearning sounded quite familiar to me across five hundred years,

wrote that when she first heard God calling her, she felt like a total loser. What had she ever done, in all her life, to warrant being talked to by God? Then God called again with a sweeter song. She tried again to shame herself, to convince God she was unworthy. But then, she wrote, "God showed me his compassion and spoke a divine truth: *I made you, dear, and all I make is perfect.*"

My task was almost done. I had a basket of rotten pears and pear parts that I would dole out to the chickens over the next few days; I didn't want to let them gorge on this rich, sweet treat. I had a small basket of whole fruits suitable for the bowl on the counter, which we'd cut into thin slices, add to elegant salads, or lay artfully on a dessert plate with blue cheese and pecans drizzled with balsamic vinegar. And then there was the bowl of pieces that would be simmered on the stove with ginger and sugar and put by as preserves for Sunday breakfasts and Christmas gifts. No part of any pear had gone to waste, not even the rotten ones. The truth was, none of these pears was perfect, and yet every single one was perfectly suited to its purpose. Perhaps perfect was not so much the quality of an object as it was a state of mind, the place of calm and beauty that arose when you accepted that imperfection was inevitable and you began to live your life in accordance with that knowledge. Then everything became luminous and precious just as it was.

Nima's Death

You, Nima, the sun, came out of your mother wet, sleek,
And drank your first miraculous yellow milk at her teat,
You played in the emerald spring grass, and slept
Curled up with your brother, Dawa, the moon.

    —From Nima's eulogy

I wanted to be a real goat farmer. To me that meant turning what was a passion and a hobby into a moneymaking enterprise that would help our small farm at least break even financially. Little did I know that my experiment with market-driven thinking, emphasizing efficiency and savings over love and care, would contribute to the painful death of one of our animals. Another lesson. Another scar.

It's not that we never killed or ate our animals. From the beginning of our goat-farming adventure, Ruth and I had one of our herd butchered each year to fill our freezer with meat that we turned into delicious stews and soups, thick spicy chilis, North African tagines, curries, pepper-encrusted chops, and lean burgers. Goat had become my preferred meat, along with the broiler chickens we raised and venison. My belief, for a long time, had been that if I was going to eat meat, I would prefer to know where it came from, what kind of life the animal led, and where and how the animal was butchered. Our "homegrown" goat and chicken meat was always firmer, cleaner, and tastier than any meat we could purchase in stores. In addition to the usually two-year-old wether we sent to the local butcher for our own consumption, we often sold one or two of our young goats to friends who wanted to start milking or wanted to raise goats for meat. If a friend or neighbor didn't present themselves to take over excess members of our herd, we sometimes sold goats to our neighbor Darrell, who in turn sold them to a livestock dealer. The dealer would pick up the animals at the farm down the road in a big trailer and take them to livestock auctions in Boston, where the goats would feed a growing number of Americans who had come from parts of the world where goat was the most widely consumed meat.

It is hard to send an animal to slaughter. Sonny was the name of the first goat we had butchered. We put him in the back of our Subaru and drove him to a nearby farm that specialized in processing local livestock. Instructions were to leave Sonny in a pen in the back of the barn. He was a small black-and-white Boer-Alpine mix, with the tell-tale floppy ears, the long, rounded forehead, and the loud voice of the Boer breed. Alpines, by contrast, had perky ears and more angular faces. Boers were bred all over the world for meat; they were bulkier than Alpines, a breed renowned for its milk. Sonny was born to our first Alpine doe, a big, feisty, black-and-white doe named Dora, whom we bred to a nearby buck named Merlin. Sonny had a brother who didn't make it. We called him (K)Not, because he got tangled in a knot in Dora's womb and was stillborn. We had to call our old-time country veterinarian, Doc Cooper, to help us with the birth. He put on a long glove, reached inside Dora's vagina, grabbed (K)Not's back feet (kids are supposed to come out feetfirst; he had been turned around in the womb), and pulled as hard as he could, with Dora straining just as powerfully in the opposite direction and grunting loudly. Out came (K)Not, a limp dark rope, which Doc Cooper flung unceremoniously on the stall floor, and then came Sonny, miraculously still alive after the prolonged trauma of the difficult birth.

Sonny was about a year old when we left him in the locked pen at the back of the butcher's barn. We knew he was scared. He shivered and his eyes were wide and he bawled. We would come back a week later to pick up the small box of ground meat, chops, and stew meat that his little body provided. That day, as we drove away to the sounds of his distress, Ruth looked at me and said, "I will never do that again."

But I did do it again, at least twice more. I brought Ms. B (better known as Ms. Barbara Stanwyck, named for her sassy, bossy personality) to the butcher, leaving her in a cage with a cement floor that still bore stains of blood from its previous occupant. Other pens were occupied by lambs, more goats, a pig, and a large cow, all scheduled to be shot in the forehead the next morning, bled, and expertly cut into edible parts that would be wrapped, labeled, put in a cardboard box, and stored in a walk-in cooler until the person who ordered them came to pick them up. I also brought Kincaid, a two-year-old wether, to the butcher. He fought me all the way, dragging his heels as I pulled him from the car to the holding pen, doing that goat thing which angry toddlers sometimes do, which is sit down and refuse to budge. In the pen he pounded the wooden sides with his hooves and horns.

After that, I couldn't do it anymore. I could not bear seeing their fear and confusion, followed by what seemed like numb resignation. Instead of taking the goats to the butcher myself, Darrell offered to do it for me for a small fee. The ethics of this might seem questionable. Ruth and I had encountered a similar situation in Bhutan, when our Buddhist friends, who vowed not to harm any sentient being, still bought meat in the market. It was the negative karma of doing the killing that was the problem. I managed to make peace with the irony of wanting to eat meat but not being able to look the animal in the eye on the way to the butcher, just as I had earlier made a shaky peace with the fact that if I was going to raise goats and chickens and eat their flesh, I had to reckon with their deaths. But becoming what I called a "real" goat farmer, that is, making a business of raising goats to sell to strangers for meat, was another story with raised stakes and a different series of ethical dilemmas.

Ruth and I discussed plans for my market-focused venture. I decided to raise baby goats for what is called the Easter Market. For the right kind of baby goat at the right time of the year, one might make a pretty penny indeed! One site I consulted gave this advice on the size and quality of animal desired for the Western or Roman Easter: "Type of goat wanted—Fleshy, milk-fed kids with relatively light-colored meat, three months old or younger." For Greek Orthodox Easter, the suggested guideline was: "Similar to Western Easter kids. A slightly larger milk-fed kid (i.e., around thirty-five pounds) is considered optimum." Other advice included: "When selling suckling lambs or kids, sell them directly off their dams. If you wean them, they will lose their bloom," and "Do not castrate males unless you have to. Intact males grow faster and more efficiently. They are preferred by many ethnic buyers. A wether is a blemished animal." Besides Easter, important goat-related holidays included Cinco de Mayo and Eid al-Fitr, the end of Ramadan when Muslims break their long religious fast. "By paying attention to these Holidays where goat meat is part of the traditional feast, goat producers should be able to increase their returns, as it is well known that goat prices increase around these Holidays because of increased demand for goat meat."

Goat gestation is usually 150 days. If I wanted to have "fleshy milk-fed kids" for sale by Easter, I had to breed my goats in October. I brought Anna, our older, experienced doe who'd been pregnant and given birth multiple times on our farm, and our beautiful all-white Saanen-Alpine mix doe, Nima, for whom being bred would be a new experience, to the farm of an older couple who lived some miles away to breed with their handsome Oberhasli male named Falcon.

It was fascinating to watch the courtship and mating process of Falcon and our does. While Anna, Nima, and I waited by the Subaru, someone fetched Falcon, who came prancing eagerly out of the barn, his big head, the dark ridge on his back, and his black mane puffed up with hormonal excitement, emanating that familiar funky smell of an older male goat. Anna was first. She and Falcon cautiously approached one another, edged sideways, came closer, moved apart. Falcon sniffed and grunted and opened his lips in a crooked poker-faced grin, showing his yellowed teeth. He flapped his lips, stuck out his tongue and drew it back, stuck it out, drew it back, bleated. Anna peed. Falcon stuck out his tongue and sampled it. "It's one of the ways he can tell if she's ovulating," Falcon's owner said. Anna raised her tail and lowered her hips. Falcon mounted her, and in moments it was done. "Should I put her back in the car?" I asked Falcon's owner. "No, wait, they need a little time together," she said, winking. They nuzzled one another companionably for a few minutes, the hormonal storm over.

Both Anna's and Nima's pregnancies went without a hitch. They grew blocky and sturdy as the months went by, their winter coats thickening, all the goats happily passing the winter in our snug barn, rambling out into the snowy pasture when possible. It seemed like things were going according to plan.

If I was going to get more serious about my goat farming and try to make some money, in addition to breeding earlier in the year I felt it was important to reevaluate all of my "inputs," one of which was hay. Our goats, like most others, "wasted" a lot of hay, pulling it from their hayrick in big mouthfuls, half of it falling to the stall floor to be trampled and peed and pooped on, building up in layers. At least twice every winter I scraped out the dirty trampled hay and hauled it to the compost pile, where it would decompose and help fertilize our summer garden. To cut back on hay wasting, I installed wire mesh that made it harder for the goats to grab big mouthfuls of hay. This alteration did keep hay off the bottom of the stalls, but it also made the bed the goats lay on less dry and fresh. I tried to keep the stalls dry and clean by sprinkling a modest layer of pine shavings on the floor each morning, but it was hard to keep up with. I'm convinced that my money-saving decision ultimately led to Nima's death.

A week before she was due, Nima was subdued and not eating. Even the handfuls of sweet grain I offered her every morning, sprinkled with vitamins and herbal preventatives of various kinds, didn't interest her. "She's probably just confused by what's happening to her body," I told Ruth. After all, it had to be weird to be growing another being inside your belly. In retrospect, I know that her logy behavior and lack of appetite were the first symptoms of an infected udder.

The night Anna and Nima were scheduled to give birth was the coldest of the year. A nor'easter, a fierce coastal winter storm, was expected to roar in, dropping several feet of snow, with temperatures in the double negative digits. I set up heat lamps in the stalls for when the babies came, the bulbs and metal shades hanging from extension cords wrapped around beams in the barn ceiling, aimed down into big plastic garbage cans I had cut doors into and layered with hay to be cozy little incubators. I readied hair dryers and stacks of clean towels. In cold like this, one expert said, you needed to get the newborns dry as fast as possible, and if they were males you must pay close attention to drying their little testicles or they would freeze.

Anna's baby came first, a great big boy we named Worm Moon after the

Baby goat incubator

full moon of March. He came out little hooves and nose first, slipping easily out of Anna's watery womb in a bloody, slimy sack. With my clean hands I pulled away the membranous covering over his face just as he opened one bright brown eye, looking straight at me. Ruth and I bundled him in a towel and lay him in a small plastic bin lined with clean towels to thoroughly blow-dry his sopping wet newborn hair before placing him in the garbage can incubator, the heat lamp casting an orange glow over his small, perfect goat body. While we waited for Nima to give birth, I cleaned up Anna's stall, putting the bloody hay and afterbirth into a bucket and setting it in a corner of the barn to take to the compost pile in the morning. Within minutes it was frozen.

Nima gave birth that night to twins whom we named Barid (cool in Arabic) and Frio (cold in Spanish). Frio was smaller, with gray-and-white markings and dark-brown socks, Barid a bit burlier and colored brown and cream. After we dried them, we put them back with their mother and helped them find her teats, at which they began to suck. But her udder looked strange—too tight, too full, too red. The babies couldn't get any milk out. Nevertheless, they snuggled close to her for warmth, stumbling back and forth from the makeshift heat-lamp incubator and their mother's warm belly.

By morning it was clear that something was wrong with Nima. The vet came to the house. She diagnosed mastitis and advised us to use home remedies, pressing warm wet cloths to Nima's udder every few hours and milking her as much as possible. What came out of her teats at these milkings was green, gooey, and foul. She did not improve. We called the vet again. With the storm then upon us, the vet was reluctant to drive all the way to our farm, so Ruth ventured out to meet her halfway, driving nearly an hour with snow slanting down, winds howling, trees dropping across the roads, power flickering out. Ruth secured a liquid antibiotic that we injected into Nima's teats, sticking a needle into the opening where the creamy milk would normally have sprayed forth.

When the storm was over the team of vets were able to drive their pickup truck into the yard, but by then Nima's udder had begun to turn black. Necrotic mastitis had set in. The vets were solicitous but also excited about the diagnosis, having learned all about it in veterinary school but never having seen it before in real life. If left untreated the udder would turn completely black, die, and fall off. They could do surgery to remove the infected udder, they said, but there was no guarantee it would save Nima. Our other option was to have them put her down.

Nima lay in her stall, her legs folded neatly under her, breathing heavily and irregularly. I gave her babies one last chance to be with their mother. They'd been separated for days as we milked Anna and

Nima and chickens

fed Anna's milk to the babies in bottles that they slurped so greedily they split the rubber teats. At their last meeting, Barid and Frio climbed on top of their sick mother and playfully nibbled at her ears.

The veterinarians, two young, strong women who'd been doing large-animal work in our area for some time, gently shaved a spot on Nima's neck and carefully injected her with a big syringe of deadly anesthetic, catching her head as it sagged and laying it down amid the hay. A candle burned on the steps to the hayloft, and a figure of Saint Francis looked down upon the scene from the top board of one of the stalls. We had named her Nima and her brother Dawa—the "sun" and "moon" in Dzongkha, a language spoken in Bhutan, where we'd spent a year living and teaching. As the vets worked, I recited a eulogy and blessing I'd written, and Ruth played a melancholy tune on the banjo:

> May you pass without more pain or fear,
> May your body continue to nourish other creatures,
> May your presence in this world not go unnoticed,
> May your life have counted for many things.

The vets hefted Nima's body onto a sled and pulled her across the snowy yard to their pickup, her big head lolling off the side of the sled and her legs sticking out at strange angles. We all worked to heave her body into the back of the cab. It felt unseemly to me, handling her like that, but it was winter, the ground was frozen, and we could not bury her on the farm; the vets would be able to cremate her body. They told us they'd been at many animal funerals, and as at the one we'd just performed, they were always moved by how much people respected and loved their animals and celebrated their lives. Once, they said, they participated in a long ritual of singing, dancing, and feasting, celebrating the death of a sheep.

Before they drove off with Nima, I asked them, "Do you think it was my fault?"

One of them looked at me quizzically.

"There wasn't enough bedding. The stall floor was wet and cold. I should have known sooner that she was sick. I bred them too early. It was just too cold. The storm prevented you from bringing medicine."

"I think your stalls looked pretty good," the vet said. "I doubt anything you did contributed to it. Sometimes they just get sick."

Despite her reassurance, I feel haunted by Nima's death, my grief the price I will forever pay for thinking I could so easily turn my beloved animals into money.

HONEY,
SWEETHEART,
DARLING

Being in a Body

"That's my last secret," I tell Ruth.

"And it serves you right," she says, laughing.

I've just confessed to her that the time I had poison ivy all over my body—between my thighs and toes, on my back, arms, neck, belly, shoulders, and face, and had to take steroids to cure it—was the result of a rendezvous with M. at the Sandy River, known for the lush poison ivy beds lining the shore.

"You had sex in the poison ivy?" she asks, clarifying my stupidity.

Years have passed. Ruth and I are still together. And we still talk about the time in our lives when we might have left one another but didn't. Every time we do, I come closer to forgiving myself and grow in compassion for Ruth and for humans in general—their precarity, their predictability, their neediness, their hungers and urges. In one recent conversation, Ruth told me one of the lasting negative impacts of my affair was a concern that I thought of her as boring and unexciting, an old lesbian fuddy-duddy. An offhand comment from a friend, that perhaps in ending the affair for good, I'd "settled" for the safety of our relationship and had not been brave or bold enough to seek "real passion" and adventure, made Ruth deeply question anew her identity, her sexuality, and her beauty, and doubt the rightness of a choice she'd made as a younger woman to become a "safe" person.

"So are you saying that the whole time I was tangled up with M. you kind of identified with her?" I asked.

"Yes! I thought you knew that. I tried for years to make nonmonogamy work, but I hurt people, and I didn't want to do that anymore. I made a choice to be reliable and loyal. So when you were attracted to M., I felt betrayed, like my decision to be a safer person had made me less sexy and unattractive to you." She cried as she remembered the woman she'd been in a previous long-term relationship with, whom she especially loved and whom she'd especially hurt.

"She and I were going to couples counseling and I made a promise not to see the woman I was attracted to until our next session, but I did anyway. I broke a promise," she said, looking straight at me with her warm, bright brown eyes. "I made a promise, and I broke it. I had an affair. That's why I tried so hard not to judge you and just let you do what you needed to do. I knew you weren't trying to ruin our relationship or hurt me. You were just trying to figure out your feelings."

Ruth has a T-shirt with an image of big-hatted, spur-jangling cowgirls dancing together under a starry western sky. The words "Don't fence me in," from the 1930s Hollywood cowboy song by Cole Porter and Robert Fletcher, float in the air, rising up from a honky-tonk piano player in the corner.

It's an old shirt, full of holes. And it's a funny shirt, with multiple layers of meaning. The figures are all women dancing together, so it is partly about women being able to love one another and not be fenced in by homophobia and prejudice. It's also about wide-open western spaces, which to me are freeing and exhilarating. The other meaning suggests, of course, that being fenced in takes away one's freedom, like, say, in a relationship. To be fenced in means you can no longer play the field, mess about, sleep around—you've got responsibilities to a partner, maybe even a family. To be fenced in means you've settled, but not by choice; you've limited your options. The song pays homage to America's love affair with the rough, independent spirit of the cowboy, who will sacrifice everything else for the freedom to be himself under the starry, unfenced sky, who will suffer any torture except, by God, a fence!

I wonder if you could fence yourself in, but not in a negative way. I remember a conversation with a friend about our lives and partners and love in general. "People say you can't help who you fall in love with," my friend said, adding, "but I disagree. You *can* help it." You can, in other words, create a boundary for yourself, a fence of sorts. You can make choices about where you want to be and who you want to be with.

Is settling in, locating yourself in a place and in a relationship, the same as giving in, acquiescing to a life you don't really want or that isn't exciting to you anymore? I wonder, looking back, if this might have been what I was struggling with in the beginning, like the goats when they first came to our farm. I was in my own unfamiliar pasture, in a relationship with a person I could potentially grow old with, in a place I could potentially live in for the rest of my life. Maybe I was a little afraid.

Like the speaker in Robert Frost's poem about fences, I know a fence is really only a fence if there is something on the other side that one wants to be either joined with or separated from. Fences can be seductive that way. They represent a challenge. Like some humans, some goats seem to think the grass is always greener, that there are more tasty morsels, more excitement and freedom, on the other side, and they will always be trying to outwit the fence. Some humans, like goats, might be too afraid to test the fence boundaries and somewhat reluctantly spend their days within them. For my part, either I have outgrown my desire to challenge the fence, or I am simply satisfied exactly where I am. I'm actually rather fond, like Frost's redneck, of the order fences bring. I like the idea of "minding a fence" and can imagine it as less of a tyrant than a wise and gentle reminder: *This is where you are meant to be. This is your place. This is your home.*

When M. unexpectedly came back into my life, I thought it was a call to revisit who I had been in my early lesbian years, and off I went, carried far and fast by a storm of hormones, surprised, grateful, and a little terrified. Even though I told Ruth about the affair, I kept it going for years, arranging clandestine rendezvous, crying and fighting with M., keeping secrets from Ruth and my friends. When I told M. that Ruth was going to leave me, she was glad that the two of us could be together. But I wondered even then whether this romantic drama could be staged on the set of real life; something important was missing—the ingredients for a long-term loving relationship, one that would last. *That* was what I had with Ruth, and what eventually drew the two of us back to each other.

What I had with M. was sex. Turning your back on it, she said, would be like spitting in the face of God. What I had with her was risky, wild abandonment, an edgy vulnerability, a sometimes violent, selfish quest for pleasure. What I had with Ruth was mutual instead of selfish. We loved each other, or were trying to love each other, no matter what. It was with Ruth that for the first time in my life I experienced what might be an unconditional love, a love that did not try to bend the other into submission, a love that did not punish or outrageously praise, a love that was grounded.

The relationship I had with Ruth was the one that offered me a real possibility of wholeness. With Ruth, the vulnerability took place in real life, not in the context of sexual fantasy. With Ruth, there was a real possibility of sexual connection, a real possibility of at-oneness with something holy, a real possibility of nurturing and acceptance. But to find all that, we had to stay together. A friend of ours wrote a book about long-term lesbian relationships. When she read from it at public events and people asked her for the secret, she told them this: There is only one difference between long-term and short-term lesbian couples; the long-term couples stay together. That's it. Their relationships aren't perfect. They don't eschew affairs. They don't have more passionate sex or less passionate sex. They don't drink more or less, or have more or less money, or vacation in Europe more or less. They just stay together.

There is lots to laugh about and understand now that the affair is past and our relationship is still strong. In conversation with a friend recently, she remembered that in her early lesbian days there were certain women, perhaps not unlike M., who cut a wide swath through the lesbian communities they were a part of. These women were popular for their sexual charisma, especially with newly out lesbians. "They just had it," my friend said. "They're sexy and smart and handsome or beautiful and make sex seem easy and fun." Lesbian communities were full of these women, she said, some of whom came to feel remorse, and others who didn't. That kind of magnetism, when women encounter it in men, my friend noted, could be predatory and abusive, but just as often, among lesbians and between men and women, it could feel bedazzling, alluring, and dangerous in just the right way.

It is too simple to say that I gave up passion in exchange for love and commitment, or that the goats and chickens were a substitute for sexual intimacy, even though that may be exactly how it seems. The deeper lessons are more complex. The world is wide and full of ways to connect. Do I feel ashamed of my affair? To admit that would be to say that I was ashamed of being human. I only regret that there was something about the thoroughness with which I abandoned my inhibitions then that has made me shy now. "You didn't do anything wrong," Ruth insists. "You were just being passionate." Just being a body. Just living in a body.

It's not over yet—our healing, our coming back to each other. Perhaps there is another ceremony we need to create for that, a third lesbian wedding—one that celebrates forgiveness and renewal, one that involves making a commitment to kindling desire anew. For now, the most profound lesson for me from the years of turmoil was when Ruth said to me, "You know, you don't have to lie to me, about anything. You can always tell me the truth." And the truth, that's real vulnerability, and that's sexy.

Honey, Sweetheart, Darling

All you need is already within you,
only you must approach yourself with reverence and love.
…all I plead with you is this:
make love of yourself perfect.

— From *I Am That: Talks with Sri Nisargadatta Maharaj*

Honey, sweetheart, darling. The words roll off my tongue, falling like rubies and diamonds into the air, spilling onto the ground. Who knew I had such jewels inside myself? Who knew that I was so full of love? I am well into the second half of my life, and this language of tenderness seems to have come upon me suddenly. One day I began uttering quiet endearments—to Ruth, to children, to cats, goats, chickens, to the Japanese beetles feeding on the rose leaves, even to the carrots I pulled out of the ground: "Oh, honey, aren't you a beauty!" Each time I hear words like these out of my own mouth, I'm surprised. After all this time, gentleness seems to finally have found a foothold within me. Few, if any, might notice any change in me, but my inner landscape feels rearranged.

Now that I am attuned to it, I hear a conversation about the power of tenderness all around me, from what might seem unlikely corners—writers, botanists, scholars, artists, medical practitioners, therapists, philosophers, activists, religious leaders, farmers, environmentalists, sociologists, and even neuroscientists. They come from their respective disciplines with different words and theories, but their voices unite in an optimistic conviction that we may be moving into what one Stanford brain surgeon calls "a new era of compassion." The more we understand about ourselves as humans, especially about the relationship of the brain and the heart, the closer we may be to understanding how we might change our unfortunate human tendency toward sectarianism and violence. The impact of these discoveries and understandings might be as radically reorienting, some say, as the eighteenth century's Age of Enlightenment in terms of changing the way humans think and act. We've been killing things, bullying and forcing and destroying things, for far too long, and, these enlightened scientists and spiritual leaders agree, it hasn't been good for us or the planet. Now might be the right time to try a different tack—loving-kindness.

Examples of this possible cultural shift had begun to serendipitously appear in my life. Not long after I turned fifty I decided to try braces on my teeth again. As a young person in the 1970s I'd gone through the routine of braces, rubber bands, headgear, and a retainer. Two of my siblings had as well. But over the years my teeth had reverted to a snaggly pattern that made me self-conscious. The orthodontist made a plaster cast of my mouth and invited me back in a few weeks for a consultation. When I returned my hopes were dashed. "I'm sorry," he said, "I'm not sure I can help you after all."

With the sculpture of my crooked teeth in one hand and X-rays in the other, he told me that because of my earlier orthodontia I had significant bone loss in my jaw. His guess was that my teeth had been moved too quickly and with too much force. If he tried to move my teeth again, no matter how gently, they might fall out. Back in the old days, he explained, that's the way orthodontists used to think: the more force you applied, the faster you moved the teeth. What they know now, he added, is that the more gently and slowly you move the teeth, the more they are likely to stay put, with minimal damage to the jawbone.

The new theory, the orthodontist said, is supported by ancient thinking and practice. Eastern philosophies such as Taoism, from which tai chi and other "soft" martial arts sprang, stress that, as illogical as it may seem to the Western mind, softness eventually triumphs over force. The orthodontist wanted to perform a demonstration of his profession's new way of thinking.

"Stand here," he said, squaring my shoulders and steadying me. He put two hands on the front of my right shoulder and began to push. I instinctively reacted with force; I braced myself and leaned in. He pushed harder. I held my ground. We both got red in the face. He gently let up.

"Okay, let's try this again," he said. I stood up straight and adjusted my shirt. Instead of two hands this time, he put one finger on my shoulder and gently pushed. I drifted backward. Because I didn't perceive his one-finger pushing method as a threat, I didn't resist as much as when he used two hands. He had moved me with softness rather than force.

Another example came from my work with a physical therapist, who helped me with chronic shoulder pain that was sometimes so debilitating I could not use my right arm. It turned out I had an extra rib that complicated things in the narrow passageways of bone and muscle in my shoulder. When the tissues in the shoulder were inflamed, a nerve bundle passing between the scalene muscles was pinched. The name for the malady is thoracic outlet syndrome. The pain started when I was in graduate school bending over books and typing a dissertation. But there were also other factors that contributed to my shoulder pain besides being a student. I was married then and my husband was teaching me to hunt. At target practice each time I fired the rifle the butt end of the stock slammed into my shoulder bone. The loss of my sister to suicide was also still heavily with me then, and the pain of that loss was boiling up out of me in fits of sadness and anger. In addition to all of that, I was also trying to figure a way out of my marriage and into a new life as a lesbian.

As I look back, I see that I was in a great deal of emotional and physical pain, pulling through by sheer force of will, along with the help of cigarettes, alcohol, and a constant stream of cruel self-talk. One of my graduate school professors had posted a sign on her door that read: "The beatings will continue until morale improves." She meant it as a joke, of course, but that is exactly the way I thought—I knew no other way to address my suffering than to abuse and berate myself. As I reflect on that time and my lack of compassion for myself, I flinch. The war on the self, which I have been so well-acquainted with, is the most insidious and devastating war. It hollows out so many people who could be making peace in the world.

The physical therapist who helped me with my shoulder so many years later applied all the regular methods—massage, muscle stimulation, and ultrasound, and at home I dutifully performed the stretches he prescribed for me. The exercises were illustrated on small pieces of paper; he had written the word "gentle" on them, reminding me to be kind to myself as I exercised. I remarked one day at his office, as I lay enjoying the tender pressure of his hands, that his methods were so subtle.

"So you wonder," he asked, jokingly, "how it can be doing any good if it doesn't hurt? We don't want to hurt you! We want to relieve your pain!" The no-pain-no-gain theory, he explained, was being discredited as a treatment philosophy in physical therapy and most other healing arts. Emily, my massage therapist, whom I also visited to keep my shoulder working, agreed. It used to be accepted, she explained, that more pressure resulted in more healing, but the thinking now was that a slight application of force achieves more cooperation between tissues in the body—the gut, skin, glands, tendons, ligaments, fascia, muscles, and nerves. I think of it as skilled diplomacy, as opposed to sending in armed troops. It seems foolish, if not heretical, to believe that tenderness and yielding could be seriously and widely embraced in our culture as virtues, and that these values might create changes in our organizations and in our practices, even in our relationships with ourselves, and yet, if I can change, then change is possible.

The desire to prove that loving-kindness is good for us as human beings has sent many contemporary researchers out to demonstrate the resoundingly positive effects of such acts as opening doors for strangers, giving a homeless person a sandwich, taking a deep breath, smiling, saying thank you, sitting by the ocean listening to the waves, going for a walk, attending church, playing basketball with your buddies at lunchtime. Current scientific research shows us that joining in community and being nice to ourselves and others lowers our cortisol levels, strengthens our immune systems, induces certain positive brain waves, releases the "love hormone" oxytocin, and even fires up health-promoting genes.

Yet, some say, for all that science has shown us about the benefits of tenderness and compassion, science as a method of inquiry might be close to reaching the limits of what it can prove in this realm. Part of what is left to know about the power of care, sympathy, and softness might lie outside of science, in the realm of imagination and faith. Another cultural consequence of a new era of compassion, some say, may be a renewed respect for these intangibles, for these things we cannot see or prove. To me this is great news. I have often felt that the positivist drive to prove a thing, especially as it relates to the heart and psyche, is a form of violence. The underlying assumption of positivist science is that if the thing cannot be proven using the empirical tools of modern science, it does not really exist. I, however, have always had a healthy regard for things I cannot see, things I can only explain through the evidence of my own experience. These experiences, be they mystical, imaginative, metaphorical, dreamlike, have been as powerful as any drug or medical intervention in my own shift in consciousness.

One such experience stands out. It was a midsummer morning. I was meditating on the grass outside our farmhouse, sitting between the pasture and the woods. The garden was crowded with brilliant yellow squash blossoms. The poppies were there too, with their papery red petals. The shaggy, dark-purple bee balm was in full bloom. Hummingbirds hung midair among the flowers. The bushes of oregano, lemon balm, and sage were aswarm with bees, as were the borage, the calendula, and the towering sunflowers. Even the fava beans still had their small white-and-black blooms on display. The pea vines, laden with sweet pods, had climbed the chicken-wire fence surrounding the garden. The tomatoes bulged out of their cages. Wind moved through the shaded cedar forest, bringing cool air to the sunny spot where I sat.

With my eyes closed, I followed the voice of the guided meditation coming to me through my earphones, focusing first on the darkness behind my eyelids or the light that came dimly through them. I imagined the colors in the garden and the shapes—the architecture of the vegetable and flower beds, the flights of the bees and hummingbirds, the swaying of grasses. The recorded voice then asked me to focus on my nose, noticing any smell or sensation in my nostrils. There was sweetness in the air—clover, flowers, grass—mixed with the pungent but not unpleasant smell of the compost pile. Then my attention went to my ears. What could I hear? Buzzing. Wings. Birdsong—a chickadee, a high-flying crow. A pine cone hitting the ground behind me. Wind. What could I taste? The morning's coffee in my mouth. What could I feel on my skin? Sunshine. Grass. An ant trekking up the mountain of my ankle. And inside of myself? Could I feel the beating of my own heart? Yes, I could. And then, it happened: sound waves, light waves, waves of consciousness, waves of energy of all kinds knit themselves into a net that gently held everything. The boundaries of my body seemed to give way and I became part of a stream of pulsing, thrumming energy. I could ride on the waves of sound, the waves of scent, the currents of wind. The bee and I, the hummingbird and I, the flower and I, became part of the same rhythm, each of us going about the business of our being, and inextricably linked.

I don't know if this was a spiritual experience or a scientifically testable one. I do know I had a powerful felt sense of being joined to all the life around me by the thinnest and most delicate of threads. That feeling humbles a person. If we are in such tender relationship to the universe, how can we not proceed mindfully, gently? If we can treat the bee with love and kindness, how can we not treat one another with the same kindness, and, perhaps most importantly, how can we not extend that kindness to ourselves?

Of course, the transition within me was not sudden at all. It was many years in formation, beginning when I was simply tired of crossing the Sandy River on the way to work each day, vividly imagining an accident—my car with me in it crashing through the bridge rails into the river below. I was tired of the bleakness of my inner landscape—unending fields of gray, hard, pocked lava that I had to labor across in searing heat. I was confused about why my life, which in actuality was one of privilege and richness, could seem so difficult and unsatisfying. Why did everything, including getting up in the morning, seem to require so much effort? Why, after all these years of trying to heal, was I still sucked dry by so much self-hatred? One bright

Baby goats resting in the spring grass

May morning when even the sunshine and daffodils and impending birth of baby goats failed to bring me the smallest shred of joy, I knew I was in big trouble.

Over the next two years, through yoga, tai chi, massage, meditation, spiritual reading, workshops in mindfulness and stress reduction, acupuncture, and well-managed antidepressants, things began to change. These practices were all acts of faith and desperation, vessels launched into the dark. At the center of all this effort was a gifted therapist who, through a relatively new practice called EMDR, guided me back to and through my sorrows. The acronym stands for Eye Movement Desensitization and Reprocessing. Central to the practice is engaging the body through bilateral stimulation. Patients can move their eyes back and forth following the therapist's finger or moving lights, or don headphones and listen to sounds that alternate from ear to ear, or, in my case, have the therapist lightly tap on alternate knees. It's not quite clear why the bilateral stimulation works, but the theory is that we experience trauma with our whole body, not just our mind. If we can't or don't or won't process the trauma physically as well as emotionally, it gets stuck in the body and manifests itself as a host of different maladies. The back-and-forth movement of the eyes, the touch on the knees, the sound in the ears, creates a rhythm that, in my case, helped me fully enter my body and safely experience the physical impact of the fear, anger, and sadness I had carried with me for so long.

I was working through the experiences that haunted me on a profound physical level. I thought of each painful episode in my past as a room. The therapist and I would enter the room together, and as I relived whatever events occurred there, her encouragement was to simply notice in my body what I was feeling and where, and let it happen. I experienced powerful urges to vomit, deep sobbing and tears, burning in my belly and throat, feelings of choking, a racing heart, waves of heat and cold, strange rapid-eye movement, pain in my back and shoulders, hands and legs that jittered and jumped and shook. In the beginning I was ashamed of these visceral physical eruptions and disgusted by what I encountered in those rooms—violence, my own abject neediness, cruelty, and betrayal. My body would stiffen as I tried to avoid the revolting images and the excruciatingly painful feelings that arose. But, the therapist reassured me, anything I saw or heard or felt in those rooms was all right. "That's right, Gretchen," she would gently repeat, "You're doing fine. Just let it happen."

The organic resolution of each issue or event we worked through came when the heavy, dark, constricted dullness in my body associated with that event began to lighten. I experienced not only a physical lifting of the weight that pressed in on me, but also a brightness inside myself manifested as images of halos and auras, and swirling upward-moving energy. Most mysterious and curious of all was that as we neared resolution of each of these episodes of trauma, a person would appear in my imagination, some version of myself perhaps, who took me by the hand and said, "Honey, you don't need to be here anymore. Let's move on. Sweetheart, come with me. We'll leave this behind." I came to call this being my friend made of light. This patient, wise, intelligent version of myself still steps out of the mist of my psyche when the fearful, angry, desperate, self-hating version of me launches an attack on the unsuspecting going-about-her-life version. With great kindness and tenderness the friend made of light might say, "That's enough now. Darling, what do you need?"

I still sometimes hear a voice suggesting a good flogging as an appropriate cure for my low morale, and though this minimizer, this bully, this psychic troublemaker still whispers in my ear, I have come closer to understanding that even I deserve not to suffer; my pain is just as in need of loving attention as anyone's pain. All suffering, after all, is suffering. The pain of the refugee, the pain of the woman punched in the face by her husband, the eleven-year-old raped by her father, the eighty-year-old who has lost his wife of sixty-three years, the pain of the suicidal college student marking his forearms with a razor blade, the mother whose child has been hit by a car, even the pain of the melancholic professor—it is all pain. To measure and compare our suffering to the suffering of others is only a way to separate ourselves—from ourselves and from each other—into isolated towers of pain and fear, rather than recognizing our wholeness and our connection to one another.

A common exercise for those wishing to cultivate a loving attitude toward life in general is to start with the self, reconnecting with the basic goodness at your core. One suggested way to do this is to imagine yourself as a child, perhaps to even look at pictures of yourself as a child, and let the tenderness you would feel for any child, any vulnerable being, well up inside you. My problem with this exercise had always been that when I imagined myself as a child I felt pity and fear, even a vague revulsion. The farm and the animals were the real beginning of the change. When the baby goats emerged covered in uterine slime and blood, so perfectly formed and completely new to the world, and were licked clean by their mother, then tottered toward her bulging udder for their first suck of milk, I cried. The first time I held an egg to my ear and heard a baby chick chirping inside, I cried. The first time I witnessed a tiny wet hatchling emerge from its shell and be gently enveloped by its mother's wing and pulled under her warm breast, I cried. It was their absolute innocence and vulnerability that moved me; these babies had never done anything wrong—they were born essentially good. *Honey, sweetheart, darling.* Those words have such a bright ring. What a miracle that they are inside of me and come tumbling out, sparkling and rich, ridiculously sweet, in the mornings when I wake to Ruth's face on the pillow beside me, when I open the doors to the chicken coop, when I offer the goats their grain, when I curl a barn cat into the crook of my arm, smother it with kisses, rocking it like a baby.

ACKNOWLEDGMENTS AND CREDITS

First, thank you to Ruth Hill, the handsome, talented, intelligent, patient, and creative woman with whom I have lived this rural life in full loving partnership. I'm so glad we met at the ends of the earth, and I'm so glad we stayed together!

Thanks to friends and neighbors whose lives have intersected with mine and whose names and stories appear in these essays: Jack Mills. Darrell, Amanda, Taytum, Dionica, and Amarell Robinson. Doug and Judy Rawlings. Dave, Jen, Xochitl, and Iona Pope. Josh and Kelly Rawlings. Marilyn Daily. Carol Scribner. Stephen and Alison Levine. Doc Cooper. Bob and Rita Kimber. Chris, Ashirah, Owen, and Bonnie Bee Knapp. Leslie, Ben, Samuel, and Abrahm Geissinger. Stephen Bien and Ellen Grunblatt and their children, Ethan and Shula. Rae Ellen and Greg Roy and their sons. Macky and Marilyn Turner and the Turner family. Rita, Elyse, Zai, and Wylder Gluck. Dave and Elaine Shipper. Kris MacCabe. All rural vets, especially those at Turner Veterinary Service in Turner, Maine. Craig Borck and his daughters. Francis Fenton and his daughter. Adam Runnells. Sudip Muzumdar. The entire queer potluck and salon gang, and my brothers and their fabulous wives.

Thanks to my writing mentors and peers, who read these essays with care and skill and offered unending encouragement: Wes McNair, Pat O'Donnell, Bob Kimber, Jayne Decker, Connie Wolfe, Susan Johnson, Elizabeth Cooke, Liz Kuhlman, and Dave Mikkelsen.

An additional thanks to Ruth, who relived this story as she helped proofread the book! To my inspiring, supportive, and hardworking colleagues at the University of Maine at Farmington, a magnificent place to teach and write, which granted me several long leaves during which I worked on this book.

Thanks to the teachers, healers, and spiritual friends who have helped me learn to trust my body and myself—who have helped me take my place at the table: Deborah Clague, Rebecca Chandler, Tim Davis, Emily Bilodeau, Mary Lello, Penny Hood, Rev. Cathie Wallace, Rev. Alexis Fuller-Wright, Rev. Doug Dunlap, Eleni Margaronis, Liz Farmer, and Dennis Flanagan.

And finally, thanks to the animals, whose dignity, grace, and beauty have offered me the most profound lessons.

Versions of these essays were originally published in the following publications: "Hunters: A Meander" in *Fourth Genre,* Spring 2019; "Tracks" in *Orion,* Jan./Feb. 2017; "Wealthy" in *1966,* Summer 2016; "Consider the Acorn" in *Orion,* Sept./Oct. 2015; "Minding the Fence" in *ISLE,* Winter 2013; "With the Animals" in *Matter Journal 14,* Winter 2012; "Acquainted with the Night" in *Let There Be Night: Testimony on Behalf of the Dark,* edited by Paul Bogard (University of Nevada Press, 2008).

Lyrics from "Talk to the Animals" (from *Doctor Dolittle*) reprinted by permission of Alfred Music Publishing Co. Words and Music by Leslie Bricusse. Copyright © 1967 (Renewed) EMI Hastings Catalog Inc. Exclusive print rights controlled and administered by Alfred Music Publishing Co., Inc. All rights reserved.

Excerpt from "Farm Country," by Mary Oliver, from *New & Selected Poems, Vol. 1,* published by Beacon Press, Boston. Copyright © 1972, 1992 by Mary Oliver. Used by permission of the Charlotte Sheedy Literary Agency.

 GRETCHEN LEGLER is the author of *Woodsqueer: Crafting a Sustainable Rural Life, On the Ice: An Intimate Portrait of Life at McMurdo Station, Antarctica,* and *All the Powerful Invisible Things: A Sportswoman's Notebook.* Her work has received two Pushcart Prizes, and her essays have appeared in the *Georgia Review, Orion, Brevity, Fourth Genre,* and other publications. She is a professor of creative writing at the University of Maine at Farmington and recently received a master of divinity degree from Harvard Divinity School. She lives in Farmington.

CPSIA information can be obtained
at www.ICGtesting.com
Printed in the USA
JSHW022159310523
42531JS00003B/5